John Ressler
9243 Hillside Trail South
Cottage Grove, MN 55016-3478

www.civilwar.org

The American Crisis Se~i~~

Books on the Civil War Era

Steven E. Woodworth, Associate Professor of H
Texas Christian University
SERIES EDITOR

~∾~ The Civil War was the crisis of the Republic's first century —the test, in Abraham Lincoln's words, of whether any free government could long endure. It touched with fire the hearts of a generation, and its story has fired the imaginations of every generation since. This series offers to students of the Civil War, either those continuing or those just beginning their exciting journey into the past, concise overviews of important persons, events, and themes in that remarkable period of America's history.

Volumes Published

James L. Abrahamson. *The Men of Secession and Civil War, 1859–1861* (2000). Cloth ISBN 0-8420-2818-8   Paper ISBN 0-8420-2819-6

Robert G. Tanner. *Retreat to Victory? Confederate Strategy Reconsidered* (2001). Cloth ISBN 0-8420-2881-1 Paper ISBN 0-8420-2882-X

Stephen Davis. *Atlanta Will Fall: Sherman, Joe Johnston, and the Yankee Heavy Battalions* (2001). Cloth ISBN 0-8420-2787-4
Paper ISBN 0-8420-2788-2

Paul Ashdown and Edward Caudill. *The Mosby Myth: A Confederate Hero in Life and Legend* (2002). Cloth ISBN 0-8420-2928-1
Paper ISBN 0-8420-2929-X

Spencer C. Tucker. *A Short History of the Civil War at Sea* (2002).
Cloth ISBN 0-8420-2867-6   Paper ISBN 0-8420-2868-4

Richard Bruce Winders. *Crisis in the Southwest: The United States, Mexico, and the Struggle over Texas* (2002). Cloth ISBN 0-8420-2800-5   Paper ISBN 0-8420-2801-3

Ethan S. Rafuse. *A Single Grand Victory: The First Campaign and Battle of Manassas* (2002). Cloth ISBN 0-8420-2875-7
Paper ISBN 0-8420-2876-5

John G. Selby. *Virginians at War: The Civil War Experiences of Seven Young Confederates* (2002). Cloth ISBN 0-8420-5054-X Paper ISBN 0-8420-5055-8

Edward K. Spann. *Gotham at War: New York City, 1860–1865* (2002). Cloth ISBN 0-8420-5056-6   Paper ISBN 0-8420-5057-4

Anne J. Bailey. *War and Ruin: William T. Sherman and the Savannah Campaign* (2002). Cloth ISBN 0-8420-2850-1 Paper ISBN 0-8420-2851-X

Gary Dillard Joiner. *One Damn Blunder from Beginning to End: The Red River Campaign of 1864* (2003). Cloth ISBN 0-8420-2936-2   Paper ISBN 0-8420-2937-0

Steven E. Woodworth. *Beneath a Northern Sky: A Short History of the Gettysburg Campaign* (2003). Cloth ISBN 0-8420-2932-X Paper ISBN 0-8420-2933-8

One Damn Blunder
from Beginning to End

One Damn Blunder from Beginning to End
The Red River Campaign of 1864

The American Crisis Series
BOOKS ON THE CIVIL WAR ERA
NO. 11

Gary Dillard Joiner

A Scholarly Resources Inc. Imprint
Wilmington, Delaware

Scholarly Resources Inc.
104 Greenhill Avenue
Wilmington, DE 19805-1897
www.scholarly.com

Library of Congress Cataloging-in-Publication Data

Joiner, Gary D.
    One damn blunder from beginning to end : the Red River
Campaign of 1864 / Gary Dillard Joiner.
        p. cm. — (American crisis series)
Includes bibliographical references and index.
    ISBN 0-8420-2936-2 (cloth : alk. paper) — ISBN 0-8420-2937-0
(pbk. : alk. paper)
    1. Red River Expedition, 1864. 2. United States—History—
Civil War, 1861–1865—Campaigns. I. Title. II. Series.
E476.33 .J65 2002
973.7'36—dc21   2002011475

For my wife

Marilyn Segura Joiner

the love of my life

And to the memory of

Charles Edmund Vetter

gentleman, scholar, fellow researcher, and

much-missed friend

ABOUT THE AUTHOR

Gary Dillard Joiner is an instructor of history and director of the Red River Regional Studies Center at Louisiana State University in Shreveport. He coauthored *Red River Steamboats* and *Historic Shreveport-Bossier* and several technical reports on cultural resources in the Red River valley. He is a member of the local board of the U.S. Civil War Center at Louisiana State University in Baton Rouge, past president of the North Louisiana Civil War Roundtable, editor of *North Louisiana History* (the journal of the North Louisiana Historical Association), and president of the DeSoto Parish Historical Society. Mr. Joiner is also a cartographer and has created geographic information systems for governmental clients and the Civil War Preservation Trust. His digital maps include various Civil War battlefields, among them Petersburg, Vicksburg, Mansfield, and Pleasant Hill. He is currently pursuing Ph.D. studies at Lancaster University in England.

ACKNOWLEDGMENTS

No author can claim that a work is solely his or hers, and this volume is no exception. It is impossible to thank and give credit to all those who have helped me, either directly or indirectly over the past several years in projects that led to this book. For those I do not mention, please forgive me. I do wish to recognize some individuals who have been of particular importance to me.

Archivists are the guardians of masses of material that almost never see the light of day. A good archivist can turn a research trip into delight. I have been fortunate to work with some of the best, particularly DeAnne Blanton at the National Archives and Records Administration in Washington, DC; Sherry Pugh at Jackson Barracks in New Orleans; and Laura Connerly at Louisiana State University in Shreveport. This book would not have been possible without them.

Historians of the Civil War are often kindred spirits, and we tend to share information in the cause of shedding new light. There are no finer researchers and writers than those working in the history of the Mississippi Valley and the region to its west. Among those whom I consider my friends as well as colleagues are Ed Bearss, Chief Military Historian Emeritus of the National Park Service; Terry Winschel, historian at Vicksburg National Military Park in Mississippi; Stacy Allen, historian at Shiloh National Military Park in Tennessee; Anne Bailey, professor of history at Georgia College and State University, Milledgeville; Arthur Bergeron, historian of Pamplin Park in Virginia; Steve Bounds, curator of the Mansfield State Historic Site in Louisiana; Scot Dearman, interpretive ranger at the Mansfield State Historic Site; Terry Jones, professor of history at the University of Louisiana, Monroe; and Steven Woodworth, professor of history at Texas Christian University in Fort Worth, Texas. All of these people in various ways have made my research journey a better one.

I also wish to recognize two historians who influenced me more than others. The first is the "dean" of Trans-Mississippi Civil War history, Ludwell Johnson, professor emeritus at the College of William and Mary. Professor Johnson's *Red River Campaign: Politics and Cotton in the Civil War* is the seminal work in the field. All others pale in the shadow of this great piece of research and writing, and every historian working in the field today owes him a great debt of gratitude.

The second historian I want to recognize is the late Charles Edmund "Eddie" Vetter, who was the chair of the Department of Sociology at Centenary College in Shreveport, Louisiana. He was a dear friend and mentor. In 1992, Eddie approached me with the idea of writing an article with him on the Red River Campaign. Two years later "The Union Naval Expedition on the Red River" was published in *Civil War Regiments* and became the kernel of this book, which Eddie and I had planned to coauthor. We were working on the early stages of research when he died unexpectedly. This study, the idea for it, the thoughts about the implications of the campaign, and the political background, particularly regarding William T. Sherman, came from my research sessions with Eddie. This work is as much his as mine.

As with any work, fact or fiction, the research and writing processes are lengthy and involve a great effort by several people. My wife, Marilyn, acted as my editor and sounding board; I could not have written the book without her. Matthew Hershey at Scholarly Resources has been my facilitator and cheerleader, and I thank him and Steven Woodworth, editor of the American Crisis Series, for their help and guidance. Finally, although great care has been taken to eliminate them, any errors in the research and writing are solely mine.

CONTENTS

INTRODUCTION

HISTORIANS AND THE general public seem to have an insatiable appetite for the American Civil War. It has been almost 140 years since the cannons last roared in anger. Still, books and articles continue to be written, reporting nuances of the war not covered previously or reexamining others. The war tugs at us like no other event in our nation's history (with the possible exception of the Second World War, since memories of its combatants are still alive). Perhaps it is the very "civil" nature of the earlier war that grips each generation—the irony of enemy against enemy as brother against brother.

The Civil War fought west of the Mississippi River, particularly in 1864, has received comparatively little scrutiny. Why? The eastern theater in Virginia grabbed the headlines of newspapers in that day and still commands a large percentage of the shelf space filled by historians and analysts of the war. Virginia received the bulk of the coverage for several reasons. The great armies contending in this theater, the Army of the Potomac and the Army of Northern Virginia, were famous. The proximity of Richmond and Washington allowed for rapid coverage by the press. That Virginia had been the home of many of the Founding Fathers, but was now the seat of rebellion, made the war stories even more poignant. As the war continued and Union victories mounted, the Northern press focused on whatever appeared to be advances by Union forces. And since it is the victor who traditionally writes the history, another reason for the Red River Campaign's neglect is that it was a colossal failure for the Union in a year of glittering triumphs on all the other fronts. It was an embarrassment for the military, heightened in December 1864 when Congress began an investigation of what went wrong.

By 1864 the war in the West had moved northward to Tennessee, and Ulysses S. Grant was a household name, thanks to his 1863 victory at Vicksburg. The war west of "the Great River" was a sideshow to larger events. Nevertheless, in the steamy spring of 1864, in the deep interior of the pine barrens and sinewy streams of the Red River valley in northern Louisiana, a drama unfolded that caught the attention of both Washington and Richmond. Among its chief characters were the brother-in-law of Jefferson Davis, a former speaker of the U.S. House of Representatives, a former governor of Missouri, and a French prince. The outcome of that drama has had a lasting impact on the war, the state of Louisiana, and the South as a region.

It began with the Union army's bold attempt to capture the Confederate capital of Louisiana at Shreveport. The promise of thousands of bales of cotton to feed the starving textile mills of New England and the opportunity to bring Louisiana and Texas back into the Union fired the imaginations of politicians, businessmen, and newspaper publishers. If successful, the campaign would have been completed just in time to affect the fall presidential elections. The prospect of putting tens of thousands of unemployed New England textile workers back on the job again was a powerful magnet for presidential politics. The Confederates were well aware of this potential and had been preparing for a possible campaign for a year, even before the fall of Vicksburg.

Several newspapers in the North sent reporters with the large commands in every theater and duly reported their successes, so veteran reporters were among those who accompanied Major General Nathaniel Banks up the Red River. Banks, considered a strong contender for the Republican nomination for president later that year, was very popular in the Northeast. New York, Pennsylvania, Massachusetts, and Maine newspapers all sent correspondents to cover his activities. Both *Harper's Weekly* and *Leslie's Illustrated Journal* dispatched illustrators and reporters. But as little happened on the trek northward into the sparsely populated reaches of northwestern Louisiana, their air of optimism faded, and on-site reports became rare. Banks's bragging that he would have an easy victory was not exciting copy for the journalists. Action made headlines; posturing by politicians was typical. Moreover, as the Union forces penetrated deeper into Louisiana, the logistical problems of getting reports out from remote areas with no telegraph lines and infrequent mail packet boat runs added to the reporters' problems of creating good stories for their papers.

As the campaign unfolded and schedules were left by the wayside, cockiness among the Union commanders, particularly Banks, Major General William B. Franklin, and Admiral David D. Porter, landed them in deep trouble. Banks chose to take the bulk of his army inland at the village of Grand Ecore in Natchitoches Parish, away from the massive fire support offered by the navy. The Arkansas arm of the campaign was completely cut off from communications with the Louisiana portion and suffered accordingly. The U.S. Navy struggled to bring a huge contingent of fighting hulls up the narrow, twisting, often shallow Red River and was forced to leave deeper-draft vessels along the way. With the Union army stretched over twenty miles on a single road where it could not support itself with needed reinforcements, Confederate forces prepared to meet Banks about forty miles south of his objective. The resulting battle near the small town of Mansfield proved to be one of the last major Confederate victories of the war. Unable to follow up on their success, however, the Confederates allowed the Federals to evacuate both their army and their navy from precarious positions deep in hostile territory.

The historiography of the campaign is filled with an odd mix of documents. The Union disaster made for poor newspaper copy, and chroniclers in that era preferred to ignore it. But there are the usual field reports and diaries of participants, several apologies for the failure, and the report of a congressional investigation into the embarrassment. *The War of the Rebellion: A Compilation of the Official Records of the Union and Confederate Armies* covers the campaign in the four parts of volume 34. The *Official Records of the Union and Confederate Navies in the War of the Rebellion* contains Union naval and Confederate army and naval information in portions of volumes 25 and 26. Testimony into the origins, conduct, and consequences of the campaign, found in the *Report of the Joint Committee on the Conduct of the War*, volume 2, *The Red River Expedition*, is of particular interest. From the end of 1864 through the spring of 1865, most of the Union cast of characters testified, including some who have escaped the greater scrutiny of history but played important roles. Chief among these is an all-but-forgotten river pilot, Wellington W. Withenbury, who, to protect his own cotton upstream, may have single-handedly sealed the fate of the Union army by convincing Banks to move inland. Most of the testimony is, of course, self-serving but highly readable. Banks was largely blamed for the disaster, and others whom he accused were vindicated.

Among contemporary accounts the Confederate field commander Richard Taylor's *Destruction and Reconstruction* still ranks as one of the most intriguing and insightful memoirs of the war. Richard B. Irwin, *History of the Nineteenth Army Corps*, is an excellent account of the largest Union field force in the campaign. Admiral David Dixon Porter, the U.S. naval commander, was a prolific writer, two of whose works provide a wealth of information: *Naval History of the Civil War* and *Incidents and Anecdotes of the Civil War*. (Readers must be warned to treat Porter with more than casual skepticism, however; the admiral was prone to self-aggrandizement and never suffered from a lack of words in describing his talents and the faults of others.) Another account that includes the naval portion of the Red River Campaign was written by the commander of the USS *Osage: What Finer Tradition: The Memoirs of Thomas O. Selfridge, Jr., Rear Admiral U.S.N.* The most noteworthy compendium of reports and articles by participants is found in volume 4 of *Battles and Leaders of the Civil War*, edited by Robert U. Johnson and Clarence C. Buel.

Without a doubt the seminal work on the campaign is Ludwell Johnson's *Red River Campaign: Politics and Cotton in the Civil War*. This brilliant piece of research and writing, first published in 1958, still withstands the test of time and revisionist historians. All students of the campaign must consider this volume the beginning of their journey into an understanding of the issues surrounding the war west of the Mississippi River following the siege of Vicksburg. Almost all subsequent books on the campaign rely on this work and the scholarship it reveals.

Among modern books on the major participants of the Red River Campaign, the commander of the Confederate Department of the Trans-Mississippi is the subject of two biographies: *General Edmund Kirby Smith, C.S.A.* by Joseph Howard Parks and *Kirby Smith's Confederacy: The Trans-Mississippi South, 1863–1865* by Robert L. Kerby. The lives of other leaders include *Richard Taylor: Soldier Prince of Dixie* by Michael Parrish; thorough documentation in *Pretense of Glory: The Life of General Nathaniel P. Banks* by James G. Hollandsworth Jr.; a more apologetic tone in *Fighting Politician: Major General N. P. Banks* by Fred Harvey Harrington; and *Admiral David Dixon Porter: The Civil War Years* by Chester G. Hearn. The best account of the Union side in the first phase of the Battle of Mansfield is found in Jim Huffstodt, *Hard Dying Men: The Story of General W. H. L. Wallace, General T. E. G. Ransom, and Their "Old Eleventh": Illinois Infantry in the American Civil War, 1861–1865*.

The vessels and tactics used by the Union and Confederate navies in the campaign are described in several important works: *The Army's Navy Series*, volume 2, *Assault and Logistics: Union Army Coastal and River Operations, 1861–1866* by Charles Dana Gibson and

E. Kay Gibson; *Lincoln's Navy: The Ships, Men, and Organizations, 1861–1865* by Donald L. Canney; *Warships and Naval Battles of the Civil War* by Tony Gibbons; *Ironclads at War: The Origin and Development of the Armored Warship, 1854–1891* by Jack Greene; *A History of the Confederate Navy* by Raimondo Luraghi; and *Warships of the Civil War Navies* by Paul H. Silverstone. The most important new information on the role of Confederate naval innovations is found in Mark K. Ragan, *Union and Confederate Submarine Warfare in the Civil War*.

What makes these men and ships worthy of further attention? The Red River Campaign of 1864 saw the greatest combined operation between the U.S. Army and the U.S. Navy to that point in the war. It taught both services lessons in what was possible in cooperation and other scenarios that were unlikely to produce success. Each one learned the strengths and weaknesses of the other, leading to modern theories of force projection. The navy and the army quartermasters brought ninety vessels up the unforgiving river. The army assembled more than 40,000 men attempting to operate in three pincers. Technological innovations included the first use of the periscope in battle and the construction of sophisticated dams to save the fleet from capture or destruction.

Twelve Medals of Honor were awarded for heroism during the campaign, and the careers of some Union naval commanders skyrocketed. David Dixon Porter later became a commandant at the U.S. Naval Academy and the second full admiral in the U.S. Navy. Many of his vessel captains rose to high ranks and achieved notoriety throughout their careers. Thomas O. Selfridge, twenty-eight years old at the time, achieved the rank of rear admiral, served as an instructor at Annapolis, and in 1895 commanded all U.S. naval operations in the Atlantic and European waters; upon retirement in 1898, he was one of the most influential officers in the navy. Ensign Henry Gorringe, captain of the *Fort Hindman*, became a career naval officer and achieved international fame in the 1880s: as naval attaché to the American embassy in Egypt, he masterminded and led the operation to bring the Egyptian obelisk known as Cleopatra's Needle to New York City, where it remains today in Central Park. Randolph K. Breese, captain of the USS *Black Hawk* during the campaign, had been with Porter prior to the attack on New Orleans in 1862, and in late 1864 and 1865, he served as fleet captain of the North Atlantic Blockading Squadron under Porter.

The most notable career casualty of the navy was that of Seth Ledyard Phelps, captain of the USS *Eastport*, whom Porter ultimately blamed for the loss of the great ironclad; Phelps resigned his commission in December 1864 but became wealthy and famous as a clipper ship captain in the China tea trade, holding the world's record for the fastest trans-Pacific sailing time by a clipper ship.

The primary Union army commanders did not fare as well; following the campaign the military careers of many stagnated or were destroyed. Banks never commanded a field force again, and his presidential aspirations died at Mansfield on April 8. Too highly ranked to be totally removed from command, he became a paper shuffler in New Orleans, though after the war he served in Congress, in the Massachusetts state senate, and as a U.S. marshal. William Buel Franklin, wounded at Mansfield, was unpopular with the Union High Command, and his military career stagnated; a civil engineer, he ran the Colt Fire Arms Manufacturing Company for twenty years after the war. John Clark, Banks's chief topographic engineer, left the army and returned to his home in Auburn, New York, where he became the city engineer; his innovative maps are still in the Cayuga County Museum in Auburn. The career of Albert Lee, Banks's cavalry chief, was ruined by his commander's accusations; he resigned his commission in May 1865 and became a successful businessman in Europe and the eastern United States.

Of the Confederates, Edmund Kirby Smith became a successful businessman and president of Sewanee College in Tennessee. He was the last full Confederate general to die. Richard Taylor achieved fame in both the North and the South during and after the war. Instrumental in ending Reconstruction and a popular lecturer, he died in New York in 1879, barely fifty-three years old, from complications of rheumatoid arthritis. He never forgave Kirby Smith for denying him total victory against Banks and the Union forces. The flamboyant Frenchman, Camille Armand Jules Marie, the Prince de Polignac, became an economist and mathematician, led French troops in the Franco-Prussian War, and was knighted for gallantry; he was presented to Queen Victoria on behalf of Emperor Napoleon III. In 1913 he died a hero to the French people. He named his son "Mansfield."

The title of this book is a quotation from Major General William T. Sherman, who had lived at Pineville on the Red River before the war and wanted to lead the campaign. When he was asked his opinion of the campaign as he was preparing for the operations against Atlanta, his response was "One damn blunder from beginning to end." It was perhaps the best critique of the Union effort ever spoken.

LIST OF MAPS

CHAPTER ONE

STRATEGIC POSITIONS PRIOR TO THE CAMPAIGN

THE WINTER OF 1863–64 was one of heady optimism for Union leaders. Their successes following the great twin victories at Vicksburg and Gettysburg in July 1863 fueled a common opinion that the end of the war was near. The Northern press carried this optimism to its readers, and the *Atlantic Monthly* proudly proclaimed in its January issue that the New Year was "the Beginning of the End."[1] *Harper's Weekly* and *Frank Leslie's Illustrated Journal* brought forth a plethora of stories and illustrations describing the seemingly endless Union advances and victories. The navy was portrayed as invincible and its primary inland fleet, the Mississippi Squadron, as unstoppable, able to pursue the enemy, wherever he might be hiding. The Northern press lionized Union commanders, even mediocre political generals.

As the winter progressed into January, Union strategists rode this wave of optimism. At their disposal was a war machine that was battle tested and becoming larger by the day. The Northern factories were producing war matériel at ever increasing rates, and these vital supplies were reaching giant supply depots prepared for field use in new campaigns. Railroads and troop transports allowed great numbers of troops to be dispatched with relatively short notice, moved or transferred from one theater to another in a matter of days.

On the other side, the Confederacy appeared to be coming apart at the seams. Its armies were shrinking by attrition. The vital supply lines from Texas and Louisiana with their huge pipeline of cattle, grain, and that most important trading commodity, cotton, had been severed after the fall of Fortress Vicksburg and Port Hudson, cutting off the grandiose-sounding Department of the Trans-Mississippi from the East. Guns, powder, and other items necessary to keep armies running were either manufactured in northwestern Louisiana and eastern Texas or smuggled up from Mexico, but they could no longer be shipped across the Mississippi River to assist the eastern armies.

Manpower was a constant concern for the South, as the relative sizes of field armies illustrate. Robert E. Lee and his magnificent Army of Northern Virginia fielded approximately 38,000 effectives against a tenacious Army of the Potomac with 73,000 men.[2] The Army of Tennessee faced 2-to-1 odds after being pushed from its sanctuaries at Chattanooga by Major General Ulysses S. Grant.[3] Confederate troops west of the Mississippi River were scattered across northern Louisiana and southwestern Arkansas and throughout eastern Texas. On paper the number of cavalry available, particularly in Texas regiments, appeared to match the hordes of Ghengis Khan, but in fact, most of these western units were dismounted and fought as infantry. Confederate troops were spread so thinly on both sides of the Mississippi River that only guerrilla-style raiders operated against the vast, numerically superior Union forces in hit-and-run attacks. When Major General William T. Sherman, posing an obvious threat and taunting the Confederates, marched his forces out of Vicksburg and crossed the state of Mississippi to attack Meridian, he met almost no opposition on the way.

It was at this point in the dichotomy of fortunes of the Union and the Confederacy that the Union High Command planned the coming year's campaigns. The number of targets thought to be worth taking occupied a short list. In order of importance they were Richmond, Atlanta, Mobile, and Shreveport.[4] Charleston, as the origin of the rebellion, should have been included, but it could not be taken until Atlanta was secured; it was already under siege from the U.S. Navy, however, and landward pressure from a fallen Atlanta would seal its fate. Richmond and Atlanta, then, were obviously the most important targets. Attacks on these cities were designed to draw out the two largest Confederate field armies and, it was hoped, lead to their destruction by splitting Confederate resources and effectively strangling major urban areas remaining under Rebel control east of the Appalachians. Mobile, the last deepwater port on the Gulf of Mexico in Confederate hands, was also a major prize. It was a constant worry to Union strategists since it was well fortified and protected by mines—called torpedoes at that time—and the large ironclad CSS *Tennessee*. Mobile offered the Confederates the potential of disrupting vital Union supply lines, either to New Orleans by possibly breaking the blockade or to the north once the drive for Atlanta began. Mobile thus figured promi-nently in the Union plans, not so much for what it was but for what it could do.

The fourth target on the list was Shreveport, the capital of Confederate Louisiana, headquarters of the Army of the Trans-Mississippi, the yard for a fledgling riverine naval force, and the nexus of a thriving small-scale military industrial complex[5] fed by regional manufacturing centers in Houston, Tyler, Marshall, and Jefferson, all in Texas. Confederate units in Louisiana, Texas, Ar-kansas, and the Indian Territories of Oklahoma and Arizona all answered to Shreveport. Located on the west bank of the Red River in extreme northwestern Louisiana, the city served as the head of the Texas Trail, the cattle and migrant road that led westward pio-neers to southern and western Texas, and was also the major route of goods and supplies coming from Mexico. Before the annexation of Texas into the Union in 1845, Shreveport had been the westernmost city in the United States. At the time of the 1864 cam-paign its population was about 12,000, including refugees from eastern and southern Louisiana and from Arkansas and Missouri. It had not yet celebrated its thirtieth birthday.

Nevertheless, Shreveport was so far removed from the fields of action that one could rightly wonder why it made the target list. Surely, if the major Confederate field commands east of the Missis-sippi were neutralized and the large urban centers brought under Federal control, any forces west of the great river would simply shrivel up and die, following the old adage "Kill the head of the snake and the body will follow." This argument was brought forth in Union high circles but was almost completely ignored until the momentum of events was such that it could not be halted.

Why Shreveport? Certainly the presence there of a Confeder-ate field army that had been largely uncontested was a major rea-son. Moreover, it was a Rebel capital, and two state capitals in exile (Missouri's at Marshall, Texas, and Arkansas's at Old Washington, both within sixty miles of Shreveport) were nearby. But the over-riding reason for the campaign was the existence of cotton.

The Red River valley in Louisiana, southwestern Arkansas, and deep eastern Texas, the greatest cotton-producing area of the Con-federacy, had given itself a grand moniker: the Upper Cotton King-dom. The rich, deep, sandy alluvial soil of the Red River was the most perfect cotton-producing region in North America. The weather in 1863 had been kind, rainy at the beginning of the growing season but not too wet; then, as the cotton plants matured, a dry spell ensured a bumper crop. By late winter of 1863–64, tens of thousands of cotton bales had been harvested by plantation slaves and processed at hundreds of local gins, then moved by wagons to landings; they were sitting on the banks of the Red River and its tributaries and distributary streams, ready for shipment southward. In addition, late cotton crops were still growing and had not yet been harvested. The existence of all this "white gold" was the lure that added Shreveport to the target list, for cotton was a great economic incentive to the North, particularly the textile mills of New England, which were starving for their staff of life.

In short, cotton—or the lack of it—played a key role in the early planning of the Red River Campaign. The Union invasion of the Lower Mississippi in 1862 had had other objectives as well; the closing of the Mississippi River to the Confederates and the capture of New Orleans, the largest city in the South, had certainly been priorities. But the chance to capture a huge supply of cotton and bring the New England mills back on line was a tremendous political opportunity.[6] President Abraham Lincoln needed New England for the 1864 elections. Its favorite sons, political generals Benjamin Butler and Nathaniel Prentiss Banks, were the senior-ranking field officers in the Union army, and both were politically ambitious. Lincoln realized he had to keep New England pacified and alleviate the cotton shortage as well as carry on the business of ending the rebellion.

The primary source of cotton was the South, and the war had cut off this source. In the textile industry, a major player in the New England economy, the lack of cotton had created massive layoffs. Of the almost 5,000,000 spindles in the mills in New England before the war, only 25 percent were operating by 1862.[7] The capture of New Orleans had yielded only 27,000 bales, a drastic reduction from the 2,000,000 bales before the invasion.[8] That New Orleans was the receiving point, not the producing center, for cotton from the Mississippi Valley and its tributaries came as a tremendous shock to the Union strategists. Cotton had to be obtained, and the general who procured it would reap tremendous political rewards. Who better to perform this civic duty than a native son of Massachusetts?

The seeds of the Red River Campaign had been planted even before the New Orleans expedition led by Benjamin F. Butler, commanding general of the Department of New England, headquartered in Boston. Politically astute, the political general from Massachusetts had higher aspirations, and his benefactors were monitoring his career for advancement. Butler was not an original thinker, but he certainly knew how to jump on a bandwagon and make the most of a situation. As the cotton sources dried up in 1861 and New England politicians, bankers, and mill owners clamored to the president for relief, it is not surprising that Butler rose to the top of Lincoln's list. The President had been led to believe—incorrectly, as shown by later events—that the German immigrant farmers of the hill country of Texas were pro-Union and would stage a revolt against their Confederate leaders if the opportunity arose.[9] Since cotton shortage could be alleviated only by liberating cotton-producing areas and bringing them back into the Union fold, Butler suggested that an amphibious invasion at some point along the Texas coast would bring about the anticipated counterrevolution by German patriots in the Texas hill country.[10]

Butler did not know that others had similar ideas, that some members of Lincoln's cabinet had been promoting it as a remedy to the faltering support for the administration among New England power brokers. At the lead in these discussions were Secretary of State William H. Seward, Secretary of War Edwin M. Stanton, and Secretary of the Treasury Salmon P. Chase. In August 1861, Major General George B. McClellan submitted for President Lincoln's review a memorandum outlining his opinions on future campaigns to be conducted by the Union army and navy. Among them, McClellan listed a project that in his words "has often been suggested and which always recommended itself to my judgment, . . . a movement . . . up Red River and Western Texas for the purpose of protecting and developing the latent Union and free-state sentiment well-known to predominate in Western Texas."[11]

Nor did Butler know that on November 12, 1861, the naval commander David Dixon Porter had submitted to Secretary of the Navy Gideon Welles a detailed plan for the rapid capture of New Orleans.[12] This plan was presented to President Lincoln just a few days later and then submitted to General McClellan with Lincoln's hearty endorsement. Porter's plan was scheduled for the following January. Butler took his idea to Secretary of War Stanton on January 15, 1862, and a few days later, Stanton asked McClellan for his opinion. McClellan turned the idea down, most likely because he wanted to lead such as invasion himself but was mired down in his own actions in Virginia.[13]

Learning of this apparent betrayal, Butler circumvented McClellan to secure the proper authorizations. He proposed that instead of landing in Texas, the expedition would cut at the heart of the Confederacy by denying the Rebels the use of the Mississippi River and capturing the great prize of New Orleans.[14] Butler, ever the opportunist, had changed his affections from the relatively easy invasion of open Texas coastal areas to a much more difficult Mississippi River attack. Consequently, when Porter's plan was approved, Butler was chosen to lead the land forces. Admiral David G. Farragut was to command the naval forces, with the brash young Porter leading the fleet of mortar schooners. As these vessels approached New Orleans, they pounded the forts below the city, neutralizing the lower defenses and forcing the metropolis into submission. New Orleans fell with ease on April 25, 1862. The late historian Charles Dufour described the fall of the great city as "the night the war was lost." This bold stroke severed the bread bowl of the Confederacy west of the Mississippi River from the main action east of the river. It would be another three years, but the beginning of the end of the war was achieved with the fall of the Crescent City.

At the same time, Lincoln was dealing with another situation upriver, this one from a political ally. Major General John A. McClernand, a political general like Butler, had been given authority to raise an army of volunteer soldiers from Illinois, Indiana, and Iowa with the seizing of Vicksburg as his objective. Fortress Vicksburg was denying the Union free access to the Mississippi River and proving its status as the "Gibralter of America." The campaign to seize the city had virtually halted, and Major General Ulysses S. Grant was gaining no ground as he occupied his men with attempts to bypass the great gun emplacements in what became known as the "water experiments." Grant viewed McClernand not as a colleague but as a threat and a distraction. Their backgrounds, styles, demeanor, and political ambitions were not compatible, and although Grant was nominally McClernand's superior, McClernand was allowed to operate under an almost independent command. Eventually Lincoln acquiesced to Grant's wishes and, after Vicksburg was invested in siege, dismissed McClernand from the campaign.

Meanwhile, Butler had begun to show his dictatorial side in dealing with the citizens of New Orleans, this at the very time Lincoln was hoping that Louisiana would be the first Southern state to be repatriated. That hope had been compromised by Butler's infantile tantrums in handling a rebellious New Orleans. Lincoln could not fire him—he was too politically powerful—but had him removed and given a field command in Virginia. Consequently, Lincoln was challenged to find a successor who would follow his ideas and not be a temperamental maverick. For practical reasons he chose another political general, Nathaniel Prentiss Banks.

Major General Banks was rakishly handsome, a fastidious dresser, and a major political heavyweight. He was honest but authoritarian, with no tolerance for those questioning his judgment, even career military officers. To his discredit, he was vain and at times showed exquisitely timed poor judgment that merited questioning.[15] Like Butler before him, Banks came from Massachusetts and clearly understood New England politics. He had grown up in Waltham and as a youth had worked in a textile mill as a bobbin boy. Banks had risen from the position of a lowly mill worker to become a self-made man (if there is such a thing in politics), serving as a three-term governor of Massachusetts. He had also served in Congress, even becoming Speaker of the House, and had aspirations of running against Abraham Lincoln in the 1864 presidential elections. He was arguably the most popular military figure from New England; the northeastern press loved him and curried his favor; the textile mill owners had in him a natural ally and were his patrons. In a region where Abraham Lincoln was at best distrusted, Banks offered his wealthy backers an alluring alternative. In return, Banks always gave preferential treatment and access to cotton brokers or factors, even to allowing them to accompany him on campaigns.

Although Banks had showed some panache in his first test of battle, against the legendary Stonewall Jackson at the Battle of Cedar Mountain, he became trapped and was rescued from capture only by the timely arrival of reinforcements.[16] His next assignment was as commander of the defenses of Washington. When Butler's position in New Orleans became untenable, Banks's choice as the replacement provided several apparent solutions. First, Lincoln could put someone in Louisiana who understood how to work politics, help to quell a volatile situation, and perhaps rejuvenate the Reconstruction process at New Orleans. Second, Banks could do a better job of cooperating with Grant in securing the Mississippi in Federal hands. Third, Banks would be able to calm down the New England mill owners and, it was hoped, increase the amount of cotton sent to the mills. Fourth, and perhaps most politically expedient, Banks would be removed far from his New England political support and thus less a threat to Lincoln in the upcoming elections just over a year away. Grant had hoped that Banks would use troops from the Department of the Gulf to assist him in reducing Vicksburg. Banks cooperated by investing Port Hudson in siege—and being ineffectual. Port Hudson would surrender to Banks only after the surrender of Vicksburg on July 4, 1863.

Major General Nathaniel P. Banks and staff. Library of Congress, Prints and Photographs Division, USZ62-7007

Pressure was placed on Banks, as it had been on his predecessor, to plant the flag in Texas, and now events outside the control of Washington or New Orleans increased that pressure.[17] Even before Vicksburg fell, French troops landed in Mexico and quickly installed Maximilian as emperor on June 7, renewing fears in Washington that the French and perhaps the British would enter into open cooperation with and perhaps even formal recognition of the Confederates.[18] Planting the U.S. flag on Texas soil therefore became a political necessity, not simply a presidential wish. Once the Mississippi was open to Federal navigation, then, letters from President Lincoln and communiqués from General-in-Chief Henry W. "Old Brains" Halleck ordered Banks to move forward. Halleck had been a supporter of the Texas invasion since 1861. Nearing the end of a long career, he was a master at delivering orders that could be read several different ways. If the recipient succeeded, Halleck would share in the glory; if he failed, the recipient would bear the sole blame.[19]

In this case, Banks seems to have agreed with Grant that Mobile was a much more important target; he later said that Halleck had pressured him into pursuing an attack on Texas.[20] Halleck had proposed an expedition up the Red River, but Banks countered that Sabine Pass at the mouth of the Sabine River would serve as a better base from which to attack Houston and move from there into the hill country of East Texas.[21] On August 31, 1863, Banks ordered Major General William Buel Franklin to load one brigade from the First Division of the Nineteenth Corps (troops that had accompanied Banks to Louisiana) onto transports and, with the accompaniment of naval gunboats, land at and secure Sabine Pass.[22] The small fleet arrived at the pass on September 7 and was met by some fifty men with five guns dug in at a mud fort. The little force neutralized two of the gunboats and forced the rest to retire. The transports never had a chance to disgorge their soldiers on the mudflats, and the entire expeditionary force was compelled to return to New Orleans.[23] Banks blamed the fiasco on the navy.[24] Neither the army nor navy was blameless, having invested little time in planning this foray, but Banks's very vocal blame of the navy caused a rift between him and Admiral Farragut and Admiral Porter. That distrust would only increase in the following months.

In late October, Banks sent Franklin on another invasion attempt, this one even less planned than the first. The idea was to march overland through the Bayou Teche country and into the prairies of southwestern Louisiana to a point somewhere on the Sabine River where the expedition could ford or otherwise cross into Texas. Franklin picked his way across south-central Louisiana, at that time very sparsely populated and consequently offering his men almost no chance to forage for needed supplies. The column made it to just west of Opelousas in St. Landry Parish and then turned around, unsure of what to do.[25]

During this trek the navy sent units up the Ouachita and Red rivers to divert attention from Franklin's column; the gunboats did little damage. There was also some action in southern Louisiana in St. Mary Parish. In conjunction with these disparate movements, an amphibious force landed at several points along the lower Texas coast. Banks reported to his superiors that "the flag of the Union floated over Texas to-day at meridian precisely" when it was planted into the sand dunes at Brazos Santiago.[26] Landings were also successful at Brownsville, Matagorda Bay, Aransas Pass, and Rio Grande City.[27] Banks instructed his occupation troops to send reports to Washington on every minor matter, and it seemed to leaders there that the undertaking was a phenomenal success. In reality, the flag of the Union was flying over uninhabited sand dunes on barrier islands and the total effect on the Confederate state of Texas was inconsequential, but the commander of the Department of the Gulf was very pleased with himself.

Banks had not informed Halleck of these actions in advance, however, and Halleck was not happy to hear of the "success."[28] The general-in-chief had indicated that Banks should attack up the Red River, and Banks had ignored those orders (or perhaps found them characteristically unclear). But Halleck was the ranking officer in the Union army and headquartered in Washington where he could influence policy and planning. Machiavellian at times, he now brought his considerable political skills to getting what he wanted.

Halleck fired off letters to Banks detailing his displeasure (forcing Banks to reevaluate his position).[29] He then wrote letters to Sherman, who was engaged in raising havoc in eastern Mississippi, and Major General Frederick Steele, the newly appointed commander of the Department of Arkansas, soliciting their opinions about a Red River expedition.[30] Steele's department adjoined the target area, and Sherman, very enthusiastic, wanted to command the force personally and operated for a time under the assumption that he would do so. He had earlier spent about eighteen months as the superintendent of the Louisiana Seminary of Learning and Military Academy in Pineville, across the Red River from Alexandria.[31] He knew more about the area than any of the officers involved and could have provided much valuable information, particularly to the navy.

Halleck next approached Grant, flushed with victory at Chattanooga.[32] Grant and Banks at this time were both in favor of a move on Mobile. Grant was formulating what would become Sherman's Atlanta Campaign. Banks could almost see what the headlines announcing the capture of a city of Mobile's stature would do for his presidential hopes. But Halleck wrote a skillful letter insinuating that President Lincoln thought a Red River expedition more politically important than the capture of Mobile and implying that Banks's coastal positions in Texas were part of the grand scheme to recover Texas. Lincoln wrote Banks a congratulatory letter on Christmas Eve, 1863, perhaps at the urging of Halleck.[33] Grant tried to lobby for the Mobile campaign over a Red River expedition by circumventing Halleck, but he failed to secure support.[34]

Grant could clearly see several uses for a Mobile campaign. It would protect his right flank and deny the Confederates the use of the deepwater port. It would free naval resources for use elsewhere. Once the troops needed for this campaign were available for further action, the distance to be traveled to join Sherman in Georgia would be relatively short. He could also clearly see the negative side of a push up the Red River. The troops would be heading in the opposite direction of his plans for attack, and if the campaign became mired, he would lose their usefulness in the East where he needed them most. Sherman wanted to command it, but Grant wanted Sherman to rip up Georgia. Even if the campaign were a success, the troops would be hard pressed to join their parent units in time for the campaign to take Atlanta. Finally, Grant could not help but see a major drawback to this Louisiana foray: what was its goal? If the expedition reached Shreveport and the Confederates did not come out and fight, where would the climax come? If the Rebels decided to fight in the pine hills of Texas east of the Sabine River, how would the army pursue them? How would the lines of supply by configured? Where would supply bases by established and would they be safe? What if tens of thousands of men were strung out deep in enemy territory and then cut off? Where would the blame be leveled?

Although these were questions that should have been asked at the cabinet level and in the general staff, Grant did not want to create a deep divide with Halleck and therefore acquiesced to his pressure. Banks also came on board when he was made aware of versions of the correspondence among the other generals.[35] Finally, Banks received several letters from Lincoln urging him to bring about elections in the free southern part of Louisiana.[36] Lincoln wanted a Louisiana congressional delegation loyal to him in the next elections. Banks thought he could turn such elections to his own benefit. By the third week of January 1864, the bobbin boy–now–general had turned his boundless enthusiasm for detail and grandiose planning to accomplishing Lincoln's wishes for a new Louisiana political order, a rejuvenation of the New England textile industry, and a preparation for his own bid for the presidency.

NOTES

1. "The Beginning of the End, A Greeting for the New Year," *Atlantic Monthly* 3 (1864): 112–22.

2. Douglas Southall Freeman, *R. E. Lee: A Biography*, 4 vols. (New York, 1934–35), 3:253; U.S. War Department, *The War of the Rebellion: A Compilation of the Official Records of the Union and Confederate Armies*, 128 vols. (Washington, DC, 1880–1901), 34:462 (hereafter cited as *O.R.*; all references are to series 1 and part 1 of the specified volume unless otherwise identified.

3. Joseph E. Johnston, *Narrative of Military Operations* (New York, 1874), 272–86.

4. Ludwell Johnson, *Red River Campaign: Politics and Cotton in the Civil War* (Kent, OH, 1993), 80.

5. Map, "Shreveport and Environs," 1864, by Major Richard Venable, CSA, Jerome Gilmer Papers, Southern Historical Collection University of North Carolina, Chapel Hill (hereafter cited as Venable Map).

6. *New York Times*, October 30, 1862.

7. Benjamin F. Butler, memorandum dated January 1862, Edwin M. Stanton Papers, Division of Manuscripts, Library of Congress, Washington, DC.

8. *De Bow's Review*, n.s. 2 (1866): 419.

9. Frederick L. Olmstead, *A Journey Through Texas* (New York, 1857), 140–41, 172–83, 358–60, 414–15, 428–41; Laura W. Roper, "Frederick Law Olmstead and the Western Texas Free-Soil Movement," *American Historical Review* 56 (1950–51): 58–64.

10. Butler memorandum dated January 19, 1862, Stanton Papers.

11. George B. McClellan, *McClellan's Own Story* (New York, 1887), 103–4.

12. Robert U. Johnson and Clarence C. Buel, eds., *Battles and Leaders of the Civil War*, 4 vols. (New York, 1887–88) 2:23–25; David Dixon Porter, *Incidents and Anecdotes of the Civil War* (New York, 1891), 63–66.

13. *O.R.* 6, 677–78.

14. Butler memorandum dated January 1862, Stanton Papers.

15. Johnson, *Red River Campaign*, 20.

16. Fred H. Harrington, *Fighting Politician: Major General N. P. Banks* (Philadelphia, 1948).

17. *O.R.* 15, 590.

18. *O.R.*, ser. 3, 3, 522; Senate Executive Documents, no. 2, 38th Cong., 2d sess., 459–60, 470.

19. Adam Badeau, *Military History of Ulysses S. Grant*, 8 vols. (New York, 1868), 2:70.

20. U.S. Congress, *Report of the Joint Committee on the Conduct of the War, 1863–1866: The Red River Expedition*, 38th Cong., 2d sess., 1865, 5 (hereafter cited as *JCCW*).

21. Ibid.; *O.R.* 26, 673.

22. *O.R.* 26, 287–88.

23. Ibid., 288–97.

24. Nathaniel Banks to his wife, dated September 22, 1863, Banks Papers, Essex Institute, Salem, MA; microfilm copy at University of Texas at Austin.

25. *O.R.* 26, 292; Richard Taylor, *Destruction and Reconstruction: Personal Experiences in the Civil War* (New York, 1890), 150.

26. *O.R.* 26, 397.

27. Ibid., 20–21.

28. Ibid., 683, 807.

29. Ibid., 834–35.

30. Ibid., 683, 807; *O.R.* 34, pt. 2, 267.

31. William T. Sherman, *Memoirs of General W. T. Sherman*, 2 vols. (New York, 1892), 1:172–93.

32. *O.R.* 34, pt. 2, 46; *JCCW*, 227.

33. Abraham Lincoln, *The Collected Works of Abraham Lincoln*, 9 vols., ed. Roy P. Basler (New Brunswick, NJ, 1953), 7:90.

34. C. A. Dana, *Recollections of the Civil War* (New York, 1898), 103.

35. *O.R.* 26, 888–90.

36. Lincoln, *Collected Works*, 6:364–65, 7:1–2, 90.

CHAPTER TWO

CONFEDERATE DEFENSES ON THE RED RIVER, 1863–64

AFTER THE SUMMER of 1863 the Confederacy west of the Mississippi River was isolated. The Union navy heavily patrolled the great river, severing all but limited contact to the east. Union armies also held strategic positions to the west. New Orleans had been occupied since 1862, and Union forces headquartered in Little Rock held northern and central Arkansas. In Louisiana, with the Union Department of the Gulf located in New Orleans, the Union army controlled Baton Rouge and the bayou country as well as prairies in the southwestern part of the state. The Confederates controlled all of Texas (except some barrier islands), most of the Indian Territory (in what is today the state of Oklahoma), southern Arkansas, and northern and central Louisiana. The Confederate area, officially termed the Department of the Trans-Mississippi, was headquartered in Shreveport, which served as the capital of Confederate Louisiana and as the nexus for the rudimentary military-industrial complex west of the Mississippi.

An understanding of the geography of the region is essential to an understanding of the defensive strategy chosen by the Confederate command. Shreveport had been in existence for less than thirty years and occupied a roughly diamond-shaped plateau river terrace of approximately one square mile. With the exception of Grand Ecore in Natchitoches Parish (about sixty straight-line miles downstream), the Shreveport terraces occupied the last high ground on the Red River before it emptied into the Mississippi River some 230 river miles downstream. The city was bordered on the east by the Red River, on the north by Cross Bayou, on the south by a shallow river overflow remnant called Silver Lake, and on the west by several parallel rows of ridges running north to south.[1] These ridges, almost the height of the plateau, were separated by valleys filled with pine forests or boggy stream bottoms. The northern portions of the ridges stopped abruptly at the narrow flood plain of Cross

15

Bayou. By 1864, Shreveport had developed a central business area intermixed with homes, and the town had begun to expand on its western side into the valley leading to the first of the parallel ridges. This low area, once a swamp created by Cross Bayou, was called St. Paul's Bottoms after St. Paul's Methodist Church located there. To the south of the town and across Silver Lake was another high plateau land consisting of rolling hills that eventually turned into the flat fields bordering the Wallace Bayou swamp.

Just below Shreveport (and within its present corporate limits) was the headwaters of Bayou Pierre, a major distributary stream flowing out and roughly paralleling the Red River until its water reentered the river just above Grand Ecore. Bayou Pierre, like most of the other water bodies in the Red River valley, had been created by a giant logjam called the Great Raft. The raft was the result of the river's sinuosity and the sandy composition of its banks: as trees collapsed into the stream from the unstable banks, the current carried them along until they collected on bars or snagged into the bed, forming an interlaced tangle of islands. Over time, other trees landed on these islands, colonizing them and creating new areas for the accumulation of debris. As the raft grew and the water coming down the stream did not diminish, parallel streams and lakes were formed. Among these were Caddo Lake, Cross Lake, Lake Bistineau, Bayou Pierre, Cross Bayou, Twelve Mile Bayou, Cane River, Flat River, Willow Chute, and Red Chute. Captain Henry Miller Shreve received a contract from the United States in the early 1830s to clear the raft and had removed most of it by the 1840s, but the tendency of the river was (and still remains) to rebuild the raft.

Approximately nineteen miles south of the original site of Shreveport was located a manmade water channel which is today called Tone's Bayou. It was created in 1851 by James Gilmer, a wealthy planter who was hostile to Shreveport. In 1850 he had brought several construction slaves called "mechanics" from another of his plantations to build a town he wanted to call Red Bluff. The town was never built, but the means to starve Shreveport of commercial traffic was. The channel Gilmer constructed, a shunt between the Red River and Bayou Pierre extending some 5,100 feet, used an ancient crossover channel that had been blocked by Henry Miller Shreve in 1843.[2] The fall in elevation from the east end to the west end was seven to eight feet, and by the time of the Civil War the waterway was a great success. It had assumed the name of a local resident, Antoine Pourier's or Tone's (a shortened form of

Antoine's) Bayou, and it drew off 75 percent of the flow from the Red River.[3]

In 1860 the state of Louisiana enacted legislation to remove the problem of Tone's Bayou. It proposed to purchase a riparian right-of-way at Scopini's Plantation northeast of the bayou and to remove a long elliptical loop from the river. The resulting work, begun in 1859, created Scopini Island, although the cut was not used until 1862.[4] The parallel streams, the manmade shunt, and the raft lakes provided navigation opportunities that would both aid and worry the Confederates in their efforts to defend the Red River valley.

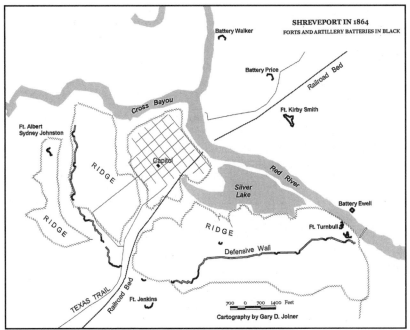

Map of Shreveport, its geography, and the inner defenses in 1864. The map is based on the Confederate engineer's by Major Richard Venable.

By the spring of 1864, Shreveport had a thriving war-based industry. With little or no help coming from east of the Mississippi River, the city had to be self-sufficient. Fortunately the region's ample natural resources and antebellum infrastructure allowed it to be so. Outlying military installations, including several in East Texas, were also directly linked to the army command in Shreveport. Arsenals, foundries, a powder mill and magazine were established in Marshall, Texas, and a powder house and warehouses in

Jefferson. Tyler housed an ammunition factory, and ordnance works were founded in Houston and San Antonio.[5] Shreveport itself boasted at least one foundry, a powder house, an arsenal, two sawmills, and corn storage sheds, all located either along the south bank of the Red River or near Cross Bayou.

This industrial base served two purposes: the first, of course, to support the Confederate army in the region; the second, to support the naval construction and repair yard in Block 66 of the original plat of the town of Shreveport.[6] The Confederates built the ironclad CSS *Missouri* here and also repaired the high-speed ram CSS *William S. Webb* after its capture of the USS *Indianola*. It was from this yard that the *Webb* would begin its famous dash down the Red and Mississippi rivers near the end of the war.[7] The yard was also the home of the tender *Mary T.*, sometimes also called the *J. A. Cotton* or the *Cotton II*.[8] The *Missouri* would be the last Confederate ironclad to surrender in home waters, the man who oversaw its construction and later served as its captain was Lieutenant Jonathon Carter, CSN. The iron armor for the *Missouri* was obtained by ripping up the rails from a segment of the prewar Southern Pacific Railroad tracks west of Shreveport.

The most secret operation at the Shreveport Navy Yard was the construction of five submarines for the defense of the Red River. One of the vessels was dismantled and shipped to Houston, but the remaining four stayed in Shreveport until the end of the war. They were built by the Singer Submarine Corporation, whose engineers had worked on the CSS *H. L. Hunley*, the first submarine to sink a boat in wartime: the Union sloop *Housatonic*. These engineers were sent to Shreveport when the siege of Charleston became a foregone conclusion. The Shreveport submarines were near sisters of the *Hunley*, having a length of 40 feet and a breadth of just under 4 feet.[9] They were never used, but that the Union navy certainly knew about them is clear from naval orders issued at the time.[10]

West of the Mississippi River, Shreveport was the only Confederate administrative center worth striking. Its importance to the Confederacy was indicated by its involvement with or proximity to governments of other Confederate states west of the Mississippi. The state government-in-exile from Missouri was located first in Shreveport and then moved to Marshall, Texas, forty miles to the west. The Confederate capital of Arkansas was located in Old Washington, seventy-five miles to the north.

On March 7, 1863, Lieutenant General Edmund Kirby Smith arrived in Alexandria, downstream from Shreveport about 112 miles, and took over formal command of the Trans-Mississippi Department.[11] His headquarters moved to Shreveport in May 1863, however, when General Banks threatened Alexandria.[12] The move was reasonable, since Shreveport's remote location provided a longer distance from a Union invasion from the south; it would also allow a shorter response time should a Union operation originate at Little Rock. The commander of the Western District of Louisiana, Major General Richard Taylor, had suggested Shreveport as a suitable site from the beginning of his tenure in the state, but General Smith initially opposed it on the advice of a personal friend (and his staff surgeon), Dr. Sol Smith of Alexandria.

Among General Smith's staff members was the recently promoted Brigadier General William R. Boggs, who had been with him in Kentucky. Boggs had graduated fourth in the United States Military Academy's class of 1853. Of his classmates, James B. McPherson, Philip H. Sheridan, and John M. Schofield all became Union generals, and John Bell Hood became a high-ranking Confederate general. (An interesting aside: at West Point, Boggs had befriended a younger man who later gained fame as an artist, James McNeill Whistler.)[13]

One of Boggs's mentors was Dennis Hart Mahan, professor of military and civil engineering. All cadets who attended the academy after 1833 and before the war studied under Mahan. Thus, virtually all Civil War engineering officers (typically the top 10 percent of the graduating class) who graduated from West Point after 1835 were inculcated with Mahan's ideas. His *Treatise on Field Fortification, Containing Instructions on the Methods of Laying Out, Constructing, Defending and Attacking Intrenchments, With the General Outlines Also of the Arrangement, the Attack and Defense of Permanent Fortifications* was first published in 1836 and used until well after the Civil War—the bible of field fortifications.[14] The similarity in field fortifications throughout the battlefields of the Civil War is a testament to Mahan's preeminence in military engineering, including those erected in Louisiana under Boggs. Encouraged at West Point to enter the engineering corps, Boggs became an engineering and ordnance officer. He spent the war as a staff officer and was never given a field command. In Louisiana, however, as General Kirby Smith's chief of staff, he was assigned the task of creating a defense of the Red River and its tributaries, especially the Ouachita and its lower portions, known as the Black River.[15]

With his evident support, Smith began to consider bringing slave labor both into public works projects and into the army as early as September 1863.[16] Boggs made an inspection trip of the valley to determine possible positions and methods of defense. To

The engineers of the Trans-Mississippi Department who served under General Boggs. *Standing left to right*: David French Boyd, major of engineers; D. C. Proctor, First Louisiana Engineers; unidentified; and William Freret. Seated are Richard M. Venable, chief topographic engineer; H. T. Douglas, colonel of engineers; and Octave Hopkins, First Louisiana Engineers. Miller, *The Photographic History of the Civil War*, 1:105

protect the Ouachita he built a fort at Trinity, near Harrisonburg; this emplacement was known as Fort Beauregard. He also began the entrenchment and fortifications of the high bluffs at the village of Grand Ecore, which served as the port town of Natchitoches, four miles to its southwest.[17] Further, after much discussion and bickering between Generals Smith and Taylor, Boggs selected a position near the town of Marksville in Avoyelles Parish for a lower Red River fortification. Fort DeRussy, named for the engineer (Colonel L. G. DeRussy) who constructed it, was located on a hairpin turn in the river where, if properly armed and manned, it could thwart gunboats. Boggs designed the fort with 40-foot-thick walls standing 12 feet high, the entire structure surrounded by a deep, wide ditch.[18] A Union boat captain, Thomas O. Selfridge, later noted in his memoirs that the fort's casemate batteries had been strengthened with railroad iron.[19] Its final armament consisted of eight heavy siege guns and two field pieces.[20]

Sketch of Fort DeRussy from the April 30, 1864, edition of *Frank Leslie's Illustrated Newspaper*. The view in this engraving is somewhat distorted by elevation. The river casemate is clearly seen in the foreground (with two large cannon ports), and the bombproof is the open area immediately behind it. Engraving in the collection of the author

Taylor, whose method of operations was movement and maneuver, had running animosity with Smith throughout 1863 and the first half of 1864. He disliked field fortifications, believing that such devices could become traps for his own men. (Later, he would contemptuously call Fort DeRussy "our Red River Gibraltar.") Instead, he wanted to build an obstruction that would allow the giant logjam known as the Great Raft to recreate itself, thinking that only a complete jamming of the river would protect his flanks from a Union naval incursion up the Red River.[21]

Rear Admiral David Dixon Porter, Union naval commander of the Red River Campaign, wrote after the war that the obstruction was located eight or nine miles south of Fort DeRussy, near the "Bend of the Rappiones," in a hairpin turn of the river.[22] It appeared to be very formidable. Heavy wooden pilings made from trees felled around the site were driven into the streambed completely across the river.[23] To these was added a second line, shorter in height. The two lines were braced together and strengthened with crossbanded ties. Attached to this structure was a raft of trees and timber which rose from the floor of the stream to the surface. In addition, wrote Porter, the Confederates cut down "a forest of trees" upstream, allowing them to pile up behind the structure, and also drove pilings into the riverbed downstream from this dam, extending 200 yards at what appeared to be close but random intervals.[24]

Boggs continued to focus on the defense of the Red River by scouting out and preparing positions. There were no defensible positions between Fort DeRussy and Alexandria, in fact, no fortifications were prepared in Alexandria until after the 1864 expedition. In late 1864 and early 1865, Forts Randolph and Buhlow were built at Alexandria, but Boggs gambled on Fort DeRussy and ample land forces under General Taylor to save the central Louisiana town. His primary mission, of course, was to protect Shreveport.

The first truly high ground upriver from Alexandria was the 120-foot bluff at Grand Ecore. Boggs was not the first military engineer to see its value. The hill and bluff complex there had been the site of a military camp and fortification during the Mexican War, one emplacement in a vital line of fortifications both guarding the Red River from the Spanish in Texas and serving as a marshaling point for the forces of General Zachary Taylor (the future president of the United States and father of General Richard Taylor). Among the young officers serving in the complex of fortifications centered in the area of Fort Jessup, west of the river toward Texas, was Ulysses S. Grant.[25] Boggs began fortifying the hills and bluffs with his usual vigor, an action Smith at first supported.[26] Again, however, Taylor did not like the idea of having his forces hemmed into the hill complex with no room to maneuver. On October 5, Smith ordered Boggs to remove the two 9-inch guns that had been placed on the bluffs, take them to Shreveport, and cease any further work on the river below the bluffs.[27]

From Grand Ecore upstream to the bluffs south of Shreveport the river narrowed, and the currents were swifter. At various points the banks rose above the surrounding land, but there was no place to construct a commanding fortified position using elevation as the central feature. The Red River valley with the river's great looping

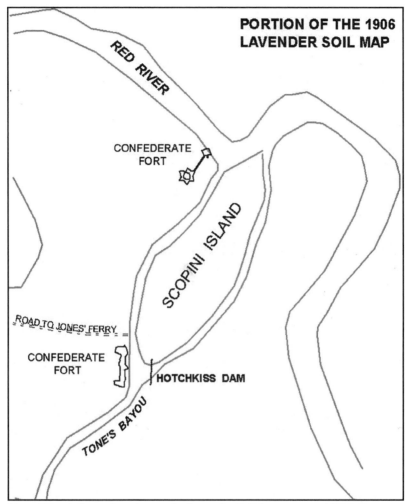

Map of Tone's Bayou based upon the Lavender Soil Survey map of 1906. Cartography by Gary D. Joiner

meanders, obscured parallel channels, distributaries, and oxbow lakes would become the next segment in Boggs's master plan.

James Gilmer's plan to starve Shreveport in 1851 now offered General Boggs the opportunity to lay an elegant trap. Since the Union fleet and army units did not pass by these structures until after the surrender of Shreveport (if at all), there is no official correspondence from the Union side describing them, yet they were perhaps, Boggs's most ingenious achievement.

To understand how his plan worked, one must first recall James Gilmer's activities. Bayou Pierre, an ancient raft channel, exits the Red River just below Coate's Bluff (in what is today the city of Shreveport) and roughly parallels the river, sometimes making great arcing meanders, until it rejoins the river just north of Grand Ecore. When cutting the shunt to make Tone's Bayou, Gilmer used the same method Captain Shreve had used to create islands in the Red River in the 1820s and 1830s. Gilmer let the force and direction of the river's current create the hydrodynamics for him. As the Confederates observed, when in operation, Tone's Bayou removed almost all of the water from the Red River into Bayou Pierre.[28]

Taylor proposed another obstruction upriver between Tone's Bayou and Coushatta Chute (Bayou Coushatta where it joins the Red River near the town of Coushatta), and Smith endorsed this venture.[29] He was concerned, however, with the effect an obstruction at the Narrows would have on his line of communications. Boggs had an additional objection to permanent obstructions in the Red River. As he told Taylor, "This will take nearly all the water from Red River above Grand Ecore, and, owing to the scarcity of wagons, will make it difficult to supply your army from this region."[30]

Nevertheless, Captain (Dr.) Thomas P. Hotchkiss was ordered by the Confederate secretary of war (certainly at the urging of Kirby Smith) to close Tone's Bayou.[31] He did so by building a dam which bore his name.[32] The dam did not, as one might think, close Scopini's cutoff. It was located near the southernmost bend of Scopini Island, the piece of ground formed between Scopini's cutoff and Tone's Bayou.

To guard this vital dam, Boggs built two fortifications, one on either end of Scopini Island.[33] The southern structure, a long artillery battery overlooking the Hotchkiss dam, had a clear field of fire across open ground to the next downstream meander of the Red River. The battery was approximately 175 meters long and shaped like a giant elongated "E." Its northern anchor was a pond that may have once been a borrow pit or a gun emplacement.[34] Lying behind this emplacement was a large infantry encampment, Camp Morgan, designed to provide garrison for the forts.[35] The northern structure was a square-star fortress (a fortification with projecting artillery placements that, viewed from above, appears as a star or snowflake) with a causeway and, apparently, a water battery. It resembled Fort DeRussy in design, though perhaps not

in scale. This emplacement guarded Scopini's cutoff and was designed to provide enfilade fire for the southern battery. The winding river would allow either fortification to assist the other with
covering fire. With Bayou Pierre on one side and the Red River on
the other, a landing force encountering fire from either battery
would disembark troops and head over land. Given the level of the
ground and the cut-in bank of the old river surrounding Scopini
Island, the troops would have to march to an all but impenetrable
river with a swift current and into the face of heavy artillery and
infantry. (The open field objective, the narrow marching front, and
almost nonexistent flanking opportunities were reminiscent of the

This photograph is the only existing scene of Tone's Bayou as it was viewed in
1864 from the Red River. Archives and Special Collections, Noel Memorial Library,
Louisiana State University, Shreveport

Chalmette battlefield and its Rodriguez Canal, the fortification line
for General Andrew Jackson at the Battle of New Orleans in the
War of 1812.) Should the Union army follow the Summer Road up
the west bank of the Red River, Taylor would be able to marshal
his forces behind this line. A portion of the artillery from the defenses in Shreveport as well as all his field artillery would have
been available to him, as well as room to maneuver to his rear.

Although there is no direct on-the-ground evidence, there must
have been an additional obstruction at Scopini's cutoff near the
northern fortification to make this scenario work, for the dam would

have had no impact on the river's flow had the Scopini cutoff been functioning normally. The blockage probably consisted of a raftlike dam, which when blown, one source states, drained the Red River "like pulling the plug out of a bathtub."[36]

Boggs, however, was not satisfied with having this Tone's Bayou defensive system stand alone. His intent was to slow the fleet down first. He knew that if the river level dropped significantly, the Union navy could not bring its heavier-draft boats up through the narrows, so he asked for and received permission to sink one vessel of the Confederate defense fleet below Tone's Bayou. The vessel chosen was the *New Falls City*, then at anchor in or near the mouth of Coushatta Chute. *Ways Packet Directory* lists it as an 880-ton sidewheel packet with a wooden hull 301.3 feet long, a beam 39.7 feet wide, and a draft of 7.6 feet—possibly the largest vessel to navigate the Red River until that time, and certainly one of the largest ever to do so.[37] It was to be not only sunk but wedged across the stream so that a sandbar would form beneath it. The Confederate engineering troops were to place the boat at the foot of Scopini's cutoff, abreast of the river, with its bow and stern resting on opposite banks. The hold was to be filled with earth to stabilize the vessel and crack its keel.[38] The result was an instant version of the Great Raft and was just as effective. Boggs also deployed a chain across the Red River at some point near his trap, possibly above the wreck of the *New Falls City*. The chain was forged at a plantation near Loggy Bayou on the Bossier Parish side of the river.[39] (A portion of it exists today and can be seen at the Mansfield State Commemorative Area Visitors' Center.)

The defensive complex Boggs was commanded to create to protect Shreveport directly was indeed impressive, considering the amount of time it took to construct, the amount of labor (both soldiers and slaves) available, and the fact that the designer was also working on other major fortification projects at various points all along the Red River, as far as several hundred river miles away.

Boggs did not build his defensive line on the central plateau of the town itself but extended his defenses outward, choosing the highest adjacent ridges, hills, and bluffs as anchor points and extending the complex across the Red River to cover the eastern approaches in Bossier Parish. On the Caddo Parish side the anchor forts were linked by defensive walls that resembled levees.[40] Boggs placed artillery batteries on hill, ridge, or bluff tops that were too small for large fortifications. The large forts were combinations of

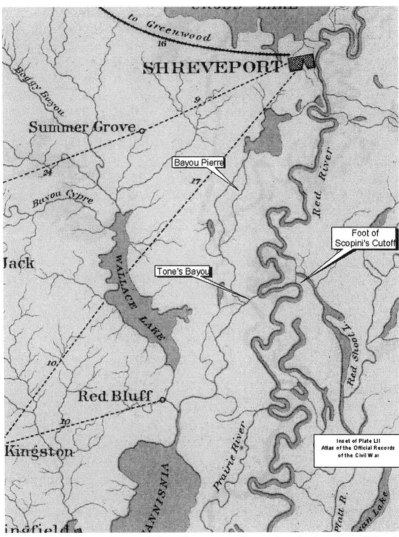

Inset detail of the Red River below Shreveport illustrating the location of Tone's Bayou, the wreck site of the *New Falls City* at the foot of Scopini's Cutoff, and the proximity of Bayou Pierre to the Red River. This map is a portion of folio Plate LII from the original atlas to accompany the *Official Records of the War of the Rebellion*. Original is in the collection of the author

construction types typical of those in Dennis Hart Mahan's text-
book, making full use of the hill lines and interior routes of communication.[41] There were three large anchor forts on the Caddo side
and one on the Bossier side.[42] Beginning at the eastern anchor on
the Caddo side, Boggs established a large fort on the first high
ground north of Grand Ecore, known as Coate's Bluff. It was named
Fort Turnbull, but its local name, attributed to General John
Magruder, was Fort Humbug because of its "Quaker guns": tree
trunks blackened to look like cannon and mounted on wagon
wheels. These were interspersed with real ordnance to give the
impression of an impregnable position. The river in 1864 came to
the foot of the bluff on which the fort was built. It was a large complex and covered several inland bluff lines. Radiating from this fort
were several artillery batteries. To the north, Battery Ewell could
provide crossfire for a position across the river.[43] Due south of Fort
Turnbull, Battery I was located on the southernmost rise of the bluff
structure. West and somewhat north of it was Battery II, situated
on the west side of the bluff complex. Battery III was located on an
extension of the fort's bluff in such a way that it could either cover
the area to the south of the defensive line or be turned to the north
to fire at targets in the river. Battery IV was placed very close to the
Confederate hospital on the high ground above it. These four batteries would most likely have been under the direct control of Fort
Turnbull.

Battery V, on a high hill behind the defensive line, could offer
fire to the south or be turned east to cover targets in the river. Battery VI and two unnumbered batteries faced south to provide support for the next anchor fort, Fort Jenkins, positioned outside the
defensive ring and occupying the highest topographic elevation in
Caddo Parish. The line then proceeded west to Battery VII, at the
southwest corner of the ridgeline extending westward from the river
at Coate's Bluff. Between this bluff and the town of Shreveport lay
Silver Lake, a shallow bog overflow from the Red River. Only one
road entered the town from the south, and Fort Jenkins provided a
frowning battlement to guard it. From Battery VII the defensive
line extended to the northwest, connecting with another ridge
aligned north to south. East of this ridge lay the marsh and the
Bottoms, a swampy area at the lowest elevation in Shreveport. Batteries VIII, IX, X, XI, and XII were all located on this ridge, Battery
XII at its extreme northern tip. Behind it to the east was a spectacu-
lar view of Shreveport; to the north lay Cross Bayou. Fording the

stream below this point would have been difficult at best, given the water's usual depth (up to 38 feet) and open position.

On the ridge running parallel to and west of that one, Boggs built Fort Albert Sidney Johnston, a long fort designed to cover Cross Bayou on the north and to prevent any attempt to attack Shreveport from the west. Any skirmish line formed west of this ridge would have met fire from the fort. Attackers from the west would have been forced to cross an opposing parallel ridgeline and then descend into a densely wooded stream bottom before rising to the fort's high ramparts.

The entire defensive line radiated from the town of Shreveport like the spokes of a wheel whose rim extended from one to three miles in a broad arc. Inside this defensive line lay the center for the military-industrial complex of the Trans-Mississippi West, the naval yard, a major infantry compound, and the Confederate government of Louisiana.[44]

In Bossier Parish, to cover the Confederate capital from the east, Boggs designed a series of four fortifications with one as an anchor, a triangular-star fort named to honor Kirby Smith. It was aligned to protect against an attack from the east, north, or southeast. South of it was a smaller square fort named Battery Ewell, and northwest of Fort Kirby Smith lay Battery Price, formed as a large lunette facing northeast. To the west-northwest of Battery Price lay another large lunette, Battery Walker, located on the river and facing north. The three northernmost emplacements on the Bossier side could provide enfilade fire for one another. The southern fort, Battery Ewell, was designed to protect Fort Kirby Smith, provide fire coverage against riverine targets, and offer enfilade fire for Fort Turnbull and its north battery.

The entire defensive ring was well laid out. Forces in place within Shreveport or in the defensive works could have moved where they were most needed in a minimum of time; even crossing troops from the Shreveport side of the river to the Bossier side was facilitated by two pontoon bridges, one near the mouth of Cross Bayou and the other adjacent to Fort Turnbull and close to Battery Ewell.[45] In short, the defenses in the Red River valley were well planned and superbly placed, considering the time available to the Confederate engineers. In less than twelve months from the time construction began, some of them would be tested by the largest concentration of Union naval forces on inland waters in North America and by land forces totaling 40,000 men.

NOTES

1. Venable Map.
2. Joyce Shannon Bridges, ed., *Biographical and Historical Memoirs of Northwest Louisiana* (Nashville, 1890; reprint, 1989), 33.
3. George W. Shannon Jr., "Cultural Resources Survey of the Port of Shreveport-Bossier, Caddo and Bossier Parishes, Louisiana" (unpublished report for the Caddo/Bossier Port Commission, 1996), 20.
4. Act 243 of the Louisiana Legislature, 1860 (Library of the Louisiana Legislature, Baton Rouge); *Bossier Banner*, May 18–25, 1860; Shannon, "Cultural Resources," 25.
5. *O.R.* 22, pt. 2, 1137–39; Waldo Moore, "The Defense of Shreveport: The Confederacy's Last Redoubt," in *Military Analysis of the Civil War: An Anthology by the Editors of Military Affairs* (New York, 1977), 396.
6. Venable Map.
7. Charles W. Read, "Reminiscences of the C. S. Navy," Southern Historical Society Papers, 56 vols., 1 (May 1876), Richmond, Virginia.
8. Caddo Parish Records, Conveyance Book N, folio 295, Shreveport, Louisiana.
9. U.S. War Department, *Official Records of the Union and Confederate Navies in the War of the Rebellion*, 31 vols. (Washington, DC, 1895–1929), 22:103–4 (hereafter cited as *O.R.N*).
10. Ibid., 103–4, 438–39.
11. *O.R.* 22, pt. 2, 781–82.
12. William R. Boggs, *Military Reminiscences of Gen. Wm. R. Boggs, C.S.A.* ed. William K. Boyd (Durham, NC, 1913), 57.
13. Ibid., x.
14. D. H. Mahan, *Treatise on Field Fortification, Containing Instructions on the Methods of Laying Out, Constructing, Defending and Attacking Intrenchments, with the General Outlines Also of the Arrangement, the Attack and Defense of Permanent Fortifications* (New York, 1863).
15. Boggs, *Military Reminiscences*, xix.
16. *O.R.* 26, pt. 2, 216–18.
17. Ibid., 322.
18. Ibid.
19. Taylor, *Destruction and Reconstruction*, 155.
20. Johnson and Buel, *Battles and Leaders*, 4:362.
21. Taylor, *Destruction and Reconstruction*, 155.
22. David Dixon Porter, *The Naval History of the Civil War* (Secaucus, NJ, 1984), 496.
23. Gary D. Joiner and Charles E. Vetter, "Union Naval Expedition on the Red River," *Civil War Regiments*, 4, no. 2 (1994): 41.
24. Porter, *Naval History*, 496.
25. Ulysses S. Grant, *Personal Memoirs of U.S. Grant* (New York, 1982), 19.
26. *O.R.* 34, pt. 2, 126.
27. Ibid., 26, pt. 2, 288.
28. Ibid., 322.
29. Ibid., 54–55.
30. Ibid., 323.
31. Bridges, *Biographical and Historical Memoirs*, 210.

32. Lavender U.S. Soil Survey Map of 1906, Archives, Louisiana State University, Shreveport (hereafter cited as Lavender Map).

33. Ibid.

34. Shannon, "Cultural Resources," 53.

35. W. W. Heartsill, *Fourteen Hundred and 91 Days in the Confederate Army: A Journal Kept by W. W. Heartsill for Four Years, One Month, and One Day; or, Camp Life, Day by Day, of the W. P. Lane Rangers from April 19th, 1861, to May 20th, 1865*, ed. Bell Irvin Wiley (Wilmington, NC, 1992), 211.

36. Clifton Cardin, *Bossier Parish History: The First 150 Years, 1843–1993* (Shreveport, LA, 1993), 62.

37. Frederick Way Jr., *Way's Packet Directory, 1848–1994*, rev. ed. (Athens, OH, 1983), 344.

38. *O.R.* 34, pt. 2, 1056–57.

39. Family diary in the collection of James Marston.

40. Eric J. Brock, "Presence of the Past: City Geared for Battle That Never Came," *Shreveport JournalPage*, November 25, 1995.

41. Mahan, *Treatise*, pl. 1.

42. Venable Map.

43. Gary D. Joiner, "40 Archaelogical Sites in the Red River Campaign" (unpublished report to the Louisiana State Department of Culture, Recreation, and Tourism, Division of Archaeology, 1997); Venable Map.

44. Edwin Bearss and Willie Tunnard, *A Southern Record: The Story of the 3rd Louisiana Infantry, C.S.A.* (Dayton, OH, 1988), 326.

45. Venable Map.

CHAPTER THREE

PREPARATIONS

LIEUTENANT GENERAL EDMUND KIRBY SMITH, commanding general of the grandiose-sounding Confederate Department of the Trans-Mississippi, and Major General Richard Taylor, head of the District of Western Louisiana, kept a close watch on Union movements in late 1863 and early 1864. Taylor's spies in New Orleans and Confederate reports elsewhere led both men to believe that Major General William T. Sherman or Major General Nathaniel Banks would make a thrust up the Red River when the spring rains made the river rise.[1]

Taylor and Smith were constantly at odds, and their frustration with each other's style is evident in contemporary reports and in postwar correspondence. In his memoir, *Destruction and Reconstruction*, Taylor refers to Kirby Smith and his large headquarters staff as the "Hydrocephalus at Shreveport."[2] Following his training under Major General Thomas J. "Stonewall" Jackson, he wanted fast-paced movement with a measure of finesse to meet the enemy. Smith wanted elaborate plans based on strong defensive points. Soon after assuming command in March 1863, he had the defenses of the valley surveyed and strengthened, and for the next year his engineers under Brigadier General William Boggs labored to prepare for the anticipated invasion. Although Taylor did not agree with fortifications in general principle, he did want Fort DeRussy, near Marksville, strengthened.[3] It had been built over his objections, but now he thought it would serve to slow—at least for a short time—any naval invading force.[4]

Taylor and Smith continued to argue over fortification placements and the number of guns from their limited artillery reserves to be placed in them. They interspersed blackened tree trunks on wheels, "Quaker guns," with real cannons in several fortifications but particularly at Fort Turnbull, the great anchor fort on the river south of Shreveport where even today the area bears the name Fort Humbug.[5] Taylor's fiery disposition made him despise the conservative plodding pace by which Smith conducted his preparations.

33

Heavily altered photograph of Major General (later Lieutenant General) Richard Taylor. Archives of the Mansfield State Historic Site, Mansfield, Louisiana. *Courtesy of the Mansfield State Historic Site*

As winter progressed, news arrived of Sherman's Meridian expedition, and the pair began to think that perhaps Mobile was the next target. Banks's men were still poised in New Orleans, and Taylor thought Banks would not move from the Bayou Teche area without Sherman's support.[6] Hopes of a reprieve seemed to evaporate, however, as news from reliable sources in both New Orleans and Vicksburg reported a huge naval buildup and the massing of Union infantry and support troops.[7]

Smith ordered his widely scattered troops into new concentration areas in early March 1864. As usual, his orders were carried out with varied degrees of urgency, with Magruder's Texas-based troops the last to be released to Louisiana soil. Smith ordered these units, consisting primarily of cavalry regiments, to gather in Alexandria.[8] He also ordered Taylor to reposition his forces. The brigade of Texans under Camille Armand Jules Marie de Polignac, a French prince and Confederate brigadier general, was ordered from Trinity, near Harrisonburg on the Ouachita River, to join the brigade of Louisiana troops led by Colonel Henry Gray at Alexandria. Major General John G. Walker's division of Texans was to operate in the prairie near the mouth of the Red River.[9] This area between Marksville and Simmesport offered good maneuvering room, assuming the troops did not find themselves trapped in the winding courses of Bayou de Glaize and other streams. The waterways that sliced through the region made organized marches all but impossible without the constant assistance of engineers.[10] At this stage of planning, only Louisiana and Texas troops were repositioned.

Meanwhile, as the Confederates arranged their forces, concepts of the expedition were coming into focus for its Union leaders. By late January 1864, Banks was pursuing his new venture with his usual boundless enthusiasm.[11] He solicited advice from Henry Halleck, the army's chief of staff, who wanted this expedition to begin. Halleck wrote letters to President Abraham Lincoln to show his support and intentions. He described his plans to his allies in New England, telling them of the possibilities of reopening their textile mills with newly acquired Louisiana cotton from the Red River valley. He corresponded with Sherman, Grant, Steele, and Porter.[12] His letters and telegrams to them varied according to what he wanted and what he expected from each individual.

Halleck wanted to be Banks's mentor in the operation and worked behind the scenes as a facilitator. The older man was in a transition phase in his career: he was about to share power with Grant, and he wanted his agenda carried out before the change was made. Lincoln had wanted the Union to mount a campaign to plant the flag on Texas soil for at least eighteen months as part of a counterrevolution. Moreover, with Banks in Louisiana, Lincoln thought he had removed his most visible Republican rival for the 1864 election from politically charged Washington, where Banks had been in charge of defenses. Banks's friends, New England bankers and textile mill owners whose support Lincoln needed if he was to win reelection in the fall, would be all too happy to put pressure on their congressional delegations to support the expedition.

Grant, Sherman, and Porter were all close friends and allies whose cooperation in large-scale projects had proved successful in several operations, particularly at Vicksburg. Sherman had a burning desire to lead an expedition up the Red River, where he had lived before the war, and lobbied Grant to put him in charge. His friend and superior was reluctant even to consider the operation, but Halleck was pushing for it to begin, the president desperately needed it, Grant lacked the authority or desire to countermand Halleck's orders and thinly veiled suggestions.[13] He was in the early process of planning the capture of Mobile and the Atlanta Campaign, however, and felt that he could not spare Sherman from those plans—though he did acquiesce to reassigning a portion of Sherman's troops to the Red River.

By the end of January, Sherman had begun his Meridian campaign, limiting the time he could contribute to planning. Halleck, writing to Sherman directly, was intimating that both he and Banks would lead the expedition when he was finished tearing up Meridian. Grant was kept out of this loop and was not told what troops, if any, from east of the Mississippi would be used. Porter had offered his full support to Sherman if the expedition were carried out. No doubt he thought Sherman would lead it and that it would be a great opportunity to work with his friend.[14]

Still thinking that Halleck might order him to be the senior field commander of the expedition, Sherman agreed to meet with Banks in New Orleans. Arriving there on March 2, he found Banks in a whirl of activity but not, in Sherman's opinion, doing what was necessary to support the pressing problems at hand.[15] Although he had completed his planning for the upcoming campaign, Banks could not devote time to explaining his ideas. Instead, he urged Sherman to remain in the city for an extra two days to attend the grand inauguration of the new governor of Union Louisiana, Michael Hahn. A disgusted Sherman later wrote in his memoirs that "General Banks urged me to remain over the 4th of March to participate in the ceremonies, which he explained would include the performance of the 'Anvil Chorus' by all the bands of his army and during the performance, church-bells were to be rung, and cannons were to be fired by electricity. I regarded all such ceremonies as out of place at a time when it seemed to me every hour and minute were due to the war."[16]

When Banks interrupted his party planning long enough to visit with Sherman, the Massachusetts political general told the great field commander that he, not Sherman, would be the overall field commander. This was so much hyperbole, since Halleck had not and never would give Banks sole authority over the expedition. Still, since Banks had been inducted into the U.S. Volunteers and promoted on the scene to the rank of major general, he and his predecessor, Benjamin Butler, outranked not only Sherman but also Grant and all other officers serving in the field at that stage of the war.[17] It forced Halleck and Grant to treat him differently from any of their field commanders, as had been evident in the Vicksburg campaign.

Sherman immediately backtracked on personally leading troops up the Red River; he wrote to his wife, "I wanted to go up Red River, but as Banks was to command in person I thought it best not to go."[18] He warned Porter, who had already committed to the campaign, that if Banks had a chance to save himself and his eastern troops, he would sacrifice the fleet to do it. And when Sherman agreed to lend the expedition 10,000 of his veterans, he placed severe limits on their use and the extent of their cooperation: his men were to accompany Porter, not Banks.[19] They were not to be used in any thrust farther than Shreveport, and most important, given Grant's upcoming projects, they were to be returned to Vicksburg no later than April 15.[20]

These limitations irritated Banks. The borrowed troops were westerners, veterans and hard fighters, to be sure, but they disregarded proper military behavior. He considered them too unruly and unkempt and displayed his open disdain by calling them "gorillas." His easterners of the Nineteenth Corps were more to his liking, cutting fine figures in parades and showing proper discipline on march. They were not as nearly battle-tested as Sherman's men, but they looked the way soldiers should look, and that meant a great deal to Banks.[21] Sherman's requirement that the troops accompany the navy also chafed at him, but at least he would not have to put up with them himself. More worrisome was the fact that it was the beginning of March, and Sherman had ordered the return of the westerners by the middle of April. But Banks often repeated to anyone who listened that he believed the Rebels would not fight him before Shreveport, if then. He expected to fight his big battle in Texas, and by that time he wouldn't need Sherman's men.[22] Sherman left New Orleans on March 3, wanting to get away from Banks and the vision of a looming fiasco. He wrote Porter, Grant, and Halleck of the decisions being made and warned Porter to be careful.[23]

Union general Frederick Steele, recently placed in command of the District of Arkansas based in Little Rock, was reluctant to participate in the Louisiana activities. Wary of the whole concept, he attempted to separate his forces from the proposed operation in all planning discussions. He tried to commit only to a feint or demonstration to draw the Confederates away from Banks, citing the need to monitor elections in Little Rock.[24] But his protests were cast aside, and when Grant became general-in-chief of the army, he ordered Steele to participate fully in the operation. On March 15, Grant telegraphed Steele in Little Rock, "Move your force in full cooperation with General N. P. Banks' attack on Shreveport. . . . A mere demonstration will not be sufficient."[25]

Banks fired off several questions to Halleck concerning overall command of the operation.[26] He wanted a clear decision from the president and the general staff as to his own authority.[27] But Halleck did not trust Banks politically and certainly not militarily.[28] He played the part of concertmaster, writing all senior commanders who would have a part in the operation, asking the extent of their intended cooperation, while Banks was conducting a similar writing campaign.[29] Adding to the confusion in planning was Halleck's talent for giving vague orders to protect himself if events took a bad turn.

Besides his misgivings about Banks, Halleck faced the almost impossible task of assigning an overall commander for the expedition. The component units spanned three departments (Gulf, Arkansas, and the Army of the Tennessee in Misisssippi), the U.S. Navy's Mississippi River Squadron, the army's Quartermaster Corps's troop transport boats, and the independent Marine Brigade.[30] Halleck's answer to this almost impossibly complex force structure was to assign no overall commander, though he did move mountains to get the campaign organized.

In March, Grant was promoted to lieutenant general, but Halleck, although Grant was now his superior, continued to play the part of the master manipulator.[31] Still with strong misgivings, Grant told Sherman that if he did not personally lead his western troops, they would probably be lost permanently from his command.[32] But of course, Grant did not want Sherman to go, so he exacted promises from Sherman that the number of Sherman's men borrowed would be minimal and that Sherman would not personally lead them, and from Banks that they would be returned to Sherman for his upcoming operations by April 15. By March 12, the day Grant was made general-in-chief, the forces were moving into position. He made no attempt to halt the operation.

On paper, the campaign appeared a surefire proposition. It combined overwhelming numerical superiority of infantry and cavalry troops, a huge naval contingent, and more than adequate logistical support, plus the blessings of the president, the cabinet, and the chief of staff of the army. The expedition would consist of a three-part pincer movement. The two southern legs would meet at Alexandria, a major road and river junction in the center of the state to which Union navy vessels had reconnoitered the river the previous year. The combined force would then proceed north to Shreveport. The northern leg was to sweep down from Little Rock and approach Shreveport from the north, effectively forcing a battle or siege with no clear route of escape for the Confederate army or the civilians caught in the trap.

The first group was to travel via navy and army vessels up the Red River to Alexandria. Porter, commanding the Mississippi River Squadron, was to bring almost all his naval assets into the Red River. It was a precursor to modern force-projection theory to supply overwhelming fire support for infantry attacking a series of fortifications located on a river. Porter boasted that he would strip the inland fleet of available hulls and guns for the expedition. A total of 210 large ordnance pieces lent credence to his word. He had promised his old friend Sherman that he would ascend the Red River "with every ironclad vessel in the fleet."[33]

The resulting fleet was a marvelous mixture of ironclads, monitors, tinclads, a timberclad, and supply vessels. These same vessels had engaged the Confederates time after time on the Mississippi, Arkansas, and Tennessee Rivers, and many had gained fame after the Vicksburg campaign. Several of the boats had been designed by James Buchanan Eads, perhaps the greatest engineer of the nineteenth century. The fleet comprised the great ironclads *Benton*, *Essex*, *Choctaw*, *Eastport*, *Lafayette*, *Carondelet*, *Louisville*, *Mound City*, *Pittsburg*, and *Chillicothe*, the large river monitors *Neosho* and *Osage*, the less impressive river monitor *Ozark*, the large tinclads *Black*

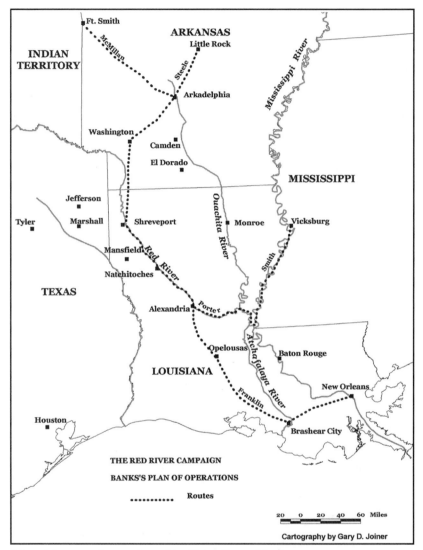

Map of the campaign as planned by Major General Banks.

Hawk and *Ouachita*, the timberclad *Lexington*, and the tinclads *Covington, Fort Hindman, Gazelle, Cricket, Juliet, Forest Rose, Signal, St. Clair,* and *Tallahatchee,* plus the previously captured ram *General Sterling Price* and the support vessels: dispatch boats, tenders, tugs, and supply boats.[34] The army's Quartermaster Corps had its own transport and supply vessels, which were to accommodate 10,000 men from two divisions of the Sixteenth Corps and one division lent by Sherman from the Seventeenth Corps seasoned veterans under the command of Brigadier General Andrew Jackson Smith.[35] There was also the independent Mississippi Marine Brigade with its rams, support vessels, a hospital boat, and approximately 1,000 marines. In all, the fleet consisted of ninety vessels, the largest congregation of inland warfare vessels in the Civil War. The most impressive was the *Eastport*, a behemoth 280 feet long and 43 feet wide (beam), drawing 6 feet, 3 inches and carrying two 100-pounder rifled cannons, four 9-inch smoothbores and two 50-pounder rifled cannons.[36]

The *Eastport* and several other ironclads were sent on this expedition because Porter had been warned of the Confederate naval presence in Shreveport, particularly the existence there of ironclads and submarines; the memory of what the CSS *Arkansas* had done to the fleet at Vicksburg remained vivid in his mind. His spies had described the CSS *Missouri* as a smaller *Tennessee* or *Arkansas* and told him that two more of the iron monsters had been completed in Shreveport and three were under construction.[37] The report was exaggerated but it was perhaps the greatest influence on his thinking. Wanting to take no chances getting caught with inadequate firepower in a narrow river, Porter would lead each leg of the journey with his largest (and thus most cumbersome) vessel, the *Eastport*, whose two heaviest guns were located in twin forward positions where they were designed to be ironclad killers.

The second pincer was to travel overland. It consisted of 19,000 infantry and cavalry from the Department of the Gulf: two divisions from the Thirteenth Corps, two from the Nineteenth Corps, and Brigadier General Albert Lee's cavalry division of 3,900 troopers. Some 2,500 men of the U.S. Colored Troops, the Corps d'Afrique, were scheduled to arrive after the main column reached Alexandria. Banks's engineers and logistics troops would move north with 32,500 combat troops (including A. J. Smith's 10,000 and the 1,000 marines) and ninety artillery pieces.[38] This huge column was to travel across the bayou country of southern Louisiana from bases near Brashear City and New Orleans and then head west to the main north-south road at Opelousas. From there it would move to Alexandria and join Porter's fleet. The combined forces were then to proceed north along the most practicable route to Shreveport, with Porter's vessels providing protection and succor for the land troops.

The third pincer, starting in two columns, was to sweep southwest from Little Rock and southerly from Fort Smith, both in Arkansas. It was to leave its bases later than the other two, since it would approach Shreveport from much shorter distances. The choice of its route was left to Steele. His first intention was to proceed southward to the Ouachita River and on to Monroe, Louisiana, then follow the bed of the Southern Pacific Railroad across northern Louisiana from east to west. The bed was part of the proposed transcontinental railroad planned before the war but still incomplete. Rails ran from Monroe eastward eighty miles to the Mississippi River opposite Vicksburg, but only the bed had been prepared westward to Shreveport. This segment ran almost due west for 110 miles and was a very straightforward approach.[39] Steele decided against this avenue of attack, however, and opted for a lengthier approach through Arkadelphia and Washington, the Confederate capital of Arkansas.[40] He may have hoped to seize the entire Confederate governmental structure in Arkansas en route. Either way, Steele would be forced to cross the Red River, whether at Shreveport itself or north of the city. This was no small feat: the river was 1,000 feet wide from the landing on the Bossier Parish side to the ferry's terminus at the wharves in Shreveport; in fact, this was one of the widest points in the entire length of the river, and in the spring the current there typically flowed at least as fast as that of the lower reaches of the Mississippi.[41] Steele would have known this, and it may have been a factor in his preparing for a line of attack from the north rather than the east. His first column, 3,600 men from the garrison post at Fort Smith on the Indian Territory border, was to march 170 miles to the town of Arkadelphia.[42] Steele would lead the main body of troops from Little Rock to join the Fort Smith column. These 6,800 men made up the Third Division, Seventh Corps, and two cavalry brigades.[43] Steele's total force would add 10,400 men to Banks's forces converging on Shreveport, making a total effective complement of approximately 42,900, excluding sailors and support personnel such as teamsters and garrison troops.

This grand scheme of overwhelming land and naval power appeared to be a truly unstoppable force, yet the very seeds of disaster lay in the initial plans. Timing was critical: all three prongs or pincers must arrive at specific points at predetermined dates for the campaign to remain on schedule. On April 15 the 10,000 best troops would be lost when they were returned to Sherman. The three groups would not be able to communicate directly with one another, and the initial distance between Steele and Banks was more than 400 miles by the shortest route. The fleet and its attached infantry would not be able to count on Banks until they all met at Alexandria. If any of the columns or the fleet were delayed, the entire plan was in jeopardy. Added to all of these uncertainties was the open distrust and skepticism of the leaders of two pincers for each other. Of the three separate groups, Porter and his borrowed infantry commander, A. J. Smith, were the only two leading officers who displayed mutual respect and were operating in their combined interest.

Still, each group began with faith that its counterparts were acting according to the schedule developed in the planning process, but none had the means to verify the actions of the others. Cynicism prevailed in all quarters. Banks's commanders viewed him as a lightweight political climber who did not have the soldiers' best interest in mind. Banks's extreme overconfidence in his own abilities and an almost total lack of understanding of the Confederate forces in the region plagued the operation from the beginning. Moreover, it would soon be evident that the lack of an overall commander would lead to the problems that Sherman foresaw.

If ever there was a campaign in the Civil War that began with strong political overtones, had major support at the highest levels in Washington, and was given more than adequate resources to make it a success, the Red River Campaign of 1964 was that operation. Conversely, if there was a campaign in which the planning factors were established to ensure confusion among the participants, animosity among the major components, and a high potential for failure, the Red River Campaign also fit that bill.

NOTES

1. *O.R.* 26, pt. 2, 117, 293–94, 341–42; *O.R.* 34, 819.
2. Taylor, *Destruction and Reconstruction*, 153.
3. *O.R.* 34, 575–76; Taylor, *Destruction and Reconstruction*, 148–49.
4. *O.R.* 34, 574; Taylor, *Destruction and Reconstruction*, 148–49.
5. Joiner, Fort Turnbull in "40 Archaeological Sites."
6. *O.R.* 34, 489.
7. Ibid., 494.
8. Ibid., 479, 494; pt. 2, 1027.

9. Taylor, *Destruction and Reconstruction*, 154–55.

10. U.S. War Department, *Atlas to Accompany the Official Records of the Union and Confederate Armies* (Washington, DC, 1891–1895), pl. 52 (hereafter cited as *O.R. Atlas*); *O.R. 34*, 599.

11. *O.R. 34*, pt. 2, 133.

12. Ibid., 10, 42, 46, 145, 267; *JCCW*, 227; various correspondence from August 20, 1863, through February 1864, Banks Papers.

13. *O.R. 34*, pt. 2, 224–25.

14. *O.R.N. 26*, 747–48.

15. Sherman, *Memoirs*, 1:425–26.

16. Ibid.

17. M. A. De Wolfe Howe, ed., *Home Letters of General Sherman* (New York, 1909), 286–87.

18. Thomas H. S. Hamersly, comp. and ed., *Complete Army Register*, pt. 1, 513; pt. 2, 5, 16, 42, 97.

19. *O.R. 34*, 168; pt. 2, 545.

20. *O.R. 34*, pt. 2, 481, 494, 496.

21. John Scott, *Story of the Thirty-second Iowa Infantry Volunteers* (Nevada, IA, 1896), 136 (hereafter cited as *32d Iowa*); Wickham Hoffman, *Camp, Court, and Siege: A Narrative of Personal Adventure and Observation during Two Wars, 1861–1865, 1870–1871* (New York, 1877), 93; Harrington, *Fighting Politician*, 152–53.

22. *O.R. 34*, 179–80.

23. Sherman, *Memoirs*, 1:425–26.

24. *O.R. 34*, pt. 2, 576.

25. Ibid., 616.

26. Ibid., 179, 266.

27. *JCCW*, 19.

28. *O.R. 34*, pt. 3, 289.

29. Ibid., pt. 2, 293.

30. Ibid.

31. Stephen E. Ambrose, *Halleck: Lincoln's Chief of Staff* (Baton Rouge, LA, 1962), 161.

32. *O.R. 34*, pt. 2, 224–25.

33. *O.R.N. 26*, 747–48.

34. Johnson and Buel, *Battles and Leaders*, 4:366; Porter, *Naval History*, 494–533, 548–53.

35. *O.R. 34*, 68, 203; Johnson and Buel, *Battles and Leaders*, 4:350–51.

36. Paul H. Silverstone, *Warships of the Civil War Navies* (Annapolis, MD, 1989), 156.

37. Jonathan H. Carter to Mallory, February 1, 1863, Carter Correspondence Book, manuscript in the National Archives and Records Administration (NARA), Record Group (RG) 45; Katherine Brash Jeter, *A Man and His Boat: The Civil War Career and Correspondence of Lieutenant Jonathan H. Carter, CSN* (Lafayette, LA, 1996), x.

38. *O.R. 34*, 167–68; Johnson and Buel, *Battles and Leaders*, 4:366.

39. *O.R. 34*, pt. 3, 601.

40. *JCCW*, 154–57.

41. Venable Map.

42. *O.R. 34*, pt. 2, 638, 707.

43. Ibid., 704.

CHAPTER FOUR

ANABASIS

THE CAMPAIGN BEGAN on March 10 with twenty-one steamboat transports packed as tightly as possible. On board were Sherman's 10,000 men and their equipment. Their departure from Vicksburg was already three days behind the timetable, creating early tension.[1] Leading these troops was A. J. Smith, known to his contemporaries as "Old Whitey" or "Whiskey." Smith was a career man who had spent twenty-three years in the dragoons, mostly in western posts fighting Indians. A short man with a scraggly beard and wire-rimmed glasses, he was a graduate of West Point but acted more like a teamster. He was exceptional at cursing and drinking, yet his men would to do anything for him and follow him anywhere.[2] Though dour and grim, he was one of Sherman's best officers. At Vicksburg, Smith was the officer Grant had ordered to usher Confederate General John Pemberton to the surrender site the previous Fourth of July. It was he who had led one of the costly attacks by the Union on the Confederate works there in May 1863.[3]

The army's transports carried Sherman's veterans down the Mississippi River from Vicksburg, arriving at the mouth of the Red River by the evening of March 11, where Porter and his Mississippi River Squadron awaited them.[4] The mouth of the Red River was complex as a result of the vagaries of the Mississippi River in ancient times. The Ouachita/Black River joined the Red just a short distance from its mouth. The Atchafalaya River, an old course of the Mississippi, exited the Mississippi near the mouth of the Red. A great sandbar buildup called Turnbull Island acted as a barrier to prevent the Atchafalaya from becoming a continuation of the Red. As it stood, some of the Red's waters flowed into the Mississippi and the rest into the Atchafalaya.[5] At times of low water, the Red built up a sandbar at its mouth, and most of its water diverted into the Atchafalaya, as was the situation in March 1864. The configuration resembled a stylized letter "H." The old course of the Mississippi was called Old River, and at its western end was the village of Simmesport. Emptying into Old River from the north at

45

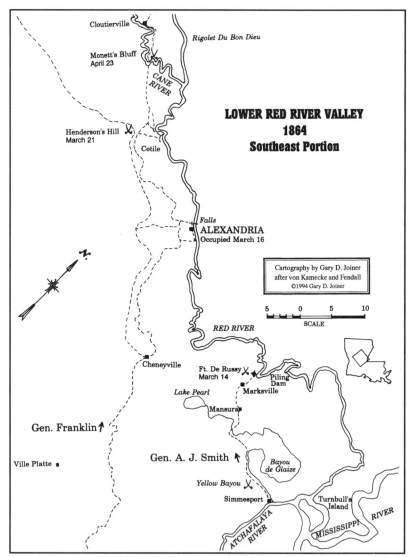

Map of the campaign in the Red River Valley in Louisiana. Battles are indicated by crossed swords.

Simmesport were Yellow Bayou and Bayou de Glaize. This jumble of ancient stream confluences was the watery morass in which the Union navy, under Porter, would operate.

Porter was the son of Commodore David Porter, hero of the War of 1812 and captain of the *Essex* in that conflict. The Union admiral was also the foster brother of Rear Admiral David Glascow Farragut, a brother of Commodore William D. "Dirty Bill" Porter, and a cousin of Major General Fitz-John Porter.[6] At the tender age of ten, Porter had gone to sea with his father as a cabin boy. During his subsequent career he had fought pirates and had seen action in the Mexican War. He was intelligent, witty, brash, courageous, and prone to self-aggrandizement. His ego was legendary, and he exuded self-confidence. Porter made decisions quickly, for better or worse. He developed a close following among his vessel commanders, and if they performed as he wished, he fostered their careers. He did not accept mistakes and could be quite vindictive if his career or his command appeared to be at risk. He operated what was in fact an independent command, answering only to Secretary of the Navy Gideon Welles. His area of operations was all of the Mississippi River valley and its tributaries above New Orleans.

Porter and A. J. Smith decided to stabilize their toehold at the mouth of the Red River. Worried about the Confederate ironclads on the Red, Porter led his fleet into the river with the *Eastport*—which grounded on the bar at the mouth of the Red. At its helm was Lieutenant Commander Seth Ledyard Phelps, a naval officer in his late twenties and one of Porter's favorite commanders. Porter had trusted the largest warship to Phelps's capable hands, and Phelps managed to haul the great ironclad over the sandbar. Other ironclads followed in case the Confederates were waiting. A. J. Smith immediately brought his transports into Old River, accompanied by the most powerful ironclad in the fleet, the *Benton*. Smith's men disembarked at Simmesport, his staging point for the attack on Fort DeRussy. Porter sent some of his ironclads up the Ouachita River to neutralize the fortification at Trinity.[7] The bulk of the fleet, however, was to proceed up the Red River to address the massive water batteries guarding Fort DeRussy and occupy the fort's attention until the army landed.[8] The plan was for A. J. Smith's men to march on the fort from the rear while Porter distracted the defenders from the front.

Some of Smith's men successfully foraged in the town. Foraging was a polite term for stealing every cow, hog, and chicken that was too slow to escape their grasp. The next day they torched a house in Simmesport, an overture to what would become their penchant for incendiary retribution during the coming campaign. "Total war" as a concept thus began in the backwaters of central Louisiana.[9]

The Confederate major general John Walker's division of Texans was guarding the lower Red River valley. Walker was the first Confederate commander to hear about the thrust into his territory, and he immediately sent a dispatch warning Richard Taylor of the incursion. The first reports he received were estimating 15,000 to 17,000 troops and thirty to forty guns.[10] These figures can be attributed to green troops who were "Seeing the Elephant"—that is, seeing battle or confronting the enemy for the first time—but Walker was inclined to believe them, and he only had 3,300 combat troops and twelve artillery pieces.[11] He sent Brigadier General William Scurry's brigade forward to occupy the Yellow Bayou forts, one named for the brigade's commander. The half-finished fort was one of those known in the valley by the insulting moniker of "Fort Humbug." Some of Scurry's pickets had been in Simmesport and were the first Confederate troops in the District of Louisiana to meet the Union thrust. The pickets either fell back in disarray or were captured.

When Walker received additional reports of how many men Scurry faced, he evacuated the forts and removed his men from the Bayou de Glaize area, fearing encirclement.[12] His three meager companies of cavalry had already been cut off with Smith's capture of Simmesport, and Walker had no way of knowing the true size of the Union force. His premature withdrawal doomed Fort DeRussy —yet it saved a full Confederate division and its artillery for later use, when they would be needed most.

A. J. Smith began probing for Walker, thinking that the Confederates must be laying a trap for him in the winding bayou country. He sent a reconnaissance patrol on the only road to Fort Scurry and captured some surprised Confederates.[13] Either Scurry's men were great actors or there were no large Rebel force concentrations to their immediate front. In any case, when Smith's patrol reported back to him, he ordered his transport vessels to unload all of his gear and then to return to Porter and rejoin the fleet while he and his men began a quick march on the Marksville road to take Fort DeRussy.[14]

The force crossed Bayou de Glaize and entered the Avoyelles prairie. Union brigadier general Thomas Kilby Smith, commanding the Provisional Division of the Seventeenth Corps, wrote to his wife that it was "one of the most beautiful prairies imaginable. High table land, gently undulating, watered by exquisite lakes[,] occasional groves, the landscape dotted with tasteful gardens and shrubberies. This prairie called Avoyelles, is settled exclusively by French *émigrés*, many of whom, as our army passed sought shelter under the tricolor of France."[15] T. Kilby Smith had just marched into a Creole area, and the Creoles had a long history of supporting other heritages for their own convenience: they had variously sought shelter either with or from the French, Spanish, and Americans.

Soon the column entered the town of Marksville, just three miles from the rear approach of the fort. The Confederate staff in Shreveport called Fort DeRussy the Confederate Gibraltar, and like its namesake, its prowess faced the water. The rear of the unfinished fort was not sufficiently fortified to withstand a large attack.

A. J. Smith decided to form the First and Second Brigades, Third Division, Sixteenth Corps, in line of battle on either side of the Marksville–Fort DeRussy road.[16] Brigadier General Joseph A. Mower, a Vermonter and seasoned veteran of Iuka, Corinth, and Vicksburg, was their very capable leader. As his men maneuvered into position and waited for the order to attack, field guns in the fort began pouring fire into their ranks.[17] Adding to this, and certainly disconcerting to the Union troops, the *Eastport*, *Osage*, *Fort Hindman*, and *Cricket* had arrived in front of the fort, and *Eastport* fired one of its 100-pound rifle shells at the water batteries.[18] The shell burst over the heads of the Confederates within the casemates, and they abandoned the position.[19]

Marine Lieutenant Frank Church, commanding Admiral Porter's 24-man bodyguard aboard the *Black Hawk*, reported two shells fired from the gunboats, and then the barrage was halted.[20] These vessels had been delayed coming to the fort for several hours when they encountered a Confederate obstruction or "raft" downstream at a sharp bend in the river which the maps called the "Bend of the Rappiones."[21] Porter had to devise a way to destroy the "forest of trees" that the Confederates had impaled in the channel and ordered Phelps to "clear that away!"[22] Phelps had the *Fort Hindman* rip the obstacles out by alternately ramming the timbers and pulling them out via the boats' hawsers. By the time the navy arrived opposite the fort, Phelps had fired a few rounds with his forward guns before realizing that they might be firing on their own men. The naval crews watched the finale of Mower's attack on the fort.

Brigadier General Joseph A. Mower. Library of Congress, Prints and Photographs Division, LC-B8172-2037

At six o'clock the order was given for Mower to charge his Third Division into the breastworks. He personally led the attack. Following Walker's decision to evacuate the area, the fort was defended only by a skeleton garrison of fewer than 300 men, who were overwhelmed in short order. Porter saw the surrender from his flagship, the large tinclad *Black Hawk*, and personally congratulated A. J. Smith. Union casualties were thirty-eight killed and wounded.[23]

Although it was in truth a glorified skirmish, the Union reports made it sound grandiose.[24] It had great significance to the campaign, because it solidified the Union position and protected its rear areas.

Mower and his Third Division men were picked up by their transports to accompany the fleet to Alexandria.[25] Porter left the *Benton* there for three days trying to destroy the fort, and A. J. Smith remained with T. Kilby Smith's men to destroy the works.[26] The *Benton* tried firing its powerful guns at point-blank range to destroy the water battery casemate but was unable to do so.[27] While conducting this effort, the ironclad began leaking through its caulking and had to be repaired. The *Banton* and the *Essex* never ascended the river farther to assist the fleet during the expedition; instead, they performed picket duty, guarding the navy's rear from some undetermined Confederate threat. A. J. Smith worked for several days trying to destroy the fortification. One night the fort's bombproof exploded in a botched attempt to set charges for later demolition, killing two Union soldiers and wounding several. A. J. Smith's men hissed and sneered at him as he rode by the next day.[28]

Porter sent his heavy monitor *Osage* to accompany Mower's transports to take Alexandria. Lieutenant Commander Thomas O. Selfridge captained the warship. Although still in his twenties, Selfridge had seen considerable action. As an officer of the USS *Cumberland* at Hampton Roads, he saw his vessel sunk by the CSS *Virginia*. Later, he was in command of the USS *Conestoga* when it was rammed and sunk by a friendly vessel. And eventually he commanded the USS *Cairo*, which struck a torpedo in the Yazoo River and sank.[29] The *Osage* arrived in Alexandria on the afternoon of Tuesday, March 15, and received the town's surrender without firing a shot.[30] Selfridge sent word back for Porter to hurry up, for he feared that once the good citizens of Alexandria realized that their population outnumbered his crew, they might capture his boat.[31] Mower's 5,000 troops landed shortly thereafter.

Porter had hoped to catch unaware any Confederate boats at the Alexandria wharves, but he had missed his opportunity by hours. The Confederates did not have heavily armed vessels at Alexandria at that time, but when word came of the attack on Fort DeRussy, Richard Taylor ordered Alexandria evacuated of both vessels and army units. (One vessel grounded on the rocks forming the rapids and was burned; it was thought to be the *Countess*, but a Confederate report shortly thereafter shows it at Grand Ecore.)

In their haste to depart, they left behind three artillery pieces, which were captured.[32] Porter brought the bulk of his fleet to Alexandria, let his men enjoy the city, monitored the slowly falling water, and waited for Banks—who was nowhere to be seen.

Porter had no way of knowing what was happening with either of the two other pincers in the plan. Steele, after trying to wiggle out of his part in the campaign, set in motion his part of the plan only after receiving, on the very day that Porter and his force took Alexandria, Grant's terse telegram ordering "full cooperation," not "a mere demonstration."[33] Porter waited in Alexandria, wondering if Banks's political machinations were taking precedence over his command obligations, thankful that Sherman had the foresight to lend him A. J. Smith and his 10,000 veterans. In fact, the Confederate cavalry knew more about Banks at that moment than his estranged cohorts did.[34]

Richard Taylor was a superb tactician and an excellent strategist. He knew how best to utilize his meager resources, and if he was left to his own devices by the command staff in Shreveport, his plans usually went smoothly. Reports were dutifully dispatched to E. Kirby Smith, but they tended to be sent shortly after an action was taken, thus minimizing the potential for interference from the commanding general and his staff, whom Taylor considered meddling know-nothings who constantly got in his way. His days in the Shenandoah Valley had taught him that rapid masking movements in the face of a numerically superior enemy were always preferable to attempting to fortify a stronghold or build one as the enemy approached. He thus had no qualms about leaving Alexandria to Union forces. He was going to pick his battlefield, and the deep cotton fields of the Red River valley in central Louisiana did not appeal to him.

Taylor needed to find a place closer to Shreveport, and it is evident from his correspondence with E. Kirby Smith's chief of staff and engineer, William R. Boggs, that both men thought the Federal forces would ascend the river and could be trapped in the Narrows between Natchitoches and Shreveport.[35] Boggs's ingenious fortifications and traps for the Federal army and navy spanned several miles of the narrow, twisting channel in that area. Taylor's plan seems to have been to draw Banks north from Natchitoches along the river road to a point of his choosing[36]—or so correspondence between Taylor and Boggs indicates.

In preparation for the anticipated invasion of northern Louisiana, Taylor had ordered supply depots positioned at several points on the main roads traversing the pine barrens of the Kisatachie Hills between the Sabine and Red Rivers and also between Alexandria and Shreveport.[37] Each depot held food, ammunition, powder, and blankets in sufficient quantities to replenish the depleted supplies of several regiments. Taylor had also scheduled his far-flung brigades to meet at predetermined places. Orders had gone out for the brigade of Texans under the Prince de Polignac to travel from Trinity, near Harrisonburg on the Ouachita River, and join the brigade of Louisiana troops led by Colonel Henry Gray, operating near Alexandria. (Gray knew the area very well. His home was located at Coushatta, a small pleasant town on the Red River between Shreveport and Natchitoches.) Gray and Polignac joined up about twenty-five miles south of Alexandria on Bayou Boeuf, where Taylor met them. He formed the two brigades into a small division led by one of his favorite lieutenants, Brigadier General Alfred Mouton, of Lafayette, Louisiana, the son of the state's former governor, Alexander Mouton.[38]

Announcing his intention to gather his forces at Natchitoches, Taylor next sent word for General Walker to join him. Walker had been waiting for orders to withdraw from his position on Bayou du Lac between Marksville and Cheneyville.[39] While Taylor was making preparations to move his force northward, around the unknowing Union troops, he received word from his Louisiana cavalry units under Colonel William Vincent that Banks's main column was moving north from Franklin. Since Taylor needed the cavalry to keep an eye on A. J. Smith's column at Alexandria, he ordered Vincent to leave the Bayou Teche area and to join Mouton. The combined Louisiana and Texas divisions gave Taylor 7,000 combat effectives.[40] Cavalry acted as the eyes and ears of the army in the Civil War, and Taylor had been moving blindly because the District of Texas commander had not yet released his Texas cavalry under Brigadier General Tom Green, and his own Louisiana cavalry had not yet arrived. Not wanting to give his position away, Taylor had no viable way of keeping track of the Union troops in Alexandria. He took his army to one of the prepared foraging depots in western Rapides Parish, this one owned by a free mulatto, Carroll Jones. Jones's place was near the village of Hinestown, about twenty-eight miles northwest of Alexandria.[41]

Four days after Taylor's call went out, on March 19, Vincent arrived. Taylor immediately dispatched the Second Louisiana Cavalry north to Bayou Rapides, about twelve miles north of his location and some twenty-two miles north from Alexandria at the village of Cotile.[42] Its mission was to keep Taylor informed of Union movements, to skirmish with the lead elements of A. J. Smith's column, and to try to slow its progress while Taylor and his two divisions proceeded north to Natchitoches. Taylor's relief at seeing his cavalry was short-lived. The horsemen arrived on the night of March 21 after riding hard or skirmishing for six days straight with little sleep. They encamped at Henderson's Hill, a toe-shaped ridge that rose above the confluence of Bayou Rapides and Bayou Cotile. The weather turned ugly and cold and they were pelted by rain and hail. Vincent's pickets, trying to keep dry, were not vigilant.[43]

Mower's force totaled approximately 1,000 men, including a light artillery battery and the First Brigade of Brigadier General Albert Lee's cavalry division.[44] Lee's cavalry was the leading element of Banks's main column, arriving well ahead of the main body. The artillery battery, which had been with the lead element of troops under Lee, had just arrived in Alexandria and, without rest, was pressed into service. Mower sought to engage Vincent's cavalry, which had been harassing the Union troops. Rapidly marching twenty-five miles in seven and half hours, Mower and his men ended their march in "knee-deep mud."[45] They captured several Confederates, including officers, and obtained the password used that night by Vincent's cavalry detachment encamped on the hill. Mower "borrowed" an officer's coat and took his regiments to the hill, led by the veteran Eighth Wisconsin Volunteer Infantry. The Eighth was famous for having a pet eagle named "Old Abe," who had given the defenders of Vicksburg fits as they tried to shoot him. Old Abe was in the forefront with his regiment now as Mower, wearing the gray officer's coat over his own uniform, gave the password during the driving storm. Just before dawn, the exhausted Rebel cavalrymen were surprised to see 1,000 rifles aimed at them and a well-soaked eagle glaring at them. Mower captured 350 Confederate cavalrymen and 400 horses while suffering no losses.[46] Taylor was once more without his eyes and ears.

Banks, a political animal to the marrow of his bones, reveled in orchestrating details, supremely confident that he was in control. To ensure that his new governor of Louisiana, Michael Hahn, was seen by the public as having overwhelming support, he had put his all into the festivities in New Orleans.[47] His military activities were thereby delayed a few days, but he was sure he could catch up and beat Porter to Alexandria.[48] Banks exuded so much confidence and moral certainty that he made his army peers shake their heads in dismay. His superiors in Washington viewed him warily, but his confidence made his Nineteenth Army Corps very proud of him.

Hahn's inauguration was held on March 5, and according to at least one soldier who witnessed it, the pageantry was magnificent.[49] Banks was very proud of himself and overcome with his feeling of success. He wrote to Halleck that the inauguration was such a spectacle that it was "impossible to describe it with truth."[50] His reports from the field in the upcoming campaign would have a similar ring.

From New Orleans, traveling eighty miles by railroad and another twenty-five miles by steamboat transports, the Nineteenth Corps arrived on March 7 at the assembly point for their overland trek, approximately five days late.[51] After a day of final preparations, Banks ordered Albert Lee at the head of his cavalry division to lead the great column on the roads that would take them to Alexandria. Moving from various outlying bases, the Nineteenth Corps assembled at Franklin in St. Mary Parish in order to follow Bayou Teche, one of the most beautiful streams in the South.[52] The column was so long, at times stretching twenty miles, that the last units would sometimes be more than a day's march behind the lead elements. Banks never considered using lines of parallel approach. To be sure, that would have been difficult if not impossible in the swamps of southern Louisiana, where roads were built on the actual natural levees of the streams; called front lands, these were the highest elevation in the countryside. But even as the column moved into the wider alluvial plains farther north, Banks never bothered to examine the possibility of shortening his column or rearranging the train's components.[53]

Albert Lee, Banks's thirty-year-old chief of cavalry for the Department of the Gulf, was a native New Yorker and a lawyer; he had moved to the Kansas Territory to practice his profession in the 1850s. In 1861 he became a justice of the Kansas Supreme Court but soon resigned from the bench to be mustered in as major of the Seventh Kansas Cavalry. The regiment operated in Kansas and Missouri for a few months and then was sent across the Mississippi River to work with Grant in the Vicksburg campaign. Lee had been chief of staff to General John McClernand at the battles of Champion's Hill and Big Black River. He was appointed brigadier in April 1863. Following his recovery from wounds suffered at Vicksburg, he was ordered to New Orleans and then undertook his Red River assignment.[54] Lee commanded 4,653 officers and troopers.[55] Interspersed with his veteran cavalrymen were recently mounted infantry operating more like dragoons than cavalry. They were new to riding and had trouble handling and tending to their horses. Lee was forced to train them on the march, a difficult task at best. When he was exasperated, Lee referred to them as his amateur equestrians. He chose Colonel N. A. M. "Gold Lace" Dudley's veteran First Brigade to lead the division, and he rode at the head of the column with Dudley.[56] The 39-year-old Dudley, a native of Massachusetts, had been with the Nineteenth Corps since January 1863. He was a veteran campaigner who had taken part in the capture of New Orleans, the defense of Baton Rouge, the siege of Vicksburg, and the capture of Port Hudson. He was a good choice to be at the vanguard.[57]

March 8 turned stormy as heavy rains blanketed southern Louisiana. The cavalry was moving over deep, rich, black alluvial "buckshot" gumbo soil which the rains turned into soup that stuck to the horses and the wagons. Without prepared roadbeds, the bottoms of the roads seemed to sink deep into the earth. The infantry, immediately following the cavalry and its wagon train, could not operate in the knee-deep muck, so departure was delayed until it stopped raining and the roads once again became firm—almost a week's time. The cavalry, moving only as fast as its wagons could follow, proceeded slowly through the sea of mud: leaving the town of Franklin on the morning of March 13, the horsemen finally rode into Alexandria at nine o'clock on Sunday morning, March 20, having covered only 175 miles.[58] After a short day's rest, Dudley and his First Brigade of cavalry accompanied Mower to Henderson's Hill.

Banks had his trusted deputy and commander of the Nineteenth Corps lead the infantry in the campaign. Major General William Buel Franklin, age forty-one, had graduated first in his class at West Point in 1843—the same class in which Grant had graduated twenty-first. (Though Franklin had a passing resemblance to Grant, his star would not rise as high or as fast.) Franklin was a topographical engineer in the army and worked in surveys on the Great Lakes and the South Pass of the Rockies. He was breveted for gallantry at

Buena Vista in the Mexican War and thereafter was put in charge
of the construction of the dome on the U.S. Capitol.[59]

After the Civil War broke out, Franklin first headed the defenses
of Washington and then led the Sixth Corps to distinction in the
Peninsular Campaign. At Fredericksburg he led the "Left Grand
Division" of the Sixth and First Corps. Ambrose Burnside, commanding the Army of the Potomac, blamed him for a large share of
that fiasco and demanded that the president fire Franklin, among
others. Lincoln's refusal prompted Burnside's relief from command,
but Franklin was never able to remove the stain of those accusations. He was not reinstated as commander of the Sixth Corps but
sent instead to the Department of the Gulf to command the Nineteenth Corps. He had participated in the ill-fated Sabine Pass operation, an attack on the Louisiana-Texas boundary in 1863, and
was now hoping to rehabilitate his career.

Three thousand of Franklin's 15,000 infantrymen had started
from New Orleans with him; the remainder, stripped from outposts
on the barrier islands of Texas, had traveled with their equipment
by troop transport boats to Berwick Bay, which lay south of the
town of Franklin, Louisiana.[60] Franklin was familiar with the area
his men were now traversing. Banks had sent him there the previous year with negligible success. As the ground dried, the column
was averaging seventeen miles a day.[61] The roads had been torn up
by the cavalry's passing, so there was no way the infantry could lose
its way.

Many soldiers wrote of the beautiful countryside they were
passing. The Teche was the stereotypical image of the South, its
great meandering bow curves and serenely slow-flowing waters
lined with huge live oaks dripping with Spanish moss. Along its
banks the sugar plantations with their great houses, sometimes
abandoned, and neglected fields reminded soldiers of the former
wealth of this once peaceful region. Near the headwaters of the
Teche the column moved into a different region, populated not by
Creoles but by Cajuns, short for "Acadians"—exiles who had settled
in Louisiana after the English expelled them from their beloved
"Acadie" in Canada at the end of the Seven Years' War. They were
not enthusiastic about outsiders occupying their lands again.[62]

The column crossed over Bayou Courtableu and passed through
Grand Coteau, Opelousas, and the old town of Washington. They
had now traversed a corner of the Attakapa prairie, former home
of the cannibal Attakapa Indians. Over low piney hills they marched

Major General William Buel Franklin. Library of Congress, Prints and Photographs Division, LC-B8172-3795

before entering a palmetto-laced swamp that covered more than thirty miles. From there the column entered the low pine hill country before reaching the Red River valley and the rich, red sandy alluvial plan that produced huge crops of cotton. Here the road led them north to Alexandria, located near the geographic center of the state.[63] The head of the infantry column marched into the town seven days behind schedule, on March 25.[64]

Banks had not endured the hazards and deprivations of the march with his infantry. He had floated into Alexandria the day before on a transport named *Black Hawk*, which was filled with reporters and cotton speculators.[65] Porter was not amused. He considered Banks's choice of conveyance an insult, for the admiral's flagship, the large tinclad also named *Black Hawk*, was his pride and joy.[66] The general's affront was not lost on the admiral or his favored captains.

Banks was dismayed by what he found in Alexandria: The navy was carrying on a bustling business in gathering, processing, and transshipping cotton. It was all legal, but Banks's cotton broker friends were angry, and he was seeing his grand scheme to be the savior of the New England textile mills literally floating down the river. Banks had arrived far behind schedule, and Porter, who had arrived at Alexandria with his forces on March 15 and 16, was like Sherman: he could not bear inactivity. With the city's surrender in hand and no sign of Banks and his legions he was not averse to procuring cotton. Speculators aside, he had naval tradition and, more important, the Naval Prize Law on his side. Federal law allowed the navy to seize as war prizes the properties of a belligerent nation and turn them over to an admiralty court, which would sell them and have the proceeds divided among the captors.[67] The admiralty court was located at Porter's home base of Cairo, Illinois. In the configuration of the law at the time, the naval personnel presenting prizes to the court received 50 percent of the total value of the captured property (Porter's share was 5 percent of the 50 percent), and the remaining 50 percent was paid into a fund, administered by the navy, for disabled seamen.[68] The law had been enacted in the early days of the republic to make it advantageous for captains of warships to seize the enemy's merchantmen and receive extra compensation for themselves and their crews. It was expanded to include war prizes of all types, as long as they had monetary value—and cotton was an extraordinarily valuable commodity in 1864. Since there was no equivalent mechanism for the army to benefit from spoils of war, there was immediate animosity between the two service arms. Army officers groused, even in official correspondence, that "every gun-boat is loaded with cotton, and the officers are taking it without regard to the loyalty of the owners. It looks . . . like a big steal."[69] Several claims were adjudicated from civilians angry over losses due to the navy's overzealous gathering of cotton.[70] Porter defended himself before Congress

Rear Admiral David Dixon Porter. Naval Historical Center photo NH 47394

and reported his efforts in his two postwar books. Selfridge later wrote in his memoirs that "incentive of prize money naturally influenced the navy to be especially active (in obtaining cotton)."[71]

Day after day while waiting for Banks, the admiral's minions were getting hands-on experience in the ways of the Southern economy. Porter sent his jack-tars out in ever increasing circles from

Alexandria to obtain the white gold. The sailors fanned out eight to ten miles on both sides of the Red River.[72] Baled cotton was brought to the wharves, and cotton waiting for processing was ginned and baled by the sailors and marines or Southerners working under the watchful eye and weapons of their Union "bosses."[73] An official congressional report quoted Porter as saying openly that "Jack made very good cotton bales."[74]

Selfridge was one of Porter's favorite commanders, and the ingenuity he showed in this venture was typical of his panache. He devised a technique, which Porter immediately had implemented by others in his command, for answering the question "How was one to know what cotton belonged to the Confederate government and what was private property?" Confederate cotton was a legitimate prize; stealing cotton from civilians was looting and punishable by imprisonment or death. If the conditions were nebulous (and they all were), Selfridge had stencils made, and sometimes branding irons, that read "CSA." The use of regulation navy paint or a fiery brand labeled the cotton for all to see as Confederate States of America property and therefore legitimate booty.

A portion of the Mississippi Squadron at Alexandria shortly before the completion of Bailey's dam. The ironclad on the left of the image is the *Louisville*; its armor plating has been removed. The monitor is the *Neosho*; note cotton on its deck. The vessel with the tall smokestacks is the *Lexington*. There are also three sisters of the *Louisville* in the photograph, one behind the *Neosho* and two to the left of the *Lexington*. *Courtesy of Rare Book, Manuscript, and Special Collections Library, Duke University, Durham, North Carolina*

Four-hundred-pound bales of cotton were not easily lugged back to the wharves. If U.S. Navy wagons and mules were not readily available, local wagons and mules were confiscated, and both animals and wagons were painted with USN. As the marked cotton was checked in by the navy quartermasters, it, too, was stenciled USN.[75] (In later congressional testimony, Colonel James Wilson stated that Porter, when asked what the letters CSA and USN meant, replied that they "stood for 'Cotton Stealing Association of the United States Navy.' ")[76] In addition, empty coal barges attached to Porter's gunboats were sent as far as twenty to thirty miles down river to be loaded with cotton. The only extant photograph of the ironclads and monitors at Alexandria show the *Neosho* in the foreground with bales of cotton stacked on its deck, for they were too large to fit in the holds.[77] Altogether, the navy gathered more than 3,000 bales of cotton in and around Alexandria.[78] The true number may never be known.

Nor will the total number of bales burned by the Confederates in retaliation, for in apparent response to the theft of cotton within a few miles of Alexandria, Taylor had his soldiers burn thousands of bales to keep them out of Union hands and pocketbooks. Wellington W. Withenbury, a steamboat pilot acting as a local expert for Admiral Porter and later General Banks, stated in testimony before Congress in March 1865, "I have no notion that a single person in that vicinity burned their own cotton. There was a great effort made to induce General Dick Taylor to rescind the order to burn cotton. He said, 'Don't ask me; General Banks is coming with his army of occupation; make your peace with him. If he respects your rights, I certainly shall.' "[79] According to Withenbury, Taylor would not have incinerated millions of dollars' worth of cotton had there not first been wholesale seizure by Banks or Porter.[80] On April 2, Banks wrote orders allowing civilians to sell their cotton to prevent it from being burned: citizens of Louisiana were to be allowed to bring in their crop to the quartermaster's office for shipment to New Orleans and sale. It was too little, too late.

When Franklin entered Alexandria at the head of the infantry column, Porter remarked on how fine they looked, even after a grueling march: "It was as fine a body of troops as were ever seen in the Southwest. Not-withstanding a march of twenty-one miles, they came in quite fresh and full of spirits. But more than a week of valuable time had been lost since the 17th instant, the day on which General Banks promised to meet the Navy at Alexandria, and the conclusion arrived at was that the General did not possess the military virtue of punctuality which the Navy had recognized in Generals Grant, Sherman, A. J. Smith, and other officers with whom they had hitherto cooperated."[81] Franklin's Nineteenth Corps, strung out fifteen to twenty miles, took the better part of two days to get in and bivouacked. The last regiment marched in on March 26.[82] It is evident from Porter's later writings that Banks and Franklin had not wanted them to appear shabby when they entered Alexandria as the conquering heroes.

Porter intimated that perhaps they looked too good—which may have been the reason they had taken so long to reach the appointed meeting place. He strongly contrasted the way the eastern troops of the Nineteenth Corps looked and behaved with his more favored western troops of A. J. Smith's command.[83] Smith's men, adept at foraging, had been living off the land. Their uniform blouses were typically soiled and torn; their military demeanor lacked the spit and polish of the eastern troops; and they had a reputation for being rowdy and undisciplined. They contemptuously called the Nineteenth Corps men "paper-collar" or "band box" soldiers for their high celluloid or thick paper collars and their appearance as members of military brass bands, of which Banks had several. The easterners, in turn, looked down upon the western rabble as a generally uncouth lot. According to Porter, when Banks first saw Smith's men, he exclaimed, "What, in the name of Heaven did Sherman send me these ragged guerrillas for?"[84]—where upon his eastern troops began calling the westerners "gorillas."[85] There were more than a few catcalls and fights—in which the westerners usually came out on top.[86]

Banks now had the two southern pincers in position, a force of 32,500 effectives and support troops situated in and around Alexandria.[87] This number included 2,500 U.S. Colored Troops of the Corps d'Afrique, which had arrived separately by transport vessels a few days after Banks. The navy's armed men-of-war and the army's Quartermaster Corps transports together totaled ninety vessels. Porter mounted 210 heavy guns, and Banks's artillery added another ninety field pieces.[88] Banks would later tell the Joint Congressional Committee on the Conduct of the War that everything seemed in place; after "one bound to Alexandria," there would be "one bound to Shreveport, one bound to the Gulf."[89] Surely, he thought, it would be an easy task.

Then politicians and cotton brokers began appealing to Banks personally, attempting to cut deals with him.[90] It appears that he

showed no favoritism but concentrated on organizing local elections and trying to placate the people bombarding him with re-
quests and demands.[91] Most of those demanding something from
Banks were local, but not all: in the midst of his business and political activity, a letter arrived on March 26 from Grant, who was
now a lieutenant general and general-in-chief. Never enthusiastic
about the campaign but never in a position to stop it, Grant gave
Banks his minimal expectations, outlining a schedule and demanding that Banks follow it. Of course, Grant had no way of knowing
that Banks had already created delays and that the troops had suffered additional weather-related hold-ups; even had he known, he
would likely have had little sympathy. Grant told Banks that the
success of the expedition was important because it would reduce
the number of Union troops needed to secure the open navigation
of the Mississippi River. He added, "It is also important that Shreveport should be taken as soon as possible."[92]

The letter included a caveat that deeply disturbed Banks: even
if for any reason there was a delay in taking Shreveport by the end
of April, Banks must return A. J. Smith's command to Sherman by
the middle of that month. Grant was emphatic, saying it must be
done "even if it leads to the abandonment of the main object of
your expedition."[93] If he *could* manage to capture Shreveport, Banks
was instructed to garrison it, retain enough troops there to keep the
Red River open to navigation, and return with the balance of his
forces to New Orleans to prepare for operations against Mobile.[94]

Banks's idea of a leisurely movement to Shreveport, such as he
had undertaken to Alexandria, thus evaporated into the sky like
the pillars of smoke from burning cotton. He also realized that anything short of taking the Confederate capital of Louisiana would
bring him political ruin, denying his presidential aspirations. Not
one to shrink from a challenge, Banks now prepared to take Shreveport. He was ready; the Red River was not.

Porter had been monitoring the river levels since the day he
arrived and did not like what he saw. Sherman, who had earlier
lived across the river from Alexandria, explained to him that the
Red River rose every spring and that this was the only time the
fleet, particularly the deep-draft gunboats, could get to Shreveport.[95]
Porter watched for the anticipated rise, but instead, he saw the river
falling, sometimes an inch per day, sometimes an inch per hour.[96]
The admiral became apprehensive, at least according to Banks. The
general said later in congressional testimony that he appealed to

Porter's lust for cotton, for surely in Shreveport there were huge storehouses filled with the white gold.[97]

Porter realized he could wait no longer and prepared to move upstream. He sent light-draft vessels forward to check the channel depth at various places in Alexandria. He secured the services of Wellington W. Withenbury, a very experienced river pilot, who advised him to take only his light-draft ironclads, monitors, tinclads, and the army transports. Withenbury told Porter about the "falls" at Alexandria, which were well known to steamboat men. They consisted of sandstone boulders, which in high water were never seen and were deep enough to cause no harm; in normal spring conditions the boulders could be navigated with care, their positions marked by swirls and eddies. When water was particularly low, however, the boulders were easily seen, which meant that the water level was just a few feet above the channel floor.[98] The twisting course through the boulders was called the Chute, swiftly flowing water that formed rapids around the sandstone (giving the parish its French name of Rapides). The falls were first described by the French explorers Le Moyne Bienville and Louis Juchereau de St. Denis before the founding of Natchitoches in the early 1700s.

Porter listened to Withenbury's counsel and then did a curious thing: he told Withenbury to take the *Eastport* over the falls.[99] Withenbury protested and suggested taking the lighter-draft vessels over first, but Porter emphatically ordered him to follow instructions. Two questions are vital to the remainder of the naval portion of the campaign. First, why was Porter adamant about leading with his largest and most cumbersome ironclad? Second, why was the river behaving as it was?

Porter, though egocentric and bull-headed, was brilliant, seasoned, extraordinarily self-confident, and certainly no stranger to command. As the most powerful and knowledgeable admiral on the inland waters of the United States, why would he make such a rash judgment? He was monitoring the river levels several times daily and must have recognized that the *Eastport*, the pride of his fleet, was also a liability in this situation. Perhaps he knew or suspected what lay ahead on the river. He had firm intelligence reports about the defenses of Shreveport. It is known that there was a double agent or Union spy operating in Shreveport in June, shortly after the campaign. It was not known when he was in place, but he certainly could have been there during or even before the campaign.[100]

Word had filtered to the army in New Orleans about Confederate submarines in Shreveport, sisters of the *Hunley*, and on June 18,
1864, Porter ordered a chain placed across the mouth of the Red
River to keep the subs hemmed in.[101] By at least March 1865, Porter
knew the dimensions of the torpedo boats and what weapons they
carried.[102] The question that may never be answered is when he
first learned about the submarines.

Photograph of the *Eastport*, perhaps on the Red River. Note the extremely low water and mud flats in the foreground. Archives of the Mansfield State Historic Site,
Mansfield, Louisiana. *Courtesy of the Mansfield State Historic Site*

At any rate, Porter did know about the possibility of as many
as five ironclads in Shreveport, described as smaller versions of
the *Tennessee* or *Arkansas*. He definitely knew that the *Missouri* was
there before the campaign, which may be why he led with the
Eastport.[103] It was his ironclad killer, and it had an excellent chance
of disabling or sinking a well-armored foe at longer distances than
his monitors or the "Pook Turtles," the nickname of the River Cities ironclads, the *Louisville* and its sisters. The huge ram on the
Eastport could deal a knockout punch at close quarters if the opportunity arose.[104] The idea of facing a squadron of up to five boats
like the *Arkansas* or *Tennessee* may have blinded him to the obvious
limitations of the giant *Eastport*.

As for the river, usually full and fast in the spring—what was
its mystery? The Confederates had set their defense plans in motion beginning March 18. The intricate series of defensive works
that Brigadier General Boggs had created in mid-1863 now became
critical sites. E. Kirby Smith ordered several things to occur in se-

quence as he and his staff anticipated the Union navy's ascent to Shreveport. First, this was the point at which he ordered the *New Falls City* brought up from its hiding place in Coushatta Chute (Bayou Coushatta) and placed at the foot of Scopini cutoff, one meander curve south of Tone's Bayou, where the engineers wedged it crosswise in the channel so tightly that its bow and stern ran up on the banks fifteen feet on each side.[105] A sandbar began to build upstream, and the engineers then poured mud into the hold and cracked the keel, making an instant dam.

It was after the placement of the *New Falls City* that other Confederate engineers used black powder to blow up the Hotchkiss dam, built the previous year—the explosion that drained the Red River "like pulling the plug out of a bathtub."[106] The river water exited its channel into the old Tone's Bayou channel and from there flowed directly into Bayou Pierre, just as planned. The bayou flowed back into the Red River a few miles above Grand Ecore, but before it did, the bayou's flood plain opened into a 19-mile-diameter circular bowl, where the bulk of the river water collected. Porter saw the river fall for several days and then rise briefly. The rise was only the small portion of the flow exiting Bayou Pierre and coming back into the river, but it encouraged him to begin sending the fleet north. Porter had again and again told anyone who would listen that he could take his fleet, and he meant *his* fleet, "wherever the sand was damp."[107] And so, with his usual braggadocio he told General Banks that he would accompany him even if "I should lose all my boats."[108] He almost did.

Following Porter's refusal to keep *Eastport* in deeper water, Withenbury reluctantly piloted the huge ironclad toward the falls.[109] The experienced pilot's concern proved correct: the deep-draft boat grounded in the chute, wedged among the boulders, and despite the efforts of tugs and the lighter-draft gunboats, there it stayed.[110] Not until three days later did the water rise enough for it to float and finally traverse the falls. While the *Eastport* was grounded, Porter did manage to move some of the lighter-draft vessels past by sending them through relatively shallow water outside the chute. Among them were the *Louisville, Carondelet, Mound City, Pittsburg, Chillicothe, Neosho, Ozark, Lexington, Cricket,* and *Fort Hindman.*[111] In fact, the *Eastport*'s bulk displaced enough water on either side to facilitate the passage of the lighter boats.

Withenbury asked Porter for permission to go to Grand Ecore aboard the *Black Hawk,* Banks's headquarters boat, and the admiral agreed. The pilot later reported to Congress that when they passed the *Eastport* on the way up the river, it was grounded again. The fleet required four days to travel 100 river miles to Grand Ecore. It moved slowly, Withenbury pointed out, because the lighter-draft gunboats had to wait for the heavier ones. Porter's fears of a potential Confederate fleet lurking around each bend of the twisting river forced him to keep the convoy in tight formation.

Among the most destructive troops in the Union contingent were the members of the Mississippi Marine Brigade—ostensibly under the command of A. J. Smith—who had looted and burned their way up the river. Porter frankly did not know what to do with them. Not only were they a discipline problem, but several were infected with smallpox. There were also persistent rumors that they were planning a mutiny because their actions were being constrained.[112] After the brigade's fast rams and support vessels moved past the falls, its hospital boat, the *Woodford*, grounded. The hull was pierced; it sank and had to be burned.[113] Banks and Porter were both pleased when orders arrived on the naval tug *Alf Cutting* that Major General James McPherson, commanding at Vicksburg, needed the Marine Brigade and its vessels to patrol the Mississippi River, since the Mississippi Squadron was not available for that duty.[114] Ellet and his marauders left Alexandria on March 27. With no one to rein them in, they wreaked havoc at every village and plantation on their way to the mouth of the river.[115]

While waiting for Porter to move the fleet over the falls, Banks ordered new elections for local officials in Alexandria and held them April 1. Again neglecting his military duties, he cajoled locals who wanted to sell their cotton, jayhawkers, and pro-Union refugees into voting. Porter called the election a farce and a humbug, adding in his congressional testimony, "We are sailors, not politicians."[116] Banks also continued to enjoy showing off his Nineteenth Corps soldiers. Marine Lieutenant Frank Church, commanding Porter's marine bodyguard detachment, wrote in his diary on March 27: "Saw the dress parade of the New York Volunteers. They were reviewed by General Banks and staff. Their bayonet exercises and charge were splendid. At 8 P.M. the Admiral was serenaded by Banks. While the band was playing [Listen to the] 'Mocking Bird' a shed fell on them badly injuring a major and two men."[117]

Banks, allowing Franklin to manage the army while he played politics, decided to ascend the river to Grand Ecore after the election on April 1. The order of march was set with A. J. Smith's veterans at the rear of the column. Albert Lee's cavalry left Alexandria and passed Henderson's Hill on March 26. Smith's men left on the evening of the 27th and the morning of the 28th, the length of the column at times stretching over twenty-five miles. Smith's contingent marched only to the steamboat landing at Cotile, about twenty-two miles north of Alexandria near Henderson's Hill, and there boarded the quartermaster transports to accompany the war fleet.[118]

Just before Banks boarded the *Black Hawk* on April 2 and headed for Grand Ecore, he wrote General Halleck one of many messages that caused concern in Washington. Banks was so self-confident, so sure that Rebels would not confront him before Shreveport, if then, that he anticipated being in the city by April 10. He told Halleck that he would then "pursue the enemy into the interior of Texas, for the sole purpose of dispersing or destroying his forces."[119] Banks reminded the chief of staff that he was well aware that Smith's troops must be returned. In this obvious move to please Grant, Banks was skating on thin ice, attempting to show Halleck that he was confident the original plan would work yet also skirting the edge of what Grant had ordered him to do—and that was not to invade Texas. Halleck shared the message with the president, who understood his staff officers' fears and commented, "I am sorry to see this tone of confidence; the next news we shall hear from there will be of a defeat."[120] Lincoln was prescient.

March and April in northern Louisiana are transitional months. The moist air streaming up from the Gulf of Mexico meets the drier air of the continental United States, and violent storms are common. The air becomes muggy and the relative humidity often 80 percent or higher. Between rains, the heat quickly dries out the Red River valley's sand and the red clay of the nearby hills. Thus, the roads on which the Union forces marched alternated between dustbins and muddy soup. Franklin marched his troops along the river road within sight of the gunboats, just as the original campaign plan had specified. Union diarists described the land changing as they neared Natchitoches. For the first time they saw rocks beside the road and hills in the near distance. Viewing the Red River, they remarked that it was appropriately named.[121] A. J. Smith's men wrote of being greeted by slaves waving and singing at some of the riverside plantations. One heard the slaves singing that it was a great day "when the Linkum gunboats come."[122]

Lee's cavalry division reached Natchitoches on March 30 and took the town simply by riding in. Franklin arrived on April 1, after marching eighty miles in four days.[123] The column set up bivouac between Natchitoches and the small village of Grand Ecore, four miles farther north on the Red River. The tiny village acted as a port for Natchitoches, for the channel of the Red River, once running alongside Natchitoches, had moved, creating the Cane River, actually a long lake. Grand Ecore was the place on the west bank of the Red River where the old Spanish Royal Road, El Camino Real, began its long route to Mexico City. The road dated back to the period when the Spanish capital of Texas was at Los Adaes, just west of Natchitoches near the present town of Robeline, Louisiana. Located on the high bluffs at Grand Ecore were the old forts of Seldon and Solubrity, where Grant had been stationed early in the Mexican War. The Confederates had fortified the place but abandoned it as the Union forces came up the river.

Porter anchored his fleet in a sheltered bend immediately downstream from the bluffs, joined by A. J. Smith's transports. Banks did not appear until late in the evening of April 3, having been delayed once more by assisting the *Eastport*, which had grounded yet again.[124] Now it was time for Banks to determine the best route for his final "bound" to Shreveport.

NOTES

1. Scott, *32d Iowa*, 130; Edmund Newsome, *Experience in the War of the Rebellion* (Carbondale, IL, 1880), 111; Walter G. Smith, ed., *Life and Letters of T. Kilby Smith* (New York, 1898), 356.

2. Smith, *T. Kilby Smith*, 356.

3. Virgil Carrington Jones, *The Civil War at Sea, July 1863–November 1865: The Final Effort*, 3 vols. (New York, 1962), 3:166; George Haven Pittman, *Memories of My Youth*, quoted in William Riley Brooksher, *War along the Bayous: The 1864 Red River Campaign in Louisiana* (Washington, DC, 1998), 38.

4. *O.R.* 34, 304.

5. *O.R. Atlas*, pl. 52.

6. Stewart Sifakis, *Who Was Who in the Union* (New York, 1988), 316; James C. Bradford, ed., *Captains of the Old Steam Navy: Makers of the American Naval Tradition 1840–1880* (Annapolis, MD, 1986), 227–49; Richard West Jr., *The Second Admiral: A Life of David Dixon Porter* (New York, 1937), 3–9.

7. *O.R.N.* 25, 787–88.

8. *O.R.* 34, 12; Ezra Warner, *Generals in Blue: Lives of the Union Commanders* (Baton Rouge, LA, 1992), 338–39.

9. Newsome, *Experience in the War*, 111–12.

10. *O.R.* 34, 599; Johnson, *Red River Campaign*, 91.

11. Taylor, *Destruction and Reconstruction*, 156.

12. *O.R.* 34, 599.

13. Ibid., 305; Scott, *32d Iowa*, 131; Newsome, *Experience in the War*, 112–13.

14. *O.R.* 34, 305.

15. Smith, *T. Kilby Smith*, 357.

16. Scott, *32d Iowa*, 132.

17. Ibid.; *O.R.* 34, 305, 338–39.

18. *O.R.N.* 26, 25.

19. Porter, *Naval History*, 397.

20. James P. Jones and Edward F. Keuchel, eds., *Civil War Marine: A Diary of The Red River Expedition, 1864* (Washington, DC, 1975), 37.

21. Porter, *Naval History*, 496.

22. Porter, *Incidents and Anecdotes*, 214–15.

23. *O.R.* 34, 305; Scott, *32d Iowa*, 131.

24. *O.R.* 34, 305, 338–39.

25. Ibid., 306.

26. *O.R.N.*, 26, 28, 30–31.

27. Ibid., 32.

28. Newsome, *Experience in the War*, 122.

29. Sifakis, *Who Was Who in the Union*, 360.

30. Johnson and Buel, *Battles and Leaders*, 4:362.

31. Ibid.; Joiner and Vetter, "Union Naval Expedition," 43.

32. Taylor, *Destruction and Reconstruction*, 181–83; *O.R.* 34, 506, 561.

33. *O.R.* 34, pt. 2, 616.

34. *O.R.* 34, 506, 561.

35. *O.R.* 26, pt. 2, 54–55, 323; Bridges, *Biographical and Historical Memoirs*, 210; Lavender Map.

36. Lavender Map.

37. *O.R.* 34, 561.

38. Taylor, *Destruction and Reconstruction*, 156.

39. *O.R.* 34, 496, 500, 578.

40. Ibid.

41. Gary B. Mills, *The Forgotten People: Cane River's Creoles of Color* (Baton Rouge, LA, 1977), 215 n.

42. Johnson, *Red River Campaign*, 96; *O.R. Atlas*, pl. 52.

43. Taylor, *Destruction and Reconstruction*, 157.

44. John D. Winters, *The Civil War in Louisiana* (Baton Rouge, LA, 1963), 330.

45. Richard H. Zeitlin, *Old Abe the War Eagle: A True Story of the Civil War and Reconstruction* (Madison, WI, 1986), 53.

46. Ibid.; *O.R.* 34, 315–16, 334–35, 463–64, 501; Taylor, *Destruction and Reconstruction*, 157; Joseph P. Blessington, *The Campaigns of Walker's Texas Division* (New York, 1875), 178; James K. Ewer, *The Third Massachusetts Cavalry in the War for the Union* (Maplewood, MA, 1903), 137–39 (hereafter cited as *3d Massachusetts*.

47. JCCW, 28–29.

48. *O.R.N.* 26, 41.

49. B. F. Stevenson, *Letters from the Army, 1862–1864* (Cincinnati, OH, 1886), 307.

50. *O.R.* 34, pt. 2, 513.

51. JCCW, 28.

52. H. B. Sprague, *History of the 13th Regiment of Connecticut Volunteers* (Hartford, CT, 1867), 186 (hereafter cited as *13th Connecticut*).

53. *O.R. Atlas*, pl. 52.

54. Warner, *Generals in Blue*, 278; Sifakis, *Who Was Who in the Union*, 233.

55. Scott Dearman, unpublished report at Mansfield, LA, State Historic Site.

56. Sprague, *13th Connecticut*, 186.

57. Sifakis, *Who Was Who in the Union*, 119.

58. *JCCW*, 28.

59. Warner, *Generals in Blue*, 159–60; Sifakis, *Who Was Who in the Union*, 142–43.

60. *JCCW*, 28–29.

61. T. H. Bringhurst and Frank Swigart, *History of the Forty-Sixth Regiment Indiana Volunteer Infantry* (Logansport, Indiana, 1888), 85–86 (hereafter cited as *46th Indiana*).

62. Taylor, *Destruction and Reconstruction*, 104–6; Orton S. Clark, *The One Hundred and Sixteenth Regiment of New York Volunteers* (Buffalo, NY, 1868), 145–47 (hereafter cited as *116th New York*).

63. *O.R. Atlas*, pl. 52.

64. *O.R. 34*, 426–27.

65. Johnson, *Red River Campaign*, 99; Joiner and Vetter, "Union Naval Expedition," 47.

66. Johnson and Buel, *Battles and Leaders* 4:366, Porter, *Naval History*, 494–533.

67. *JCCW*, 18, 71, 74, 224–25.

68. Johnson, *Red River Campaign*, 101.

69. *O.R. 34*, pt. 2, 655.

70. *O.R.N. 26*, 412.

71. Thomas O. Selfridge, *What Finer Tradition: The Memoirs of Thomas O. Selfridge* (Columbia, SC, 1987), 96.

72. *O.R. 34*, pt. 3, 18.

73. *JCCW*, 18, 82, 90, 224, 283, 288.

74. Ibid., 303.

75. *JCCW*, 18, 82, 90, 224, 283, 288.

76. Ibid., 11.

77. Photograph in the Lord-Eltinge Collection, Duke University, Raleigh, North Carolina.

78. Winters, *Civil War in Louisiana*, 331.

79. Ibid., 285.

80. Ibid.

81. Porter, *Naval History*, 499.

82. *O.R. 34*, 426–27.

83. Porter, *Naval History*, 499–501.

84. Ibid., 501.

85. Scott, *32d Iowa*, 136.

86. Ibid.; Harrington, *Fighting Politician*, 152–53; Hoffman, *Camp, Court, and Siege*, 93.

87. *O.R. 34*, 167.

88. Ibid., 168.

89. *JCCW*, 400.

90. *O.R.* 34, pt. 3, 4.
91. *JCCW*, 281, 335.
92. *O.R.* 34, pt. 2, 494, 610–11.
93. Ibid., 610–11.
94. Ibid.
95. *JCCW*, 281–83.
96. Porter, *Naval History*, 500.
97. *JCCW*, 8–9; *O.R.N.* 26, 50.
98. *JCCW*, 282.
99. Ibid.
100. *JCCW*, 285, the spy was possibly Withenbury. Also, there was an agent in place in 1864 and 1865, *JCCW*, 529. *O.R.N.* 20, 103–4.
101. *O.R.N.* 26, 438–39.
102. Ibid., 22, 103–4.
103. *JCCW*, 287.
104. Silverstone, *Warships of the Civil War Navies*, 156.
105. *O.R.* 34, pt. 2, 1056–57; Lavender Map.
106. Cardin, *Bossier Parish History*, 32.
107. *JCCW*, 8–9.
108. Ibid., 275; *O.R.N.* 26, 50.
109. *JCCW*, 282.
110. Ibid., 282–83.
111. *O.R.N.* 26, 50; *JCCW*, 282–83.
112. *JCCW*, 322.
113. Ibid., 7, 322.
114. *O.R.* 34, pt. 2, 735; Warren D. Crandall, *History of the Ram Fleet and the Mississippi Marine Brigade in the War for the Union on the Mississippi and Its Tributaries: The Story of the Ellets and Their Men* (St. Louis, 1907), 378.
115. *JCCW*, 322; *O.R.* 34, pt. 2, 746, 768.
116. *JCCW*, 280.
117. Jones and Keuchel, *Civil War Marine*, 41.
118. Scott, *32d Iowa*, 135; Ewer, *3d Massachusetts*, 139; Richard B. Irwin, *History of the Nineteenth Army Corps* (New York, 1892), 294 (hereafter cited as *19th Corps*).
119. *O.R.* 34, 179–80.
120. John G. Nicolay and John Hay, *Abraham Lincoln, a History*, 10 vols. (1890; reprint, New York, 1909), 8:291.
121. Clark, *116th New York*, 149–55; Elias P. Pellet, *History of the 114th Regiment, New York State Volunteers* (Norwich, 1866), 190–91 (hereafter cited as *114th New York*).
122. William H. Stewart Diary, Southern Historical Collection, University of North Carolina, Chapel Hill, 17; Thomas J. Williams, *An Historical Sketch of the 56th Ohio Volunteer Infantry* (Columbus, OH, 1899), 66 (hereafter cited as *56th Ohio*).
123. *O.R.* 34, 428, 445; Bringhurst and Swigart, *46th Indiana*, 86.
124. *JCCW*, 282, 286.

CHAPTER FIVE

THROUGH THE
HOWLING WILDERNESS

BANKS'S PROGRESS TO Grand Ecore had been relatively easy, though time consuming. It was April 3, and in twelve days A. J. Smith's 10,000 men were scheduled to depart from his command. The fact that they were attached to the fleet and not under his direct authority eased the pressure somewhat. The army faced a major problem, and Banks had to make a decision quickly. What was the best avenue of approach to Shreveport? The maps carried by his staff were different from those of the river pilots. Some showed roads not marked on others. The same was true for lakes, villages, and town locations. Streams were shown flowing in different directions; their size varies and often the same stream might have several different names.[1] Brigadier General Charles P. Stone, Banks's chief of staff, consulted with Withenbury, the river pilot who had taken on the additional role of adjunct adviser to Banks.

Withenbury later testified before Congress that he had examined Stone's maps and given Stone copies of his own, showing where towns and roads were located.[2] Stone asked him about the location of a place called Pleasant Hill. Withenbury showed him the location on Stone's map, where the place name was not labeled. Stone argued that it was not there, and Withenbury assured him it was. The argument occurred because Stone had been given a report that Albert Lee's cavalry had engaged the enemy at a place called Pleasant Hill, whereas the skirmishes actually took place at White's Store and at Crump's Corners, both south of Pleasant Hill.

The army was using LaTourette's Map of Louisiana, published in 1853, which portrayed the entire state on a single large sheet and displayed very little detail.[3] Union topographical engineers, under Colonel John S. Clark, had altered the map to identify features as they saw them. (Clark was adept at making maps that Banks, untrained in military mapmaking, could understand; Clark's maps were beautiful, using watercolors and colored inks and pencils.[4]) Banks and his staff regarded the LaTourette Map as gospel, but it was not as reliable as it should have been, and it was not a substitute for field intelligence provided by cavalry. Two maps in the National Archives by a Major Houston of Banks's staff, dated 1864, show two additional roads drawn in as single lines closely following the Red River, one on the east bank and the other on the west.[5] These were obviously drawn either at the close of the campaign or soon afterward, and one was the route that Richard Taylor and William Boggs expected the Union forces to take. Certainly Porter, and probably Banks, would have tried the river route and discovered a serviceable road if not for the convincing recommendations of the riverboat pilot.

Withenbury, a twenty-year veteran pilot on the Red River, had piloted steamboats since shortly after Henry Miller Shreve cleared the logjam called the Great Raft and opened the waterway to navigation. Withenbury had made numerous trips up and down the river and had seen every feature on and near it. He also had a financial interest in cotton grown along the river near Alexandria and Shreveport, for which he had collected $4,413.73 from the Confederate government.[6] Although he proudly proclaimed himself to Porter, Banks, and members of Congress as "a Union man" from Connecticut, he was in fact a businessman dealing in the most lucrative commodity of the South. (After the campaign he was listed as a claimant to some of the cotton confiscated by the navy.) He knew from his long experience on the river that the two roads Houston would later sketch did, in fact, exist. They were called the Winter Road and the Summer Road. The Summer Road on the west bank was used only when the terrain was dry; the Winter Road, on the west bank, was open year round. Withenbury also knew that he could expect his cotton to be safe only if the army did not ascend the river with the navy. That he did not want to see his cotton destroyed or captured perhaps explains what he did next.

When asked about the roads leading to Shreveport, Withenbury pointed to and described in great detail the two road networks shown on the LaTourette map, both of which bowed far away from the river, forming an irregular parenthesis. The Fort Towson Road, to the east, was an old military road that led inland from Campti, a few miles upstream, to the town of Minden, almost due east of Shreveport. In the LaTourette map the road ends there. In fact, however, it continued near the present town of Hope, Arkansas, to the Confederate capital of Arkansas at Washington before following

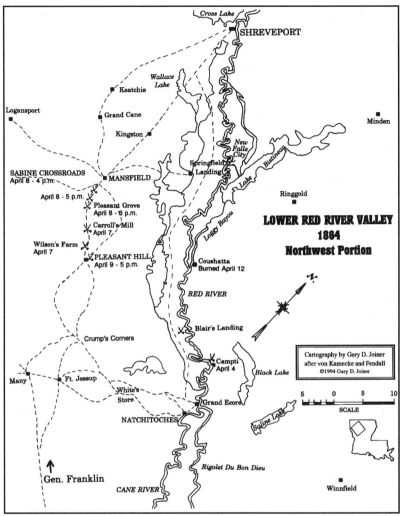

Map of the campaign in the Red River Valley in Louisiana. Battles are indicated by crossed swords.

the great bend of the Red River to Fort Towson in the Indian Territory; this old fort monitored the Union forces at Fort Smith. The river pilot told Congress, "I pointed out on the [LaTourette] map precisely all the roads."[7] Withenbury knew, however, that Banks would not use the eastern road. He told the general it would take three extra days to move around the lakes on that side; he acknowledged to Banks that the roads would be better on the east, but he was much more specific about the roads to the west.

When questioned about the western inland road, Withenbury testified before Congress that he had told Banks the Pleasant Hill to Mansfield Road would take the army away from the river and the protection of the navy until they reached Shreveport. Porter pleaded with Banks to let him make a reconnaissance upriver for two or three days, but the general was watching the calendar and thought the delay would be a total waste of time. Banks decided to move his army west by the inland road.

Porter, of course, had to take the river route, and once he began his move toward Shreveport, he wrote his friend Sherman that he saw the road and the fields filled with corn and herds of cattle grazing near the west bank of the river: "It struck me very forcibly that this would have been the route for the army, where they could have traveled without all that immense train, the country supporting them as they proceeded along. The roads are good, wide fields on all sides, a river protecting the right flank of the army, and gunboats in company."[8] But by then it was too late. Withenbury had changed the course of the campaign in a single night. Because Banks, eager to take Shreveport and claim his glory, trusted the river pilot as a parishioner would a priest, the pilot denied the Union army the support of the great guns on the warships and gave it a sense of false security. If there were no roads beside the river, ascending to Shreveport, the Confederates could not flank Banks though the piney wilderness that he saw from the heights of Grand Ecore. Withenbury thus saved his cotton and, except perhaps in Porter's eyes, was still a good Union man.

Banks seems to have been totally satisfied with Withenbury's information; he wrote his wife the next day that "the enemy retreats before us and will not fight a battle this side of Shreveport, if then."[9] Given the meager information at hand and his belief that there were only two roads, Banks made the correct choice between those alternatives; however, even considering the severe time limitation placed upon him by Grant, his refusal for either a naval or cavalry reconnaissance of the area to his north and west was unforgivable. On April 3, Banks sent a portion of Oliver Gooding's cavalry brigade on a reconnaissance up the east side of the river to Campti, where they captured a few prisoners, including two men from John Marmaduke's division. The cavalrymen learned from the prisoners that most of Major General Sterling Price's Confederate army was at Shreveport.[10]

Colonel John S. Clark, Banks's aide-de-camp and topographic engineer, reported to Franklin his estimates of enemy strength based on intelligence reports and the interrogation of the captured Confederate soldiers. On April 7 he discussed the possibility that Marmaduke's cavalry was heading for Missouri, that at least some of Sterling Price's forces were in Shreveport, and that Tom Green's Texans and the Louisiana forces were somewhere to the north. Clark estimated that Confederate forces to their front included as many as 5,000 infantry and cavalry in Texas with the Confederate commander of the District of Texas, Major General John Magruder; 5,000 with Price in Arkansas; and an additional 10,000 troops already positioned in Louisiana. He estimated the total number of effectives in their front to be 20,175, with seventy-six artillery pieces. He also reported to Franklin that the Union forces would consist of 15,000 to 18,000 infantry and cavalry, since the Marine Brigade had been released to other areas of operation.[11]

Franklin was handling the day-to-day affairs of the army while Banks made himself busy organizing another election at Grand Ecore and bribing the villagers with vows to protect their cotton.[12] But politics were not his only interest here. Other tasks also occupied him as well. Banks spent a considerable amount of time making sure his supply train was fully stocked with ten days' provisions for the march. His train included 300 wagons for Albert Lee's cavalry division, 700 wagons for William B. Franklin's infantry, and at least another fifty for the artillery and A. J. Smith's men.[13] (It was considered an exorbitant size; the Army of the Potomac at that time had 4,000 wagons while engaged in the Wilderness Campaign and, at its largest, 7,000 wagons.)[14] The train was a major component of the grand plan for the eventual cooperation of the army and navy. It allowed the army to act independently until its needs could be replenished by the supply vessels.

Once Banks had determined to take the inland route, he and Porter agreed to meet at a point opposite Springfield Landing in northern Desoto Parish on April 10.[15] The landing was about sixty miles by road and slightly over one hundred miles by river from Grand Ecore. It was located just four miles from the Red River on a narrow channel connecting Bayou Pierre Lake and Lake Cannisnia (today called Smithport Lake).[16] Banks was to leave Grand Ecore on April 6 and Porter on April 7.[17] At Springfield Landing or near it, Porter's fleet and the army transport vessels would replenish

Banks's supply trains before the two groups made the final approach to Shreveport.

Withenbury did not accompany Porter upriver, and since the admiral had been upstream only as far as Alexandria in 1863, Grand Ecore was his point of deepest penetration into the Red River valley. He would not know the territory he was to travel, yet he had to consider which vessels could best be used on the river above his base of operations in Natchitoches Parish. The *Eastport* had become such a liability that Porter decided to leave it at Grand Ecore. All

The monitor *Neosho*. Miller, *The Photographic History of the Civil War*, 6:147

the maps showed the river between Grand Ecore and Shreveport to be winding and contorted. This stretch was in fact called the Narrows by river pilots. Porter correctly assumed that if the *Eastport* grounded in a tight bend, he might not be able to get it out. Deciding to compose his final assault force of the lightest-draft gunboats, he chose six vessels: the monitors *Osage* and *Neosho*, the timberclad *Lexington*, and the tinclads *Cricket*, *Fort Hindman*, and the ironclad *Chillicothee*.[18] The admiral made the *Cricket* his flagship. The gunboats accompanied twenty army transports loaded with supplies and T. Kilby Smith's small division of about 2,300 men from the Seventeenth Corps for protection.[19] Porter thus had his portion of the force defined and hoped that the army was using as much forethought.

Banks had the order of march just the way he wanted it. The cavalry would form up and ride out on the morning of April 6. It would take well over a day for the entire column to be moving on the road. Lee's cavalry was to be followed immediately by its 300 wagons, at the insistence of Franklin, so as not to delay his own supply train.[20] The wagons of the column were protected by the 2,500 U.S. Colored Troops of the Corps d'Afrique, some of whom were with Lee but most with the main supply train. Immediately following the cavalry's wagons and guards were the 15,000 infantry under Franklin. Banks and Franklin rode at the head of this contingent, whose order was two divisions of the Thirteenth Corps, then one division of the Nineteenth. Because of the narrow roads, the men were never able to march more than four abreast.

Behind this long line of infantry were the 700 wagons of its supply train.[21] When Banks had taken such care in defining the marching order, he neglected to note that 300 wagons to the front of the main infantry column and another 700 wagons to the rear would effectively box the marchers in: they would have difficulty assisting the cavalry to their front and would not easily be able to fall out or retreat with such a massive train behind them. Moreover, Bank's decision to use only one road set the stage for disaster. It may be said in his defense that he trusted his advisers to be correct in their assessment of the terrain ahead, and they showed him only the one road on their maps. The fact that he did not allow his cavalry to fan out ahead and seek other routes, however, qualifies as one of the greatest blunders in the Civil War.

Following the 700 wagons of the infantry's supply train were A. J. Smith's 7,500 men of the Sixteenth Corps. Relegated to eat the dust of the entire column, they delayed leaving Grand Ecore until the next day. The column's only flankers, a single brigade of cavalrymen under Colonel Oliver Gooding, never fanned out ahead as a screen but covered the column's rear and, when possible, its left flank.[22] Artillery dedicated to each of the infantry components traveled with them.

The column of men and matériel resembled a giant accordion, stretching out at some points, squeezing impossibly tight in others, at times not moving at all. The cavalry was not allowed to move far ahead and conduct its mission. Lee was repeatedly told to protect his own wagons and was not allowed to place them with the infantry's train. Banks's "bounds" had become a creep. Frustration was rampant, and the terrain they entered did little to ease the men's attitudes. The land traversed by the Union soldiers on their way to Grand Ecore had been remarkable for its flatness; the soil was either the rich, black alluvium of the deep delta or the reddish sands that gave the Red River its name. Now, as the column turned westward and left Natchitoches, the relatively easy traveling in the river valleys lay behind them. Red sand was replaced by red clay which, though hard when dry, turned slick and stuck to everything when moist. Wet clay made movement tiring and footing treacherous. The giant stretches of cotton-bearing land that the troops had grown accustomed to seeing were gone, replaced by yellow pine trees growing so thick in places that there was no undergrowth. At times landscape seemed like a long green cathedral, the road its only aisle. One Union cavalry trooper called the area a "howling wilderness."[23]

After a torrential rain on April 7, a reporter writing for the *Philadelphia Press* remarked that the narrow road seemed "more like a broad, deep, red-colored ditch than anything else."[24] He added that he had "ridden for fifty miles into the heart of this pine country, and from the beginning to the end of the journey there was nothing but a dense, impenetrable, interminable forest, traversed by a few narrow roads, with no signs of life or civilization beyond occasional log-houses and half-cleared plantations. . . . Such a thing as subsisting an army in a country like this could only be achieved when men and horses can be induced to live on pine trees and resin."[25] The forest became oppressive with its terrible sameness. The men found very little water that was not falling from the sky. Once it hit the earth, the rainwater became as bright red as the ditch they were marching in—and equally appealing.[26] When rain pelted down, the column stretched out even farther; the pace had slowed to a crawl, and tempers flared toward the rear. The western soldiers thought it was the easterners' inability to march and conduct a campaign that was the problem.[27]

As the Federal soldiers picked their way west and then north, Taylor finally began receiving some much-needed reinforcements, although not all that he needed and requested. About the time Lee felt the first raindrops, the Confederate major general Tom Green was crossing the Sabine River into Louisiana at Logansport in DeSoto Parish, bringing several regiments of Texas cavalry to Taylor's aid, once he was allowed to leave Texas soil. The fearless Green was a dynamic commander whose men would follow him anywhere. As a young boy he had fought at the Battle of San Jacinto, and he had helped usher in the independence of Texas, making him a living legend in his home state.[28] His cavalrymen and mounted infantry were famous for their individuality and the variety of their weapons and gear. Some were disciplined cavalry troopers, but many others were not; most brought their own weapons, but some had to be given guns when they arrived. Most wore bandoliers and carried bowie knives for close-in fighting. Many wore sombreros and sported drooping handlebar mustaches. They rode with abandon and could be compared to Russian Cossacks.[29] Their regimental leaders were Arthur Bagby, August Buchel, Xavier Debray, William Hardeman, Walter Lane Likens, James Major, Alexander Terrell, and Isham Chisum Woods. Perhaps the most unusual of these commanders was Colonel August Buchel, late of the Prussian army, who now commanded a regiment of cavalry raised from the Texas hill country town of New Braunfels. Because the German immigrants felt they were fighting for their new homeland, they were particularly enthusiastic warriors. Their presence made Lincoln's hope of a German-Texan counterrevolution ring hollow.[30]

After a short rest at the village and college campus at Keachi, Green's men joined Taylor at Pleasant Hill and then rode ahead to find out the location and activities of the Union forces. But Taylor did not have all the available forces at his disposal. In Shreveport, the Confederate strategic plan was becoming clearer. He had requested as many regiments as possible to be sent to him from Arkansas, and E. Kirby Smith was vacillating. He knew that Steele was coming down from Little Rock; at the same time, he knew that Banks posed by far the greater threat, so he ordered most of his Arkansas infantry under Major General Sterling Price to come to Shreveport so that they could be sent out in any direction as needed. These forces were small divisions operating under the command of Brigadier Generals Mosby Parsons and Thomas J. Churchill. To cover the void left by the units departing from southwestern Arkansas, Smith ordered Confederate forces under Brigadier General Samuel Maxey to leave the Indian Territory and move into Arkansas to assist Price in holding off Steele.[31] His deployment effectively denuded Texas, New Mexico, and Arizona of Confederate troops, leaving only 4,600 effectives in the entire region, most of them gathering in eastern and southeastern Texas to be ready if Banks captured Shreveport.[32]

Taylor was apprehensive and wanted to fight Banks farther south. He expected both Parsons and Churchill to join him south

of Shreveport in DeSoto Parish, but Kirby Smith delayed them while
they waited for their ammunition supplies, and without adequate
forces Taylor could not make his move. He bitterly laid his rein-
forcement and supply problems squarely at Smith's door in Shreveport and would continue to blame him for all the logistical and
remote command failings of the campaign to the day he died. Taylor referred to Kirby Smith not only as that "Hydrocephalus in
Shreveport" but also as a "pompous potentate presiding arbitrarily
over an empty empire."[33] Even though Tom Green had been de-
tained not by orders from Shreveport but by his department commander in Texas, Taylor assigned that delay, too, to his list of
grievances against Smith.[34]

Adding to this animosity was the highly charged political atmosphere in Shreveport, where the commanding general's staff
officers were trying to advance Smith's reputation and their own.
The chief instigator among Smith's cronies was the departmental
surgeon Sol Smith, a medical doctor from Alexandria who had been
with Kirby Smith from the beginning in Louisiana. Against Taylor's
advice, he had persuaded the general to make Alexandria his headquarters; only when the 1863 invasion made the central Louisiana
town untenable was it moved north. Sol Smith was rabidly antago-
nistic to Richard Taylor, going so far as to blame him for the Union
invasion.[35] Some officers and civilians in Shreveport loyal to Taylor reported to him that reinforcements were being delayed in order to let Kirby Smith look good by saving Taylor should the latter
get into trouble fighting Banks. Taylor, with his usual abruptness,
confronted Kirby Smith in heated correspondence.

Brigadier General William Boggs, no fan of Sol Smith (after the
campaign, the surgeon replaced Boggs as chief of staff in the department), and Taylor had to fight a political backstabbing war at
the same time as they were encountering a legitimate military action in their front. According to Boggs, Sol Smith persuaded Kirby
Smith that he should take the bulk of the army, including Taylor
and his growing number of infantry and cavalry regiments, against
Steele first, even though Banks at that time was closer.[36] Kirby Smith
met with Richard Taylor at Mansfield on April 6, and during a
heated meeting, Taylor objected to every plan Smith recommended.
Nothing was decided and Smith gave Taylor no specific orders.
Smith suggested that they go against Steele, or that they gather all
their forces behind the defenses in Shreveport, or even that they
should perhaps evacuate Louisiana and Arkansas and fight it out

Lieutenant General Edmund Kirby Smith. Archives of the Mansfield State Historic Site, Mansfield, Louisiana. *Courtesy of the Mansfield State Historic Site*

in East Texas. Taylor was appalled.[37] When Kirby Smith left the meeting without providing specific orders, Taylor was free to do what he wanted—or so he thought.

On April 8, instructions arrived for Taylor from Shreveport, but they were so obscure as to be almost unintelligible. Taylor was to fight a battle in a place that could easily be supplied. Taylor was not to fight on April 8, as it had been declared a National Day of Prayer.[38] Boggs may have been correct in thinking that Sol Smith was behind the vacillations. Kirby Smith did withhold the Arkansas

and Missouri troops for a time, and he would have looked the conquering hero if Taylor had been hard pressed against Banks.[39] His
letter arrived too late to have any effect on events, however, and
Taylor probably would have ignored it if he had had the chance.

While the Confederates were gathering, and waffling, the Union
column was feeling its way west and then north. Albert Lee led the
column westward from Natchitoches through the rolling red clay
hills on the track that had been the Spanish Royal Road. About
twelve miles west of Natchitoches they passed near the old Spanish capital of Texas at Los Adaes and then turned north at a stagecoach road intersection at which stood White's Store. (Today this
site is in the town of Robeline at the intersection of Louisiana State
Highway 6, the Royal Road, and Louisiana State Highway 120.)
Some of the men fell out of the column and bought almost everything the storeowner had. On their return, they would burn the
store down.

Just north of the store the terrain opened briefly into bottom-
land with small streams where canteens could be filled; then it
climbed back into the seemingly endless hills and ridges. Lee
pushed up the road to another store at Crump's Corners (today a
location near the intersection of Louisiana Highways 120 and 175
at the village of Belmont).[40] Four days earlier, Lee's men had encountered Confederate cavalry pickets who were waiting for them
near the store. He brushed them aside; at the intersection of the
road that would lead him north the next day, he halted the column
for the night. The pickets were part of Tom Green's advance troops,
sent to find the enemy and then report back. Refugees the column
met on the road told Union officers that the Rebels were massing at
a place called Sabine Crossroads and that it "was the point where
the rebels said they were going 'to begin to bury the Yankees.' "
The officers laughed the information off as so much braggadocio.[41]
The next day, April 7, appeared to Lee and the other commanders
much like the 6th. The Confederates had not shown any interest in
doing anything but light skirmishing. Maybe Banks was right; perhaps the Rebels wouldn't fight them until Shreveport, if then.

Colonel John Clark rode at the head of the column with Lee
and observed the advance that morning.[42] Lee had set out early
with three of his four brigades (Gooding was still occupied with
flanking duties). Of his ten regiments of cavalry, half were mounted
infantry but not accomplished horsemen, and most were untested
in battle.[43] The road ran almost due north for about twelve miles

with very few curves and almost no homesteads. At noon, Lee reached the sleepy little village of Pleasant Hill. Clark later reported that the cavalry, with its wagon train in tow, ran into four regiments of Green's cavalry at Wilson's farm, three miles north of Pleasant Hill.[44] There, Green chose to change his tactics and charge the Union cavalry. The Confederates occupied a large field beside the road to Lee's left and were also in dense woods ahead on his right. Though Lee could not accurately estimate their numbers, he formed his men on both sides of the road and set up his howitzers to provide support.

Green charged and forced the Union right back several yards, the Rebels attacking with their customary yell. The first brigade of infantry came up and fired a volley into the rank of Confederates, who then fell back into the field. The trees on Lee's right still contained an unknown number of Rebels keeping up a withering fire, and there was no way to charge them in the dense woods. But the Confederates fell back, and Lee had held his ground; his cavalrymen had not folded and had behaved well in the face of a forceful attack.[45] Union casualties were 70 killed and wounded in an action that lasted half an hour.[46] While the fight was unfolding, the column ground to a halt. Franklin and Banks were well to the back of the action and did not ride forward, since neither had expected organized opposition.

Both Lee and Clark tried to explain to Franklin what had happened and how things had changed, Lee by messages and Clark in person. Lee was concerned that for the first time the Rebels were operating differently. Rather than being seen as ghostly riders in the distance, this time they had massed and were waiting in an area of their choosing. And since they were cavalry, and no infantry had appeared, this area was perhaps just the first of the Confederate positions on this road. Lee requested that his wagons be moved back with the infantry's train and infantry, and that perhaps a division be brought forward to assist him.[47]

Franklin denied him out of hand. Then Clark, who had seen the skirmish and was in complete agreement with Lee, tried to intercede. Franklin again refused to reposition the train or more reinforcements forward, telling Clark "he must fight them alone—that was what he was there for. It might require the sacrifice of men, but in war men must be sacrificed." Clark, trying to placate both generals, told Franklin that he would go back and tell Lee to press forward. Franklin assured Clark that Lee would get infantry support if he really needed it—but Franklin would decide if he really needed it. Franklin then told Clark to inform Lee to "keep your train well up," as he fully expected to reach Mansfield the next day.[48]

Clark next went to Banks to plead his case, and Banks ordered a single brigade of infantry to be moved ahead of the wagon train to support the cavalry. The brigade was to come from the command of Brigadier General T. E. G. Ransom, who led the Thirteenth Corps component of the expedition. Ransom, from Illinois, was a fierce fighter, and Banks could not have picked a better man; his mistake was in not putting the entire Thirteenth Corps detachment forward. Ransom, not sure what was expected of him, chose to follow the order to the letter and sent only Colonel William J. Landram, commander of the Fourth Division of the Thirteenth Corps, and Colonel Frank Emerson's First Brigade of the Fourth Division, consisting of only about 1,200 men.[49]

Clark rode back to Lee, told him what Franklin wanted, and gave him the news that he could expect some infantry support—a brigade that was meant to salve what Banks and Franklin thought were Albert Lee's jittery nerves. Neither expected any opposition for days. Only the cavalry leader and the cartographer saw what had happened at Wilson's Farm, and both knew that Franklin and Banks were detached, stubborn, and almost immovable in their plans—now that they had plans. Lee later told Congress that he was laughed at for insisting that they would have a fight before they got to Shreveport.[50] Nevertheless, the cavalry began to move ahead more tentatively.

Richard Taylor now had good cavalry and in sufficient numbers to perform the tasks for which they were designed. Tom Green's orders were not to bring on a full-scale battle but to delay Banks until Taylor was ready to meet him. Forcing Lee to move his men out of column and into attack formation, deal with the Texans, and then re-form into column bought Taylor time. When the Confederates melted away into the forests, Lee thought he had whipped them soundly and that they were not up to professional military standards, whereas in fact they were very well disciplined and had completed the task assigned them. Wilson's Farm would not be the only site of such incidents.

Lee picked his way another three miles beyond Wilson's Farm and decided to halt for the evening. He had marched fifteen miles, fought a small battle, and thought his men deserved a rest. But Franklin sent word forward that Lee was to take his cavalry unit as far forward as possible, with his train and artillery, so that the infantry would have room to move at the next morning without waiting for the cavalry train.[51] This order may have been a slight aimed at Lee by Franklin for questioning him earlier in the day, it may have been retribution for Clark's bypassing Franklin when he sought help from Banks. In any event, Lee returned his men to their saddles and began moving up the narrow road again. The pine trees rarely gave way to open pasture, and there was very little water. Lee was clearly disgruntled as the cavalry slowly rode another four miles to Carroll's Mill. This gristmill on a small stream served the surrounding area and was one of the first in the region to use a waterwheel. As Lee's cavalry neared the mill, Green's Texans made another demonstration that forced them to come into battle order. After a brief skirmish in the diminishing twilight, the Rebels again melted into the woods. Lee finally halted for the night and posted pickets.

Early in the morning of April 8, Franklin went to Banks and told him of the day's plans: he intended for the column to shorten its length by letting the head of the column have a short day and the rear a much longer one. Lee's and Ransom's men were to move to a position about three miles south of Mansfield and then halt. The Thirteenth and Nineteenth Corps and the infantry supply train were to move about ten miles north of Pleasant Hill and bivouac for much needed rest. A. J. Smith's 7,500 men were to encamp at Pleasant Hill. This plan would force Smith's "gorillas" to march twenty-one miles. He made it to within two miles by nightfall, and there his weary men bedded down for the night.[52]

Landram began his march at three o'clock the morning of April 8 in order to catch up with the cavalry as ordered. At sunrise, Lee moved his cavalry out with Thomas Lucas's brigade in the lead.[53] Almost immediately, they encountered Green's Texans. Lee had to abandon the idea of having his cavalry probe their way on horseback. He ordered Lucas to dismount one of his cavalry regiments and deploy them as skirmishers, with two regiments of Landram's infantry as reinforcements.[54] Green slowed them every foot of the way, trying to buy time for Richard Taylor and determine what reaction the men in blue would have to his deliberate withdrawal. Two brigades of Emerson's division were brought up to speed the column's progress.

Ransom began the day's march at 5:30 A.M. at Pleasant Hill and five hours later reached what he thought was Bayou San Patricio

Brigadier General T. E. G. Ransom. Library of Congress, Prints and Photographs Division, LC-B8172-1581

but was actually Ten Mile Bayou. He stopped according to his orders after covering ten miles, and his men were moving into camp when Lee asked for relief for Emerson's exhausted men. Franklin ordered Ransom personally to go forward with Joseph Vance's brigade to see what was happening and to make sure that Emerson's men came back to the main column. Franklin still did not want a large body of infantry operating with the cavalry.[55]

With constant skirmishing, a frustrated Lee pushed the Confederate cavalry screen back six miles on the morning of April 8. Sometime between noon and one o'clock, he and his men emerged from a thick woods and found themselves at an intersection of their road with one that went to the Texas line at Logansport. It was called Sabine Crossroads. The Confederate cavalry that had been a constant menace for the last two days seemed to disappear. Lee, at the head of his column, moved another three-quarters of a mile to the edge of a huge clearing, 800 yards deep and 1,200 yards across, at the slope of a ridge called Honeycutt Hill.[56] Confederate skirmishers were there in force, but as Lee and Landram moved forward, they gave way, and the Union cavalry and infantry units moved to take the ridge. As Lee crested the hill, he saw the bulk of the Confederate army west of the Mississippi drawn up in line of battle all across his front on both sides of the road and extending down and past his right flank.[57]

NOTES

1. *O.R. Atlas*, pl. 52.
2. *JCCW*, 286–87.
3. La Tourette's Map of Louisiana, NARA, RG 77, folio M72 (hereafter cited as LaTourette Map); *O.R. Atlas*, pl. 52.
4. Earl B. McElfresh, *Maps and Mapmakers of the Civil War* (New York, 1999), 162–70.
5. NARA, RG 77, folios M103-1 and 2.
6. Senate Documents no. 987, 62d Cong., 3d sess., 256.
7. *JCCW*, 286–87.
8. *O.R.N.* 26, 60.
9. Nathaniel Banks to his wife, April 4, 1864, Banks Papers.
10. *JCCW*, 192.
11. Ibid., 194.
12. Ibid., 281.
13. Ibid., 32, 58, 323.
14. Author's interview with Edwin C. Bearss, Chief Military Historian Emeritus of the U.S. National Park Service, June 7, 2001.
15. Ewer, *3d Massachusetts*, 201, 276, 323.
16. *JCCW*, 201, 276, 323.
17. *O.R.* 34, 284; *JCCW*, 323; *O.R.N.* 26, 51.
18. Johnson and Buel, *Battles and Leaders*, 4:363.
19. *O.R.N.* 26, 51; *JCCW*, 201, 323; Newsome, *Experience in the War*, 124.
20. *JCCW*, 32.
21. *O.R.* 34, 284, 322, 331, 428, 446; *JCCW*, 32, 58.
22. Irwin, *19th Corps*, 296.
23. Ewer, *3d Massachusetts*, 142.
24. *Philadelphia Press*, April 25, 1864.

25. Ibid.

26. Scott, *32d Iowa*, 135–36; Pellet, *114th New York*, 193.

27. Scott, *32d Iowa*, 136; Harrington, *Fighting Politician*, 152–53; Hoffman, *Camp, Court, and Siege*, 93.

28. Taylor, *Destruction and Reconstruction*, 178; Francis R. Lubbock, *Six Decades in Texas* (Austin, TX, 1900), 536.

29. Taylor, *Destruction and Reconstruction*, 158; *O.R.* 34, pt. 2, 1029; Johnson and Buel, *Battles and Leaders*, 4:369; Lubbock, *Six Decades in Texas*, 534–36.

30. Taylor, *Destruction and Reconstruction*, 158; Lubbock, *Six Decades in Texas*, 536.

31. *O.R.* 34, 479; pt. 2, 1056, 1062–63; pt. 3, 745, 761.

32. *O.R.* 34, pt. 3, 800.

33. Taylor, *Destruction and Reconstruction*, 153; Johnson, *Red River Campaign*, 111.

34. Taylor, *Destruction and Reconstruction*, 159; *O.R.* 34, 479, 517.

35. *O.R.* 34, 512–13, 517, 519.

36. Ibid., 521–22.

37. Taylor, *Destruction and Reconstruction*, 159; *O.R.* 34, 480, 485; Johnson and Buel, *Battles and Leaders*, 4:371.

38. *O.R.* 34, 528.

39. Ibid.; Boggs, *Military Reminiscences*, 75–76.

40. *O.R.* 34, 520; Taylor, *Destruction and Reconstruction*, 158.

41. Ewer, *3d Massachusetts*, 152; Brooksher, *War along the Bayous*, 80.

42. *JCCW*, 194.

43. *O.R.* 34, 449; *JCCW*, 185.

44. *JCCW*, 185.

45. *O.R.* 34, 450, 616–17; *JCCW*, 58.

46. *JCCW*, 194.

47. Ibid., 32, 59, 88, 194.

48. Ibid., 194.

49. *O.R.* 34, 167, 290; pt. 3, 72; *JCCW*, 29, 59–60, 194–95.

50. *JCCW*, 64.

51. Ibid., 58–59.

52. Irwin, *19th Corps*, 300; *JCCW*, 30.

53. *O.R.* 34, 290.

54. Irwin, *19th Corps*, 200.

55. *JCCW*, 32, 61–62, 68.

56. John G. Belisle, *History of Sabine Parish Louisiana* (Many, LA, 1912), 159.

57. Irwin, *19th Corps*, 299; *O.R.* 34, 291, 456; Taylor, *Destruction and Reconstruction*, 160–61; *JCCW*, 60–62.

CHAPTER SIX

I WILL FIGHT BANKS IF HE HAS A MILLION MEN

RICHARD TAYLOR WAS ready for the Union column, thanks to the time bought for him by Tom Green. After his frustrating meeting with Kirby Smith on April 6, Taylor had seized the initiative to prepare for the coming battle. He was furious with the commanding general for not specifically allowing him to fight the battle at the time and place of his choosing and with all the forces available.[1] During early April, as Smith vacillated, Taylor wrote his commander concerning the need to do *something*: "Action, prompt, vigorous action, is required. While we are deliberating the enemy is marching. King James lost three kingdoms for a mass. We may lose three States without a battle."[2] Fortunately for Taylor, Kirby Smith's response was so vague that there was time and room to prepare for Banks.

On April 7, Taylor rode south on the road to Pleasant Hill and found Green and his cavalrymen annoying the Federals. After making sure that the Union column had halted at Carroll's Mill, Taylor rode back the seventeen miles to Mansfield. He had told the Texan to harass the Union forces as much as possible until he met the main body of troops, who would be waiting for him.[3] The next day Taylor planned to stop Banks and chose as his ground the great field at Honeycutt Hill. This was an ideal spot because any place north of this position offered the enemy a choice of three roads to Shreveport.[4] The eastern road would allow the Union column to link up with the navy. The other two roads also posed problems for the Confederates: the western road passed through the Wallace Bayou swamp, and the center road stopped at a ferry landing with no place for the Confederates to maneuver. Taylor had no other clear choice for his stand. Had the Union troops taken the river road from Grand Ecore, Boggs's traps would have awaited them. Taylor now had to work with the terrain at hand.

After arriving in Mansfield on the evening of the April 7, Taylor began issuing orders to his commanders. He sent a courier to Keachi to summon Price's men to Mansfield. The 4,400 troops had to force march twenty miles beginning at dawn on the 8th. Provost guards were sent to Mansfield to keep the roads clear and to preserve order. Houses were commandeered for hospitals, and a wagon park was created to funnel supplies to the troops. Walker and Mouton were ordered to break camp north of Mansfield and concentrate their forces at the field.[5] To cover himself, Taylor's last official act that evening was to send another courier to Kirby Smith in Shreveport at nine o'clock: "I respectfully ask to know if it accords with the views of the lieutenant-general commanding that I should hazard a general engagement at this point, and request an immediate answer, that I may receive it before daylight to-morrow morning."[6]

This was a clear offer to allow Kirby Smith to make a decision. It was also highly improbable that Taylor would receive a reply before the appointed time. Mansfield was more than forty miles south of Shreveport; the rider arrived late at night, and unless a staff officer awakened the commanding general, his response would arrive long past daylight. Taylor did not expect an answer and, anticipating a battle the next day, told his friend the Prince de Polignac, "I will fight Banks if he has a million men."[7]

At 9:40 A.M., Taylor sent another message to Shreveport: "I consider this as favorable a point to engage the enemy as any other."[8] The clearing formed a giant "L" with the long axis facing east and the short axis facing south.[9] The Shreveport-Natchitoches stagecoach road entered the clearing at the vertex and ran to the southeast. Forests bordered the clearing on the west and north along ridgelines. After a gentle drop to a shallow stream, the ground rose again to a ridge forming a smaller "L" in the same configuration. The southeast side of this ridge sloped into a shallow saddle before rising gently to Honeycutt Hill, which was mostly covered in trees. On its southeast slope was an orchard that gave way to open pasture bordered by a shallow stream that separated it from another field. Southeast of this field stood a band of trees, and behind these woods was the crossroads. From the southern tip of the first ridgeline to the stagecoach road and then continuing to the easternmost tip of the clearing, Taylor's battle line ran more than three miles.

Looking at the battlefield today, the visitor is struck with the question, "Why didn't the Confederates place their men on the highest ridge, Honeycutt Hill?" But there have been two changes in the battlefield since 1864: the clearing is now in forest, and wooded Honeycutt Hill has been cleared. Taylor wanted his men with the forest to their backs. He did not want Banks to see how many men he had. He positioned his artillery to focus on the point at which the Union forces would exit from the woods and enter the field. He also needed the three-mile front to position his regiments. There is no doubt that Taylor expected Banks to act rashly and to charge his center position, at which time his two broad wings would converge on the Union center.

Taylor began placing the Confederate forces in position. On his far right, separated from the main body by several hundred feet, were two regiments of Green's cavalry under Brigadier General Hamilton P. Bee. To their left were two brigades of Texas infantry from Major General John G. Walker's division. Brigadier Generals William Scurry and Thomas Waul led these brigades. Between them was an artillery battery, and another battery occupied both sides of the stagecoach road. Here the "L" turned east with the third of Walker's brigades, this one led by Colonel Horace Randal. Next in line were the Texas and Louisiana troops under Brigadier General Alfred Mouton. Positioned on Randal's left was the brigade under Brigadier General Camille Polignac, and to his left was the brigade under Colonel Henry Gray. An artillery battery in front of Mouton's troops was the closest artillery to Honeycutt Hill. Separated by several hundred feet and to the left of Gray was the bulk of Green's cavalry in three tiers. They were the last to arrive and were placed to hold the most endangered flank.[10]

Green and his cavalrymen had done their tasks admirably. Not only had they slowed Banks's column until Taylor was ready to receive it, but they were also able to tell Taylor what units were located within the Union column and where they were, at least to the depth of the main supply train. Taylor had thought that he was fighting the Nineteenth Corps and that A. J. Smith's 10,000 men were guarding Porter and the fleet.[11]

Taylor approached Mouton and Gray, riding up and down the line of Louisianians. He promised them they would draw first blood in honor of protecting their home state.[12] These units, battle-hardened veterans of the Eighteenth Louisiana Infantry, the Twenty-eighth Infantry, and the Consolidated Crescent regiments, would take the brunt of the initial fighting. With Green's arrival, Taylor's force was complete. (Price's forces were still en route, and Taylor did not know

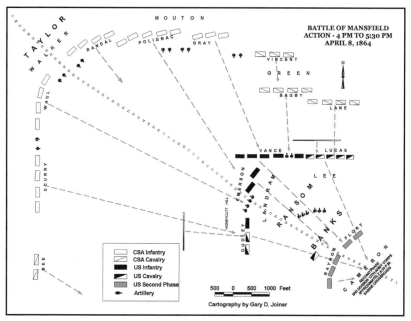

Map of the Battle of Mansfield on April 8, 1864.

when they would arrive or what shape they would be in.) He now
had approximately 5,300 infantry, 500 artillerymen, and 3,000 cavalry on the field.[13] Almost all the cavalrymen were to fight dismounted as infantry. An unknown quantity of other troops were
also on the field for the Confederates that spring day; there may
have been from several hundred to several thousand of them in the
field.[14] Taylor's report refers to them as "reserves" or the home
guard. These were exchanged soldiers, veterans of Vicksburg, not
yet legally paroled. If the Confederates lost and these men were
captured, they could be executed by the Union forces. They were
never carried on the rolls or lists of battle units, but they were there
fighting for their state and their country. Diary entries and postwar compilations suggest that they filled in the ranks of units before the battle. Taylor made adjustments to the line, most notably
moving Randal's brigade from its original position south of the road
to north of the road.[15] With the line now in its final position, the
Confederate troops saw the first Union troops come out from the
woods shortly after noon.

Colonel William Landram's small Fourth Division of the Thirteenth Corps had fought Green's cavalry for two days. The men
were tired, wary of the Texans, and frustrated by the constant

change from marching in column to deploying for battle, only to
have a short exchange and then watch the Rebels retreat. Lee and
Landram saw the Confederates form skirmish lines in the open field
on the southeastern slope of Honeycutt Hill. Landram had only
one brigade and did not believe he had enough men to take a hill
that size. He wanted reinforcements, so he ordered his second brigade forward.[16] The Confederate cavalry broke from the skirmish
line and disappeared over the hilltop. Annoyed at this continued
tactic, Lee and Landram followed with their regiments arrayed
behind them, and, reaching the hilltop, were the first to view the
massed Confederate regiments drawn up in line of battle across
their front and to their right. Lee estimated that Taylor had between
15,000 and 20,000 troops.

Banks, annoyed by the almost constant starting and stopping
of the column, rode forward to see what Lee and his amateur equestrians were doing. As he left Franklin's side, Banks told his army
commander that he would return if there was no heavy fighting.
Franklin answered, "There will be no fighting."[17] Banks and his
staff, passing the wagon train, artillery batteries in limber, and then
the infantry units, arrived at the base of the hill about 1:00 P.M. to
find his forward infantry and cavalry units skirmishing with Confederates. Banks sent for Lee and asked him to describe the situation to their front. Lee later testified before Congress that he told
Banks, "We must fall back immediately, or we must be heavily reinforced. I said the enemy must have 15,000 or 20,000 men there;
four or five times as many as I had."[18] Lee described how he had
his men deployed, and Banks approved, then told Lee that he would
order the infantry to move forward.

Banks then sent George Drake, his assistant adjutant general,
back down the column with a message for Franklin: "The commanding general desires me to say that the enemy are apparently prepared to make a strong stand at this point, and that you had better
make arrangements to bring up your infantry, and to pass everything on the road. The general will send again when to move. He
thinks you had better send back and push up the trains, as manifestly we shall be able to rest here."[19] Another message followed
almost immediately, this one telling Franklin to begin moving his
men forward as quickly as possible.

The first message is astounding. Either Lee did not communicate the seriousness of the threat poised in front of them, or Banks did
not take the threat seriously. Banks told Lee that infantry support

was being called forward, yet he told Franklin to "make arrangements" to bring the units up once he was told when to move. Perhaps the answer lies in the last line: "manifestly we shall be able to
rest here." Banks still did not believe the Confederates would fight
him.

Landram's second brigade arrived on the hill about 3:30 P.M.
He now had 2,400 infantry in place.[20] Lee placed his men in a smaller
replica of the Confederate L-shaped line. He positioned Ormand
Nims's artillery battery on the stagecoach road with Emerson's infantry brigade protecting them. Landram's second brigade took up
positions behind a rail fence perpendicular to Emerson's line. Lee
then placed Colonel Thomas Lucas's cavalry brigade on his right
flank, facing Green's cavalry, and "Gold Lace" Dudley's small cavalry brigade on the left flank. Lee ordered the Chicago Mercantile
Battery and the First Indiana Battery to set up at a residence called
the Fincher House, located behind and down the slope from the
infantry and cavalry. There they would be able to provide fire support for either the Federals' front or their right flank. As these units
came into place, the cavalry's supply train pulled up to the crossroads about one-half mile behind the front line, where the wagons,
their teamsters, and guards from the Corps d'Afrique halted. Once
again, the 300 wagons blocked the road.[21]

About 4:00 P.M., Lee rode back to the crest of the hill after con-
ferring with Banks. Thinking the infantry he requested would soon
arrive, he was stunned to be given an order by one of Banks's staff
aides to move immediately on Mansfield. Lee was incredulous; he
said there must be a mistake and immediately rode back to Banks,
who confirmed that the order was correct. Lee later explained, "I
told him we could not advance ten minutes without a general engagement, in which we should be most gloriously flogged, I did
not want to do it."[22] Banks then agreed to delay the advance and
sent a courier to Franklin with the message ordering the infantry
up.

Richard Taylor watched the sun sink lower into the western
sky, knowing that he had only about three hours of daylight left.
He had counted on Banks to be impetuous and act rashly, but this
scenario was not happening. As his men watched, more Union regiments were arriving, and their line was getting stronger by the hour.
The Confederates had to act or they would lose the initiative. There
is some question as to whether Taylor ordered Mouton to attack or
told him they would soon attack. The reason for the confusion is

the order in which the Confederate units began their charge: rather than having the entire line moving in unison, Mouton advanced his regiments in echelon, staggering their lines. The result was high casualty rates, for the Union troops could focus on specific regiments as they came close to the Union positions. It was not a tactic that Taylor usually employed. But Mouton's men had been waiting for their chance for most of the day, and their charge, as recorded by both sides, was magnificent.[23] The division's officers rode their horses, however, in order for their men to see them more easily, and their bravery led to catastrophic results.

On Honeycutt Hill, Ransom had now joined Lee and Landram. When Mouton's men moved forward, Ransom ordered his five infantry regiments facing the Louisianians to leave the fence and engage them in the field. The two sides met at close range and fired volleys.[24] Losses were heavy, and as Mouton's attack faltered, the Union infantry began picking off the mounted officers, with Mouton one of the first casualties. Shortly after he fell, the commanders of the Eighteenth Louisiana Infantry, the Twenty-eighth Louisiana Infantry, and the Consolidated Crescent regiments were also killed. One-third of Mouton's men were killed or wounded in the attack.[25]

Mouton was shot in the back several times while ordering his men to stop firing on Union troops who were trying to surrender; some of the Union infantrymen picked up their guns and fired at the general. Mouton's men then fell on the blue regimental line with a vengeance before the Confederate line stalled, and the accurate Union fire pushed it back to about 200 yards from Ransom's right flank.[26] Within minutes of the beginning of the assault, Tom Green was the senior Confederate officer on Taylor's left wing.[27]

To Mouton's left, the Texas cavalrymen made their entry on foot, putting the five Union regiments in danger of being flanked. The five regiments of Lucas's cavalry, likewise fighting on foot, were also in danger of being turned. If these units folded, the entire Union line risked being enveloped. Mouton's right was anchored by Randal's Texas brigade, holding the center of the Confederate line. As this brigade marched out in echelon, the men found themselves squeezed between Polignac's charge and the road; they were forced to march slower.

From horseback, Taylor watched the Texans and Louisianians engage the enemy. He was smoking a cigar and had one leg crossed over the saddle.[28] As soon as he saw the Union forces occupied with the first wave, he ordered Walker to unleash his Texans on the Federal left. The Texans, who had been watching the action on the other side of the field, were anxious to attack and did so in rapidly advancing solid lines, not echelon formations.[29]

R. B. Scott and his Sixty-seventh Indiana Infantry was at the vertex of Lee's "L," to the right of Nims's battery on the stagecoach road. Scott saw the Texans coming at his position and later wrote that they ran toward the Union line "like a cyclone. Yelling like infuriated demons."[30] The Texans ripped through "Gold Lace" Dudley's Third Massachusetts Cavalry and began to push the Union line in on itself. Nims's battery kept up a deadly fire until three of its guns were captured, turned around, and used on former friends.[31] The Twenty-third Wisconsin and Sixty-seventh Indiana were crushed. Ransom ordered the Eighty-third Ohio, the last infantry regiment on his right flank, to move in support of the left.[32] Those men, however, were already being flanked by Green's Texans, and when they shifted to their new position, they found that the left flank did not exist.[33] Ransom then ordered them back to support the Chicago Mercantile Battery.[34]

Ransom ordered his adjutant, Captain Cyrus Dickey, to instruct Landram to retreat on the same line as the Eighty-third Ohio. Dickey started out and was shot in the head; hence, the order was not carried out, and most of the right-wing regiments were surrounded and forced to surrender. Two regiments, the Forty-eighth Ohio and the 130th Illinois, simply ceased to exist; there were not enough survivors either to rally or even formally surrender.[35] Ransom described his Thirteenth Corps as being caught in a nutcracker. Shortly after Dickey's death the entire Union line collapsed.[36] Ransom rallied his men through the woods and around the Chicago Mercantile Battery, which was pouring accurate fire into the Confederate ranks. Ransom was mounted so that his men could see him in swirling fight, and as he ordered the remnants of his Thirteenth Corps into their new positions, he fell from his horse, hit in the knee by shrapnel.[37] Some of his men lifted Ransom on their shoulders and took him to the rear. Brigadier General Robert Cameron's Third Division finally made its way around the cavalry train and set up between the battery and the copse of trees standing in front of the crossroads.[38] The head of the wagon train was at the crossroads. In thirty minutes of fighting, the Union advance had been crushed. Ransom was wounded, and both of Landram's brigade commanders, Emerson and Vance, had been wounded and captured.[39]

Confederate brigadier general and French nobleman Camille Armand Jules Marie, Prince de Polignac. Photograph from a painting. Archives of the Mansfield State Historic Site, Mansfield, Louisiana. *Courtesy of the Mansfield State Historic Site*

Franklin came to the front with Cameron, and as they formed their line behind the artillery battery, the remnants of Dudley's cavalry tried to rally to the new line. Lieutenant Colonel Lorenzo Thomas of the Third Massachusetts Cavalry yelled to his men to "try to think that you are dead and buried, and you will have no fear."[40] Franklin, making an accurate assessment of the situation to his front, ordered Brigadier General William Emory to form his First Division of the Nineteenth Corps in line of battle behind him on the first good position he could find.[41] Emory, coming forward from Ten Mile Bayou, picked a point about three miles behind the initial line on a stream called Chapman's Bayou with a ridgeline lying behind it. There he waited.

As Cameron's men solidified their line, they were met with a crashing charge—not by the Confederates but by the fleeing Union survivors of the opening phase of the battle. A northern reporter described the scene: "We found ourselves swallowed up, as it were, in a hissing, seething, bubbling whirlpool of agitated men."[42] The rout was endangering both the men running and the men of Cameron's division. Soldiers were shedding guns, knapsacks, and any gear that slowed them down.[43] The Confederates behind them were still giving the Rebel yell, and the cacophony at the crossroads was maddening.[44] Franklin, unhorsed by the mob, fell and broke his left arm.[45] Banks tried to rally his men. No one doubted his personal courage, but he was ineffective; he shouted, "Form a line here. I know you will not desert me," but desert him they did.[46] The wagons could not be turned around, so the teamsters cut the lines to ride the horses and mules away from the disaster. The Corps d'Afrique added to the tide of men in retreat. The wagons acted as a barrier to any organized retreat, and no artillery limbers could pass the train, so they were captured piece by piece. Franklin was taken away to safety as Cameron tried to hold the line, but after only about twenty minutes his position collapsed as well.[47] He had only five regiments; flanked on both left and right, his men joined the exodus of blue trying to reach safety somewhere behind them. It was by then about 5:30 P.M., and the sun was low in the western sky.

Emory was coming forward from Ten Mile Bayou when he began to encounter trickles, then masses, of Union soldiers, running or riding toward him and then past him.[48] This slowed his division's progress tremendously. He stopped at a house on a ridge overlooking the small creek called Chapman's Bayou. Next to the house was an orchard which, although there are no local records to state why, Emory called Pleasant Grove.[49] He positioned his men in front of the creek, correctly assuming that this was the only water for miles around and certainly the only water between him and Ten Mile Bayou, itself little more than a small creek, seven miles behind him. His fresh troops stood their ground better than their predecessors. The Confederates had lost unit cohesion in the wild assaults leading to the third Union position of the day, and the final attack was made as a mad rush. They hit Emory's entire line in a massive assault and, even though they were exhausted from continuous fighting, managed to push the Union troops behind the creek and claim the water for themselves.[50]

Emory redeployed his men on the low ridge above the bayou. The Rebels made a last push up the ridge in the waning light but failed to dislodge the Union infantry; Emerson held the ridge against the Confederate mob. Fighting ended with the darkness. The Union soldiers could hear their wagons being moved to the north, cavalry units rallying to bugle calls, and companies being mustered for formation in the darkness.[51] As the fighting was winding down, Taylor received the reply to his letter to Kirby Smith from the previous night. Smith told Taylor to avoid a general engagement. Taylor sent the courier back to Shreveport with a message for the commanding general: "Too late, sir, the battle is won."[52]

The losses that day were high for both sides. Landram's Fourth Division of the Thirteenth Corps, the first line of Union infantry in the battle, lost almost half of its 2,400 men; 25 killed, 95 wounded, and 1,015 reported missing. Many of these missing were killed in the opening minutes of the battle, and hundreds had been captured within the first half-hour.[53] Cameron's Third Division lost 317 of its 1,200-man roster. Lee's cavalry division lost 39 killed, 250 wounded, and 144 missing. Emory's division lost 347 killed, wounded, and missing of its 5,000 men. The total Union losses were 113 killed, 581 wounded, and 1,541 missing—2,235 official casualties from a force of 12,000 participating in all three phases.[54] But Taylor reported taking 2,500 prisoners.[55] Moreover, the number of dead was certainly higher than Union officers' estimates. They left their dead and wounded on the field to be cared for by Confederate doctors, though some Union doctors remained to help.[56] An examination of individual regimental records increases the total casualties: 240 killed, 671 wounded, and 1,508 missing or 2,419 casualties.[57]

Confederate losses were listed as approximately 1,000 killed and wounded of 8,800 combat soldiers. A few Confederates were taken prisoner, but the number missing was insignificant. Two-thirds of these were from Mouton's division and were captured because of the echelon attack, as is easily proved by comparing Walker's fewer casualties.[58]

Taylor lost many of his favorite commanders that day, but he had stopped the Union advance on Shreveport and was confident that early the next morning he would crush Bank's Nineteenth Corps. At 1:30 A.M., April 9, Taylor penned a letter to Walker telling him what they would do the next day. The plan was simple: at dawn his force would sweep over the ridge, led by Missouri and Arkansas troops to give the Texans and Louisianians a much-needed rest. Taylor ordered Green to take his cavalry to the Blair's Landing road to cut off the Union retreat and try to keep reinforcements from joining Banks. Brigadier General Mosby Parsons's division of Missouri infantry was to form the left wing, Brigadier General Thomas Churchill's division of Arkansas infantry the right wing. Because the road was so narrow, Churchill's men were to wheel around in the woods and attack the Union forces on their left flank.

Taylor told Walker that the only troops they faced were those of the Nineteenth Corps, consisting of about 7,000 men, many of whom were raw recruits "who will make no fight. Yankees whom we have always whipped."[59] If Banks pulled his men back during the night, the Confederates would pursue them and push them behind Pleasant Hill, forcing them to return to Natchitoches. Taylor also believed it impossible for reinforcements to reach Banks before late in the day but cautioned that they must fight him quickly, for Confederate intelligence reported troop transports coming up the river—Admiral Porter's force of six warships and twenty troop and supply transports coming to meet Banks at Springfield Landing. Taylor emphasized to Walker the importance of halting Banks's advance, stating "the safety of our whole country depends upon it."[60] With the letter completed, Taylor slept a few hours on the battlefield. He would be ready for Banks in the morning.

Throughout the night the Confederates could hear the clanking and rustling sounds of troops being repositioned. What they did not know, but Taylor suspected, was that Banks was withdrawing to Pleasant Hill. Taylor did not know that A. J. Smith's 7,500 men, who now formed the rear of the Union column, had encamped at Pleasant Hill that night. Taylor's battle plan for the next day was set, but the location would be fourteen miles down the road rather than over the ridge to his front.

NOTES

1. *O.R.* 34, 512–13, 517, 519.
2. Ibid., 522.
3. Ibid., 528.
4. Johnson, *Red River Campaign*, 129.

5. Taylor, *Destruction and Reconstruction*, 159.

6. *O.R.* 34, 526; Taylor, *Destruction and Reconstruction*, 161.

7. Taylor, *Destruction and Reconstruction*, 161.

8. *O.R.* 34, 526.

9. Map of Mansfield battlefield, dated April 1864, by Major Richard Venable, Gilmer Papers.

10. *O.R.* 34, 563–64; Taylor, *Destruction and Reconstruction*, 162; Blessington, *Walker's Texas Division*, 185–86.

11. Richard Taylor to Major General John Walker, Mansfield, 1:30 A.M. April 9, 1864, Walker Papers, Southern Historical Collection, Wilson Library, University of North Carolina, Chapel Hill.

12. Taylor, *Destruction and Reconstruction*, 162.

13. Ibid.

14. Author's interview with Steve Bounds, manager of Mansfield State Historic Site, October 10, 2001. Diaries and letters in the site's collection indicate that large numbers of parolees fought in the battle.

15. Taylor, *Destruction and Reconstruction*, 162; *O.R.* 34, 564.

16. *O.R.* 34, 464; *JCCW*, 61.

17. *JCCW*, 10.

18. Ibid., 60.

19. Ibid., 30.

20. *O.R.* 34, 167, 264, 266; Irwin, *19th Corps*, 303.

21. *O.R.* 34, 464; *JCCW*, 61.

22. *JCCW*, 61; Johnson, *Red River Campaign*, 134.

23. *O.R.* 34, 564.

24. Ibid., 266–67, 295–96, 300–301; Irwin, *19th Corps*, 304.

25. *O.R.* 34, 564; Mary L. B. Bankston, *Camp-Fire Stories of the Mississippi Valley Campaign* (New Orleans, LA, 1914), 152–53; John Dimitry, "Louisiana," in *Confederate Military History*, 12 vols. (Atlanta, 1899), 10:140–41; Napier Bartlett, "The Trans-Mississippi," in *Military Record of Louisiana: Including Biographical and Historical Papers Relating to the Military Organization of the State* (New Orleans, LA, 1875), 13:42.

26. *O.R.* 34, 266–67, 295–96, 300–301; Irwin, *19th Corps*, 304.

27. *O.R.* 34, 564.

28. Bartlett, "The Trans-Mississippi," 13.

29. *O.R.* 34, 564.

30. R. B. Scott, *The History of the 67th Regiment Indiana Infantry* (Bedford, IN, 1892), 71–72 (hereafter cited as *67th Indiana*); *O.R.* 34, 462; Frank M. Flinn, *Campaigning with Banks in Louisiana, '63 and '64, and Sheridan in the Shenandoah Valley in '64 and '65* (Lynn, MA, 1887), 108.

31. Scott, *67th Indiana*, 462; Flinn, *Campaigning with Banks*, 108.

32. *O.R.* 34, 266–67, 300–301; T. B. Marshall, *History of the Eighty-third Ohio Volunteer Infantry, the Greyhound Regiment* (Cincinnati, OH, 1913), 134 (hereafter cited as *83d Ohio*).

33. Marshall, *83d Ohio*, 134.

34. Jim Huffstodt, *Hard Dying Men: The Story of General W. H. L. Wallace, General T. E. G. Ransom, and Their "Old Eleventh" Illinois Infantry in the American Civil War (1861–1865)* (Bowie, MD, 1991), 177.

35. John A. Bering and Thomas Montgomery, *History of the Forty-Eighth Ohio Veteran Volunteer Infantry* (Hillsboro, OH, 1880), 132; Belisle, *Sabine Parish*, 161.

36. Huffstodt, *Hard Dying Men*, 177.

37. Ibid., 179; *O.R.* 34, 273–74, 292, 302; Irwin, *19th Corps*, 304.

38. *O.R.* 34, 274–75.

39. Ibid., 274–75, 292, 301; Irwin, *19th Corps*, 304.

40. Ewer, *3d Massachusetts*, 156; *O.R.* 34, 273–74.

41. *O.R.* 34, 257, 273–74.

42. *Philadelphia Press*, April 25, 1864.

43. *O.R.* 34, 273–74; Ewer, *3d Massachusetts*, 149; Scott, *67th Indiana*, 72; Hoffman, *Camp, Court, and Siege*, 89; John M. Stanyan, *A History of the Eighth Regiment of New Hampshire Volunteers* (Concord, NH, 1892), 409.

44. *O.R.* 34, 273–74; Ewer, *3d Massachusetts*, 149.

45. *O.R.* 34, 273–74; medical certificate in William B. Franklin Papers, Division of Manuscripts, Library of Congress, Washington, DC.

46. *O.R.* 34, 273–74; Ewer, *3d Massachusetts*, 149; Scott, *67th Indiana*, 72; Henry M. Shorey, *The Story of the Maine Fifteenth Volunteer Infantry Regiment* (Brighton, ME, 1890), 83–84 (hereafter cited as *15th Maine*).

47. *O.R.* 34, 257; Ewer, *3d Massachusetts*, 155; Flinn, *Campaigning with Banks*, 109.

48. *O.R.* 34, 391–92; Harris H. Beecher, *Record of the 114th, New York N.Y.S.V.: Where It Went, What It Saw, and What It Did* (Norwich, NY, 1866), 311 (hereafter cited as *114th New York*).

49. Belisle, *Sabine Parish*, 163.

50. *O.R.* 34, 392, 421–22, 429, 606–7, 616–17; Taylor, *Destruction and Reconstruction*, 164; Clark, *116th New York*, 155–57; Williams, *56th Ohio*, 66.

51. *JCCW*, 218; Hoffman, *Camp, Court, and Siege*, 91; Pellet, *114th New York*, 202.

52. Sarah A. Dorsey, *Recollections of Henry Watkins Allen* (New York, 1866), 263.

53. *O.R.* 34, 167, 263–64, 273.

54. Ibid., 263, 421.

55. Taylor, *Destruction and Reconstruction*, 164.

56. Benjamin A. Fordyce, *Echoes: From the Letters of a Civil War Surgeon*, ed. Lydia P. Hecht (N.p., 1996), 248.

57. Casualty lists and reports at Mansfield, LA, State Historic Site; Steve Bounds Interview, September, 15, 2001.

58. *O.R.* 34, 553; Bartlett, "The Trans-Mississippi," 13:42.

59. Taylor to Walker, April 9, 1864, Walker Papers.

60. Ibid.

CHAPTER SEVEN

THE SAFETY OF OUR WHOLE COUNTRY DEPENDS UPON IT

BANKS WAS VERY PLEASED with Emory's stand as night fell on April 8. He considered the ridge a wonderful place to defend and sent an aide back to Pleasant Hill to order A. J. Smith to bring his Sixteenth Corps forward.[1] Franklin, nursing his broken arm, pointed out that Smith would have just reached Pleasant Hill and could not likely get back to the ridge before the next morning. Even if he could, would his men be in any shape to fight after covering twenty-two miles in one day and immediately marching fourteen miles overnight? Franklin also pointed out the lack of water. Banks asked the opinion of his friend General William Dwight, a brigade commander in Emory's division, who advised Banks to retreat to safer ground and to do so promptly. Banks agreed, and at 10:00 P.M. the army began its retreat.

Banks allowed the Thirteenth Corps to lead, followed by the cavalry, then the Nineteenth Corps. Dwight's brigade brought up the rear, guarding against Rebel attack. The column moved slowly, picking its way through stragglers and hampered by the infantry's trains. The head of the column reached Pleasant Hill at 8:30 A.M. on April 9.[2] After daylight, some Confederate cavalry began harassing the rear of the column, mostly worrying stragglers and disrupting the 153rd New York Infantry. A. J. Smith began hearing rumors that the Thirteenth Corps had been cut to pieces early that morning. As small groups of weary men walked, mounted riders trotted, and teamsters bullied their teams into the village, Smith knew the rumors were true.[3] He ordered the Second Brigade, Third Division, of his Sixteenth Corps, commanded by Colonel William Shaw, to take up a position on the road west of the village. Hampered by the bulk of the column, which was now streaming into the village, Shaw's men were forced to abandon the road and make their way through the dense woods.[4] Shaw reported to Emory, who told him to relieve Brigadier General James McMillan's brigade.

McMillan had picked a good location south of the road and formed his men perpendicular to it. On the north side of the road was a small hill that overlooked the position.

Shaw relieved the brigade and set up in line of battle three regiments of Iowans on the south side of the road and one regiment of Missourians plus a four-gun battery on the north side.[5] The nearest friendly troops, a quarter-mile away, were New Yorkers led by Colonel Lewis Benedict. Dwight's brigade was positioned parallel to Benedict and on the north side of the road with his units facing north. This left both of Shaw's flanks exposed and Dwight with his left wing facing 90 degrees to the expected angle of attack. Benedict was positioned astride the Logansport road.[6] The bulk of A. J. Smith's men were located in and around the village of fifteen or sixteen buildings on the tallest of the gently rolling ridges. Banks set up his headquarters on the east side of the village in the largest residence, the Childers House, which stood near the intersection of the road that led to Blair's Landing.[7] Shaw's brigade was in line of battle over a mile to the west from the bulk of the Sixteenth Corps, which was in and near the village.

Pleasant Hill, established in the 1850s, contained a store, a recently built Methodist church, the Pearce Payne College (its two unfinished brick buildings designed to be wings of a larger structure), and about a dozen houses.[8] The village was situated on the east side of a large cleared field that ran along the stagecoach road. To the west was a stand of dense pine trees and beyond them a very large open field. (This basic configuration remains today, though with more wooded area and less pasture. Only one original structure remains on the battle site.)

Before dawn, Taylor ordered his men to probe the ridge at the previous day's fighting, and they soon found that Banks had pulled out. In his message to Walker earlier that morning, Taylor had told the Texan, "Arkansas and Missouri will lead the fight this morning. They must do what Texas and Louisiana did today [yesterday]."[9] During the remainder of the day, the plan he had outlined the night before was followed. Taylor and Green led the Texas cavalry down the road with orders for the infantry to follow. Six miles northwest of Pleasant Hill they found a large number of prisoners being herded back to the Confederate lines by Texas cavalrymen. These men were part of the 165th New York, a Zouave unit (elite troops patterned after the French North African "Foreign Legion") from Dwight's brigade. Seeing the Zouaves still dressed in their bright blue and red uniforms of baggy trousers and short jackets, one of Green's men said the war must be almost over because "Lincoln was now reduced to sending his women to fight."[10] About 9:00 A.M., Green's cavalry came into contact with McMillan's and Shaw's troops just as the former were to be relieved by Shaw. Taylor thought they were a rear guard protecting the trains. He had no way of knowing that Banks had pulled out the night before.[11] Taylor ordered the cavalry to reconnoiter the Union position.[12]

About 1:00 P.M., Churchill's men arrived some two miles west of Pleasant Hill.[13] Taylor talked to Churchill and found that the Arkansans had marched forty-five miles in the last thirty-six hours and were exhausted. Taylor told them they should rest for a short time and be ready to lead the attack.[14] He then decided that all his infantry units required rest to perform at optimal ability, so he delayed his attack for three hours with orders for all units to rest for two hours.[15] He knew he was wasting valuable daylight, but he also knew his men were in no condition to fight.

When the cavalry scouts reported the basic layout of the Union forces, Taylor used the concept for battle he had created the night before, with one slight variation: Churchill would sweep to the Confederate right over a mile into the woods. On his right would be three regiments of cavalry to cut off the Union retreat. Churchill would then extend past the Union left, wheel around to his left, and reinforce the main line of attack from behind the Union line. This move would effectively sever communications between Churchill and other Confederate units. Walker would form in line of battle south of the road and begin his advance when he heard Churchill's assault. Walker was charged with linking his right flank with Churchill's left. Once it appeared that the Union forces had been drawn south of the road by the combined infantry attack, cavalry under Bee and Buchel were to charge down the road and through the village. Two more cavalry units under Major and Arthur Bagby were to seal off the Blair's Landing road. Mouton's division, now under the command of Prince Polignac, was held in reserve. Taylor told his men to rely on the bayonet, "as we had neither time nor ammunition to waste."[16]

Meanwhile, Banks and his commanders in the village were idle and bored. Some officers were sleeping or playing cards; some were reading to fill their time. There was no sound of action in the distance, and few believed there would be action that day; other than skirmishing down the road. Banks sent Porter a message telling him about what had happened at Mansfield and that he intended to resume the advance to Shreveport that evening.[17]

At 3:00 P.M. Churchill and his men headed down the road for two miles and then began their trek though the dense woods. He formed them in line of battle with Brigadier General Mosby Parsons's division on the right and his own division, composed of Brigadier General James Tappan's brigade and Colonel Lucien Gause's brigade, on the left. The forest immediately posed problems to the two divisions. The dense woods did not allow a view of more than a few feet ahead. The terrain was hilly with steep slopes and ravines that broke the line of approach, making it difficult for the men to walk abreast. As they swept to their right, Parsons's left flank came in contact with Federal units, so the entire force moved even farther to the right. With each of these problems, forward progress became more difficult to determine.[18]

After the Missouri and Arkansas troops disappeared into the woods, Taylor began a countdown to the battle. He gave Churchill an hour and a half to get into position. At 4:30 P.M. a twelve-gun battery opened up on the Union four-gun battery with Shaw's men to the north of road. The distance between the two batteries was about 800 yards. Within thirty minutes the counter battery fire had become so intense that the Union battery was withdrawn for its own safety.[19] As the Union battery withdrew, Churchill's men were heard yelling, signaling the beginning of their attack. Walker's Texans, recognizing the signal for their advance, at 5:00 P.M. began their charge.[20]

Green saw the Union battery limbering up. Believing that the forward Union units were collapsing under the weight of the Confederate artillery barrage, he ordered Bee to charge.[21] Bee charged his men across an old track and was met with a furious volley from Shaw's brigade. One-third of Colonel Xavier Debray's regiment died in the assault. Colonel Augustus Buchel forced the now advancing Union infantry back to its original line and then fell, mortally wounded. Debray's horse was hit and fell on him. He survived by losing his boot; having slightly injuring his ankle, he limped back to his line using his sword as a cane.[22]

Walker's men marched against Shaw's brigade, exchanging volleys as they approached. Shaw's men were only thinly protected in a band of trees and behind a rail fence and had no flank support. Walker's men drove through the Thirty-second Iowa just as Major's

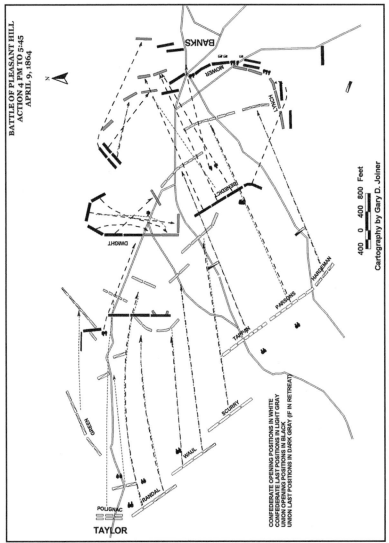

Map of the Battle of Pleasant Hill (battle positions) on April 9, 1864

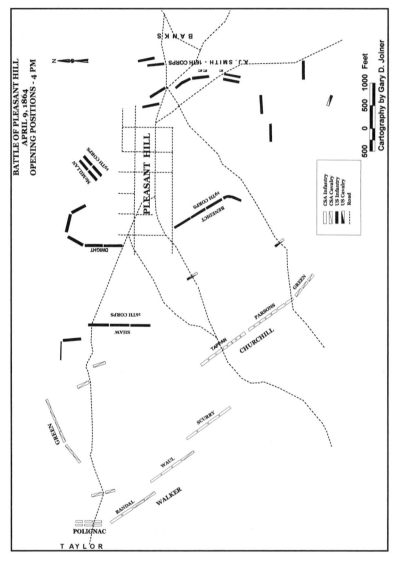

Map of the Battle of Pleasant Hill (opening positions) on April 9, 1864

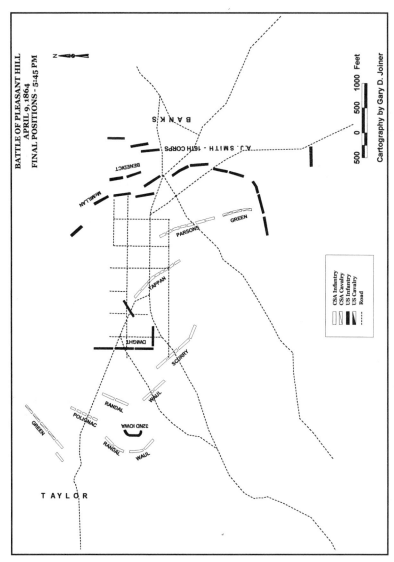

Map of the Battle of Pleasant Hill (final positions) on April 9, 1864

cavalry, fighting dismounted, attacked the Union brigade's right flank.[23]

Churchill's divisions believed they were abreast of the Union line. They could hear the cannonade to their left rear. They saw a Union line ahead of them in a field, in the center of which lay a dry, tree-filled streambed. This was Benedict's brigade. Most of the enemy was in the thicket, and Churchill charged them. Unable to fire their muskets in the thick undergrowth, the Confederates used their weapons as clubs. The four regiments collapsed as a line and each was routed. The three New York regiments broke first; the Thirtieth Maine retreated only after it was almost enveloped. Benedict was killed shortly after he told the Maine troops to pull back.[24] Flushed with this victory, Churchill's men captured an artillery battery and aimed for the village. They did not notice A. J. Smith's men ahead and to their right. Churchill had wheeled too soon and had come into the Union lines almost in front of the Union left flank. It was a terrible mistake.[25]

When Benedict's brigade collapsed, there was no support on any side for Shaw. The Thirty-second Iowa at the center of the line stubbornly refused to leave and bent itself into a semicircle. Walker, wounded, was carried to the rear. Taylor called in Polignac's weary reserves as Major's dismounted cavalrymen swept the regiment's right. Shaw urged Dwight to move in to help, but Dwight refused to move, saying he had no orders to do so. A. J. Smith ordered Shaw's brigade to withdraw, and three regiments did so, but the steadfast Thirty-second Iowa was surrounded and cut off.[26] Dwight decided that if he did not act, orders or not, he would suffer the same fate as Shaw. He ordered two of his regiments to cross the road and set up on the south side. General Emory then ordered McMillan's brigade, which had been relieved by Shaw and was being held in reserve, to fill the void created by Dwight. The men marched into a hailstorm of shells from both sides.[27] A soldier of the Thirtieth Maine wrote that the "air seemed all alive with the sounds of various projectiles."[28]

At that point in the battle, both sides thought the Confederates were winning handily. The Union right and center had all but collapsed, and the left seemed to have evaporated. The one large contingent of the command thus far not engaged was the bulk of the Sixteenth Corps, and those troops were waiting for their chance. The Fifty-eighth Illinois, which had been concealed in a copse of trees, began pouring accurate fire into Churchill's men. Other regiments of Lucas's brigade joined in, and A. J. Smith then ordered his entire line to charge the Confederates. Churchill's men still had forward momentum and had reached the eastern side of the village.[29] They fell back to the stream bottom where they had found Benedict's men, and the fighting became especially brutal; just as before, they used muskets as clubs because of the dense undergrowth.[30] With Parsons driven back, Tappan was forced to retreat; otherwise, his flank would be exposed, and Smith's "gorillas" would drive a wedge between the two formations. As they withdrew, they ran into Scurry's brigade of Walker's division of Texans and were thrown a tight position. Taylor had to send both Randal's and Waul's brigades to Scurry's aid before he was enveloped.[31] The two armies mutually separated at the end of the battle, which thus ended in a tactical tie as darkness fell.

During the battle the Confederates had forced the Union lines to bend back on the left and then had blown through the Union center, only to have their own right wing compromised at great loss. Taylor's plan had worked as it was designed to except for the unknown quantity of the Union Sixteenth Corps. Banks rode up to A. J. Smith and shook his hand, saying, "God bless you, General. You have saved the army."[32] A. J. Smith had little to say to Banks and went back to see to his troops' welfare and to make them ready in the event of another Confederate attack. He did not attend a conference of Union commanders who met with Banks to decide their next course of action. The dead of both armies lay on the battlefield that night, and the wounded of both armies could be heard pleading from no-man's-land for help and water, but neither side could afford to offer assistance.[33]

It was in the midst of this chorus of misery, that Banks decided on his next course of action. He wanted to try again to take Shreveport and had told A. J. Smith of this intention.[34] In preparation, the commanding general ordered Albert Lee to bring what was left of his trains back to Pleasant Hill. Banks met with Franklin, Dwight, and Emory to seek their counsel. Franklin later told Congress that he held no hope for success in another battle; he was so disgusted with Banks's leadership that he was "certain that an operation depending on plenty of troops, rather than upon skill in handling them, was the only one which would have a probability of success in his [Banks's] hands."[35] Both Franklin and Emory thought the most prudent option would be to take the road to Blair's Landing and link with Porter and the fleet, since the supply transports held all the equipment and food the army needed. But Dwight suggested that the army retrograde to Grand Ecore because no one had heard from Porter, and they did not know whether Taylor's forces had captured or destroyed the fleet.[36] Banks listened to his friend and confidant over the objections of the two more seasoned generals; at Grand Ecore he would determine what to do. The night was filled with the sound of the army packing and preparing to leave the way it had come. Lee was ordered to turn his train around again. For the second time in two days the dead and wounded were to be left on the field where they lay.[37]

A. J. Smith was furious when, after midnight, he found out about Banks's plan. He stormed up to Banks to protest the action, stating the reasons for not retreating. First, he was angry at the thought of not burying his dead and leaving his wounded for the Confederates to tend to, if indeed they could or would do so; it was a matter of honor not to leave his men on the battlefield. Second, his 2,500 men with Porter would be at risk without the benefit of support. Banks said no on both counts. A. J. Smith then pleaded to stay behind with his men to tend to the dead and dying. Banks refused this as well, saying that there was no water for the troops, and they must return to Grand Ecore. The lack of water was certainly true, but Banks would too often use it as the primary excuse for the upcoming retreat.[38]

A. J. Smith next made a visit to Franklin. Still seething at Banks's very evident incompetence on the battlefield and his callous disregard for the dead and wounded, Smith asked Franklin to place Banks under arrest and take over the command of the army, assuring him the full support of the Thirteenth, Sixteenth, and Seventeenth Corps. Franklin, himself still disgusted with Banks, considered this possibility but then replied, "Smith, don't you know this is mutiny?"[39] Since mutiny was a hanging offense, the generals dropped the conversation.

Union losses at Pleasant Hill by regimental tally were 289 killed, 773 wounded, and 1,062 missing for a total of 1,605.[40] Confederate losses were 1,200 killed and wounded and another 426 taken prisoner.[41] The twin battles fought over two consecutive days had left dead and wounded over a twenty-mile line, with the vast bulk of these on the two battlefields. Homes, schools, and all other available buildings were pressed into service as hospitals, and Confederates and Federals were treated side by side for several days afterward.[42] The Union trains provided much-needed supplies, but food was unavailable for three days, and the Confederate physicians were quickly overwhelmed with the numbers of wounded to be tended.[43] Many Federal soldiers, though, later wrote of the kind care they had received in the homes of people in DeSoto Parish.[44]

The Confederates buried their dead first, the Mansfield dead in the town's cemetery. Officers were placed in adjacent graves at the crest of the hill on which the cemetery was located; other Confederate dead were buried in makeshift graves near where they fell, for reburial later.[45] Some of the Union dead at Mansfield were also buried near the town's cemetery, men who died while under medical care. Two trenches were dug near the second phase of the Mansfield battle, and hundreds of Union soldiers were buried in those mass graves.[46] At Pleasant Hill, of 400 Union wounded, more than half died.[47] It took well over a day to bury Confederate dead near the village's cemetery.[48] Union dead at Pleasant Hill were buried in a makeshift graveyard to the rear of the Pearce-Payne College, some in individual graves and others in common trenches.[49] Captured Union officers and soldiers were taken first to Shreveport, and then to prison at Camp Ford in Tyler, Texas.[50]

Among the Confederate prisoners held at Grand Ecore was David French Boyd, one of Taylor's engineers, who had been Sherman's best friend when he was superintendent of the Louisiana Seminary at Pineville. Boyd was kept aboard the *Polar Star*. On April 14, Boyd smuggled out a letter to Taylor, telling what he had discovered at Grand Ecore.

> GRAND ECORE
> April 14th, 1864
> General Taylor,
> Com. of Confederate Forces.
>
> General:
>
> Two iron-clad gunboats were lying at the mouth of Red river on 7th inst: The Essex at Fort DeRussey on 7th. The Benton at Alexandria on 8th; and on 12th a brigade of infantry, and one of cavalry, and four (4) light batteries at Alexandria (last is the statement of a private (Zauker [?]), who left that place on 12th inst.

At Grand-Ecore four (4) heavy iron-clad *Three* (3) of *Nine* (9) guns, and *One* (1) monitor of *Two* (2) guns [the *USS Osage*]. Some Four (4) transports also.

Mostly the whole of Banks' Army is here (Grand-Ecore). A pontoon bridge spans the River; and a large forage train is encamped on East Bank, half (1/2) mile below the town; and evidently some cavalry and infantry are encamped on that side.

The enemy is said to be fortifying in rear of Grand-Ecore. They are foraging a great deal on East Bank. Some twenty (20) transports are *above*—between Grand-Ecore & Coushatta; and from the best information I can receive, they are protected by three (3) heavily plated gunboats, one (1) monitor and another, a *Ram,* and six (6) Tin-Clads; and it is certain that a large body of infantry is aboard the transports—probably the whole of one (1) Division, belonging to 17th Army Corps, commanded by Kilby Smith. [He was correct.]

The River is falling slowly—about four (4) inches last night (13th inst.). Scant six (6) feet of water is on the Falls. *Move heaven and earth to close up Scopini's Cut-Off!* [Boyd underlined this entire sentence and double underlined the last portion] A fall of two (2) feet more in the River would ruin the enemy. If the Fleet is lost, General Banks considers himself ruined. He has been heard to say so. He is certainly much disturbed.

If Plaisance [a small village south of Grand Encore] could be seized, and your 24 pounders and 30 pounder Parott placed there, I think you wd reap a rich harvest, th' your Battery was finally lost. Such a movement—if Plaisance were tenaciously held—would completely paralyze General Banks.

I have just now heard from a reliable source that there are but three (3) regiments & a squadron of Cavalry (Whites), and some negro troops (number not known) at Alexandria. To that number add about 500 Whites sent down on 13th. Three (3) boat loads, about 1500 men, came up from Alexandria on 12th.

I wd have put-down this information *neatly* in a letter; but as the returning surgeon will be most likely required to carry out no letters but those examined & approved by the

Federal authorities, I have thought it best to resort to this means of communicating with you.

I hope you will give our enemies another good thrashing. They acknowledge themselves badly whipped.

We have now been on this Boat Ten (10) days, and many men are sick. I am well, and in good spirits, but bitterly regretting that my ignominious capture has prevented my participating in your glorious victory.

Resp'y
D. F. Boyd[51]

The letter, written in the margins of a newspaper, was placed in Taylor's mailbox in Shreveport, but he did not see a copy until the 1870s. Boyd had no way of knowing that the dam had been blown at Tone's Bayou, apparently on or soon after March 18, 1864; the river did not return to its main channel course until 1873. In the summer of 1864 the W. P. Lane Rangers, a Texas cavalry unit, came to the site and crossed Bayou Pierre in short order, but it took them half a day to cross Tone's Bayou.[52]

The Union army, having halted Confederate attacks for three straight days (including the short battle at Wilson's Farm), now moved back on the road to Natchitoches and then to Grand Ecore. It had sustained heavy casualties but was still very much a viable fighting force. The average soldier was disgusted with Banks and had very little confidence in his ability as a commander. This was never more certain than with the Western troops. The easterners had seen Lewis Benedict, one of their favorite commanders, killed and T. E. G. Ransom, now almost a legend among Illinois troops, wounded and carried off the field. The Nineteenth Corps commander had a broken arm from being knocked off his horse by his own men during the rout and was seen wearing a sling by all the troops he passed. What had they gained for their hard marching and for fighting a determined, almost maniacal foe? Nothing.

Although the Battle of Pleasant Hill was a Northern tactical tie, Banks's decision to retreat to Grand Ecore effectively turned the engagement, and eventually the entire campaign, into a strategic defeat for the Union. The forward elements of the navy were left without support and had to fend for themselves. Yet Banks's army had not been shattered, and his senior commanders wanted to press ahead. His excuse of a lack of water was real in the army's immediate location, but he made the retreat to Grand Ecore more for a sense of security than to slake the thirst of the column.

NOTES

1. *JCCW*, 77.
2. *O.R.* 34, 392, 422.
3. Scott, *32d Iowa*, 136–37.
4. Ibid., 136–46.
5. *O.R.* 34, 354.
6. Ibid., 354, 423.
7. Map of the Battle of Pleasant Hill showing locations of buildings and streets as well as unit dispositions, Mansfield, LA, State Historic Site; map of the Red River Campaign by Col. John Clark (no. 8), John Clark Collection, Cayuga County Museum, Auburn, NY; Map of Pleasant Hill by Major Richard Venable, Gilmer Papers.
8. Pellet, *114th New York*, 193–94; Beecher, *114th New York*, 308; S. F. Benson, "The Battle of Pleasant Hill, Louisiana," in *Annals of Iowa* (Des Moines, 1906), 7:500; Henry H. Childers, "Reminiscences of the Battle of Pleasant Hill," *Annals of Iowa*, 7:514–15; *DeSoto Parish History; Sesquicentennial Edition, 1843–1993* (Mansfield, LA, 1995), 104.
9. Taylor to Walker, April 9, 1864, Walker Papers.
10. Blessington, *Walker's Texas Division*, 193.
11. *O.R.* 34, 607.
12. Ibid., 565, Blessington, *Walker's Texas Division*, 194; Hamilton P. Bee, "Battle of Pleasant Hill—An Error Corrected," *Southern Historical Society Papers* 8 (1880): 184–86.
13. *O.R.* 34, 566, 605.
14. Taylor, *Destruction and Reconstruction*, 166; *O.R.* 34, 566, 605.
15. *O.R.* 34, 566, 605.
16. Ibid., 567.
17. *JCCW*, 176, 218; *O.R.* 34, 308; pt. 3, 99; *Philadelphia Press*, April 10, 1864; Frank Moore, ed., *The Rebellion Record: A Diary of American Events, with Documents, Narratives, Illustrative Incidents, Poetry, Etc.*, 12 vols. (New York, 1862–71), 8:549–50.
18. Taylor, *Destruction and Reconstruction*, 167; *O.R.* 34, 602.
19. Taylor, *Destruction and Reconstruction*, 166–69; *O.R.* 34, 567, 608, 617.
20. *O.R.* 34, 567, 608, 617.
21. Taylor, *Destruction and Reconstruction*, 166–69.
22. X. B. Debray, "A Sketch of Debray's Twenty-Sixth Regiment of Texas Cavalry," *Southern Historical Society Papers* 13 (1885): 158–59.
23. Scott, *32d Iowa*, 140, 180–83.
24. *O.R.* 34, 430–31; Scott, *32d Iowa*, 198.
25. Ibid., 392; *JCCW*, 218.
26. Scott, *32d Iowa*, 145–47; Taylor, *Destruction and Reconstruction*, 169; *O.R.* 34, 355–56, 361, 363, 366, 369, 423–24.
27. *O.R.* 34, 392–93, 417–18, 423–24.
28. Shorey, *15th Maine*, 85.
29. *O.R.* 34, 341–42, 345–46, 350; Shorey, *15th Maine*, 97.

30. Shorey, *15th Maine*; *O.R.* 34, 317, 328, 350, 373.

31. Taylor, *Destruction and Reconstruction*, 168–69; *O.R.* 34, 605.

32. *O.R.* 34, 309.

33. Johnson, *Red River Campaign*, 163.

34. *JCCW*, 13, 62, 195–96.

35. *JCCW*, 35, 221–22.

36. Ibid., 189.

37. Scott, *32d Iowa*, 230–35; Hoffman, *Camp, Court, and Siege*, 96–97; *O.R.* 34, 309.

38. *O.R.* 34, 309; Scott, *32d Iowa*, 230–35; Hoffman, *Camp, Court, and Siege*, 96–97; Johnson, *Red River Campaign*, 163–64.

39. *O.R.* 34, 309; Scott, *32d Iowa*, 230–35.

40. Losses calculated from documents at Mansfield, LA, State Historic Site.

41. *O.R.* 34, 309; Taylor, *Destruction and Reconstruction*, 167, 171.

42. Ben Van Dyke, "Ben Van Dyke's Escape from the Hospital at Pleasant Hill, Louisiana," rev. S. F. Benson, *Annals of Iowa*, 7:524.

43. Shorey, *15th Maine*, 105.

44. Benson, "Battle of Pleasant Hill," 501; Scott, *32d Iowa*, 152.

45. Silas T. Grisamore, *The Civil War Reminiscences of Silas T. Grisamore, C.S.A.*, ed. Arthur W. Bergeron Jr. (Baton Rouge, LA, 1993), 151.; Liz Chrysler, "The Battle of Pleasant Hill—From a Boy's Point of View," *Mansfield Enterprise*, May 17, 1977.

46. Map in the archives of Mansfield, LA, State Historic Site.

47. Benson, "Battle of Pleasant Hill," 503; Shorey, *15th Maine*, 107.

48. Grisamore, *Civil War Reminiscences*, 151; Chrysler, "Battle of Pleasant Hill."

49. Shorey, *15th Maine*, 107.

50. Benson, "Battle of Pleasant Hill," 503; Shorey, *15th Maine*, 107; Amos J. Barron, "History of Pleasant Hill, Louisiana" (manuscript in the archives of Mansfield, LA, State Historic Site, 1969), 4.

51. David French Boyd to Richard Taylor, April 14, 1864 in the archives of Jackson Barracks, New Orleans.

52. Heartsill, *Fourteen Hundred and 91 Days*, 211.

CHAPTER EIGHT

STEELE'S DILEMMA

FREDERICK STEELE THOUGHT he knew more about campaigning in Arkansas than Grant did. Central Arkansas had many of the same characteristics as northern Louisiana. It was hilly and barren with little population; in the spring, rains turned the few roads into bottomless muddy troughs. Steele had to contend with regular Confederate troops to the south and west, hostile Indians in the west, guerrilla units called "partisan rangers" operating freely in the countryside, and jayhawkers, ostensibly pro-Union but mercenary enough to work for the highest bidder.[1] Moreover, he was reluctant to participate in any venture with Banks, and he said so.

Grant forced him to cooperate, however, and Steele obeyed. His orders were to take a force down to Shreveport and work in concert with Banks and Porter. How this would be accomplished was left up to Steele and his staff. Steele at first planned to move southwest from Little Rock and approach the Ouachita River somewhere between Hot Springs and El Dorado. From there he would descend to Monroe, Louisiana, which was also located on the Ouachita River. It was a straightforward line of travel that would be devoid of Confederate units until he reached Louisiana. If he did not cross the Ouachita River sooner, he would do so at Monroe and follow the uncompleted bed of the Southern Pacific Railroad west in an almost straight line, crossing few streams until he reached the Red River opposite Shreveport. If he crossed north of Shreveport, he would be able to approach the town from the same side of the river. If he approached via the railroad bed, his artillery could harass the town while Banks attacked from the south.[2]

For some reason, Steele decided instead to veer more to the southwest. His forces would assemble at Arkadelphia and go on to Washington, the capital of Confederate Arkansas, about seventy miles north of Shreveport, and then move south to the city. It was a variant of Banks's plan to meet at Alexandria after Franklin marched west, then north, and A. J. Smith and Porter came up the Red. Once Steele began the march, his faith in the timetable Banks had set

was the only guidance he had. There would be little or no communication with either Banks or Porter.

On March 17, Steele ordered Brigadier General John Thayer,
the commander at Fort Smith, to march his troops to Arkadelphia,
where he was to join Steele's column coming from Little Rock. Steele
gave Thayer until April 1 to march the 170 miles. He then ordered
the commander of the small garrison at Pine Bluff to send scouts to
watch for any movement by Confederate forces to the south. Steele
took the Third Division, Seventh Corps, and two brigades of cavalry from Little Rock on March 23. His force consisted of 6,800 men,
and Thayer added another 3,600, making a main column of 10,400.[3]
Each man was loaded down with full equipment for a campaign
and forty rounds of ammunition. Steele's men, who had been per-
forming garrison duty traveled nine miles the first day. The next
day they reached the Ouachita River at the hamlet of Rockport,
which they found deserted. Although they easily crossed the shallow river, they stopped to throw up a bridge in case rains made the
stream rise. This activity slowed them, and for the next three days
the column marched at a leisurely pace to a point a few miles outside
Arkadelphia. The advance elements entered the town on March 29.[4]
The Confederates seemed to be ignoring them.

Edmund Kirby Smith's district commander of Arkansas was
Major General Sterling Price, who had been a brigadier general in
the Mexican War and had served as governor of Missouri. Price
had seen his territory shrink drastically since the Union forces had
taken Little Rock, and his numbers were small—just five brigades
of cavalry but mostly tough veterans—concentrated in the southwest portion of the state. His brigades were separated when Steele
began his expedition. Two were east of the Saline River—one near
Monticello and the other near Elba—and east of the Ouachita River,
approximately halfway between the towns Pine Bluff and Camden.
Of the other three, led by Brigadier General John Marmaduke, two
were with Marmaduke at Camden—one under Brigadier General
Joseph Shelby, the other under Colonel Colton Greene—and the
third, W. L. Cabell's, west of Washington on the Red River.[5]
Marmaduke's brigades totaled 3,600 men.

Marmaduke's intelligence gathering was suffering from a time
lag. On March 25 the brigades were dispatched to specific points,
only to discover that Steele's column was already approaching
Arkadelphia. Marmaduke had intended to harass the Federal column from both front and rear and then attack its supply trains with

a third brigade from the flanks. When the cavalry reached its objective at Tate's Bluff, however, they found only hoofprints and wagon tracks. Marmaduke then decided to make a dash for the Little Missouri River and contest the crossing with all of his brigades.

Steele had made excellent time reaching Arkadelphia, but when he arrived for his expected link-up with Thayer, Thayer was missing. After waiting for three days as his men rested, Steele became anxious and finally felt he could wait no longer. On April 1 he moved his men out of the pleasant little town and headed toward Washington. Cabell's brigade began skirmishing with the Union column almost immediately. That night Marmaduke ordered Greene's brigade to take up a position on the Washington Road near the Little Missouri River.[6] The next morning Cabell's brigade was ordered to join Greene. Marmaduke's plan to hold at the Little Missouri crossing seemed to be working. As the two brigades prepared to hold their position, however, word came that the Union column had turned toward Elkin's Ferry, bypassing them.[7]

Steele seized and then began fortifying the ferry landing, mounting artillery on all the approach roads. Shelby's brigade attacked the rear guard with spirited cavalry charges. On April 3 and 4, Steele's column crossed the Little Missouri with Shelby harassing it from the rear. Marmaduke then attacked the column while it was most vulnerable, crossing the river; he charged with 1,200 men and drove several regiments back. The Union soldiers stopped running when they found the main concentration of Union troops, and Marmaduke was forced to withdraw. Shelby joined the other two brigades that night, and the three withdrew to Prairie d'Ane, where the Confederates had built earthworks. Marmaduke received reinforcements from the Indian Territory on April 6 in the form of Brigadier General Richard Gano's brigade.

Steele finally received news from Thayer, who was trying find him as his column marched from Hot Springs. Steele halted his troops to give Thayer time to catch up. A spring rainstorm meanwhile deluged the camp area, destroyed the corduroy plank roads, and threatened to float the pontoon bridges away.[8] Steele's men repaired the damage on April 8 and 9 while the battles of Mansfield and Pleasant Hill were being fought. Steele, of course, knew nothing about Banks's fortunes or Porter's problems. When Thayer arrived, Steele's men were very unimpressed by their reinforcements. The second column seemed to consist of every kind of soldier possible, even Indians, and had a variety of bulky wagons and other transportation that had been scavenged along the route.[9] But despite their many conveyances, they had no supplies; Thayer had apparently expected Steele to resupply him. Since Steele's men had been consuming supplies at a fast pace while waiting for Thayer, he was forced to request supplies from Little Rock, dispatching an empty supply train. His quartermasters were told to resupply the column with thirty days' half-rations for 15,000 men.[10]

On April 10, Steele moved across Prairie d'Ane, pushing two of Marmaduke's brigades before him. Shelby and Thomas Dockery stiffened their positions by late afternoon, and a larger engagement occurred. Both sides brought up artillery, and the battle escalated until nightfall. The lines were so close that Union troops reported seeing the glowing matches the Confederates used to light cannon fuses.[11] April 11 saw little fighting: that afternoon, Steele tried to force the Confederates out of their lines by making a grand show of his line of battle, but the Confederates would not budge, and Steele returned to his camp of the previous night.[12] Under cover of darkness, Price withdrew his men about eight miles toward Washington, abandoning without a fight the earthworks his men had held.[13]

Price had made a blunder, but he was surprised by Steele's next move. On the morning of April 12, Steele's men occupied the trenches, but shortly thereafter, the column reversed its direction and marched for Camden, the most convenient place to set up a supply base. Price had no way of knowing how short of supplies Steele was or that until supplies arrived, the combined Union column could not move on to Shreveport. Steele's men marched toward Camden on April 12 and 13. On the 13th the rear guard was repeatedly attacked by fresh reinforcements that Price had received: the remainder of the division from the Indian Territory, including Colonel Tandy Walker's Second Indian Brigade of Choctaws. These troops harassed the Union column, slowing it down to give the remaining Confederates time to join in the assault, after which they made a combined attack on the rear guard of Thayer's division. They were finally repulsed after most of the column turned back to help the beleaguered Frontier Division. The Confederates broke off the engagement, and the march resumed. Pouring spring rains once again slowed the column.

Steele was forced to lay corduroy road before the wagons and artillery could pass through the rain-soaked bottomlands. On April 14, after an exhausting march through the stream valleys of

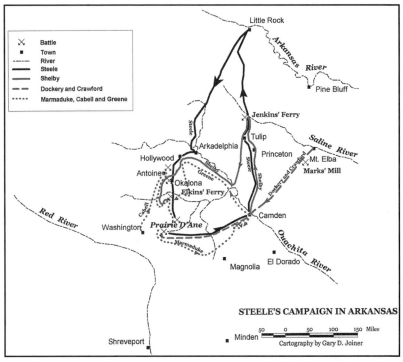

Map of Arkansas portion of the campaign, sometimes called the Camden Expedition.

the Camden road, Steele received word from scouts that a large Confederate force was assembling between him and his future supply base: Marmaduke had marched his entire division sixty miles around Steele's flank to take up a position across the road fourteen miles from Camden. Since Steele had enough men to push the Confederates aside, his intent was not to deal a death blow to this enemy obstruction but to get past it and enter Camden, where he could dig in until his supplies arrived.

Five days earlier, after the Battle of Pleasant Hill, Kirby Smith had met with Richard Taylor at Mansfield to discuss the situation. Smith affirmed his support for Taylor—it would have been very difficult to do anything else after the two battles—but did not want Taylor to pursue Banks, believing that the Union column could still follow the navy to Shreveport. Besides, he wanted Taylor close to Shreveport in case Steele moved past or around Price and Marmaduke—though Taylor was insistent that neither Steele nor Porter could or would attack Shreveport with Banks's main column out of the picture.[14] Smith stayed with Taylor at Mansfield until April 11, then returned to Shreveport and ordered Taylor to move his army from Pleasant Hill to Mansfield. When Taylor did not comply, Smith returned to Mansfield on April 13. Taylor brokered a deal that he thought was practical: he offered to lead his infantry against Steele until that Union column was either destroyed or forced to retreat; then he would return to fight Banks with both his and Price's forces. Smith agreed to this arrangement, and on April 14, Taylor sent three divisions to Shreveport, those of Walker, Churchill (commanded by Tappan), and Parsons. Polignac's small and hard-fought division was sent south to track Banks and make him think that Taylor was still in pursuit.

Taylor himself rode to Shreveport the next day to lead his three divisions north and found an unpleasant surprise: he learned that Steele had turned his column toward Camden, about 110 miles from Shreveport. Smith then announced that he, not Taylor, would pursue Steele.[15] He dismissed Taylor from Arkansas action, telling him that he could either remain in Shreveport or harass Banks at Grand Ecore.[16] Taylor, livid, returned to his troops. Smith, promising Taylor that he would return his infantry through Minden to Campti once Steele posed no further threat, marched his men out of Shreveport on April 16.[17] Walker was sent thirty miles to Minden and then north on the Fort Towson Road, to guard against Steele's trying to link up with Banks, another thirty miles, making a single day's march of sixty miles.[18] Smith moved north to Calhoun, Arkansas, only a few miles from Price's position. He planned to block any chance of Steele's combining with Banks or Porter and to destroy the northern column, leaving Little Rock and even eastern Arkansas devoid of Union presence. He could then grandly march into Little Rock as the conquering hero.

Steele reached Camden the same day Smith left Shreveport. He was desperate for supplies. Camden was well fortified, but if he could not feed his 15,000 men, the earthworks were useless to him. The next day Steele dispatched a supply train of 198 wagons to forage for corn and whatever other food could be acquired by any means. He sent along two cannon and 200 men of the First Kansas Cavalry (Colored). The train moved west about eighteen miles and then scattered on various roads to forage. Most were successful in retrieving corn. On the morning of April 18 the train reassembled for the return to Camden. They had moved about four miles when they were met by reinforcements, including 375 infantry and ninety cavalry with two small mountain howitzers.[19] A force of 1,000 men and four field guns now accompanied the wagons.

Marmaduke sought to attack the supply train and set out with 2,000 men, planning to hit the Union column simultaneously from the front and the right flank. When he received word of the reinforcements, however, he halted, asking Price for permission to bring his entire force to interdict the supply train. Permission was granted, and after another flanking march he set up a trap at a community called Poison Springs. Price sent reinforcements and before the supply train arrived, Marmaduke had 3,100 men waiting for it.[20]

When the supply column came in contact with the Confederates, Colonel James Williams of the First Kansas Cavalry ordered the wagons as close together as possible, hoping to protect them. He then moved his regiment to the front and along the flanks of the train, facing outward, and the infantry to the rear, also facing outward.[21] The Confederates attacked the right flank first and the Union troops were so spread out trying to protect the 198 wagons that reinforcements could not reposition to counter new threats. Marmaduke then hit the train from the front, and the black cavalrymen broke and ran into the woods. The Confederates gave chase and cut them down.[22]

Williams believed that Steele's men in Camden would hear the commotion and rush to their aid. When no help came, the Union infantry and the remnants of the cavalry routed, and the Confederates captured the train. The Choctaws chased the survivors through the woods. The Rebels took 170 wagons and burned twenty-eight others. They also captured the four cannon with ammunition and powder, plus 100 prisoners.[23] Marmaduke suffered 115 killed, wounded, and missing. Union losses were 301 killed, wounded, and missing—182 of the total from the First Kansas Cavalry.[24] The Rebels seemed to relish killing the black troops, at least according to Cabell.[25] The survivors straggled back into Camden, without any wagons or field pieces and with 300 fewer men.

Steele hunkered down in Camden waiting for supplies from Little Rock. He could do little else. On April 18 a messenger arrived with word that Banks wanted Steele to join him; Banks said he had won at Mansfield and Pleasant Hill but had withdrawn to Grand Ecore for supplies.[26] On April 22, Steele wrote Sherman that he could not confront all of Kirby Smith's forces if Banks were defeated.[27] Steele then send a courier to Banks to say that he probably could not link up with the southern column because he had received word that 8,000 Confederate infantry had just reinforced Price. Steele's letter rambled about possible lines of approach, each of which he dismissed.[28] In fact, Steele had no idea what he should do next. The Confederates would decide for him.

Kirby Smith arrived at Calhoun with three divisions of infantry on April 19 and immediately took command of field operations. He ordered James Fagan's division and Shelby's brigade to place themselves between Steele and Little Rock and, while doing so, to attack Steele's supply bases on his main line of retreat. Smith also ordered Parsons and Churchill to Camden from their western Arkansas positions, and by the next day they had moved to Magnolia, about half the distance to Little Rock. Fagan was to cross the Ouachita River; the movements of Parsons and Churchill were designed to make Steele believe that the main attack would be on his fortified position at Camden.[29] Four days later, Fagan arrived at El Dorado on the Ouachita. Learning that Steele's supply train was returning to Camden under a heavy guard, he then headed northwest to intercept it. Forty-five miles of fast marching placed Fagan on the Saline River at Mount Elba, where he allowed his exhausted men to bivouac at midnight. At dawn the next morning, Fagan moved to Marks' Mill, located on an intersection on the road between Camden and Pine Bluff. Finding no trace of the supply train at the intersection, he prepared to attack when it arrived.

Steele's supply train, commanded by Lieutenant Colonel Francis Drake, was heading southwest from Pine Bluff. At its core were 240 wagons filled with the required half-day rations for 15,000 men, plus other supplies. Guarding this train were three regiments of Union infantry, a total of 1,200 men, and 240 cavalry troopers.[30] (Oddly, for a column heading potentially into harm's way, there was also a large number of hangers-on, including 300 escaped slaves.) They encamped near Marks' Mill on the evening of April 24 without knowing that Fagan was just down the road. Drake apparently did not feel the need to post pickets.

At dawn, before the supply column could reach the Saline River, Fagan hit it with two brigades. A third, Cabell's brigade, formed in the woods parallel to the road, hit the column in the flank, and chased Steele's men from the train and into the woods on the opposite side. Realizing that Union infantry was massing to attack one of his flanking regiments, Cabell then ordered an about-face and fell upon the Union troops, thus avoiding a trap. His men fought hand to hand for one and one-half hours, until Confederate reinforcements arrived to crush the Union line. As the Union troops were pushed back to fighting among the wagons, Shelby's brigade arrived after a ten-mile march. At this point, Drake was wounded, and two Union regiments surrendered.[31] The Confederates then directed attention to the third regiment, which was still holding out, and soon conquered it as well. The Confederates next attacked the cavalry that had been conducting rear guard duty several miles behind the train. The Union horsemen were driven off, and Fagan owned the day and the supply train.[32] The Southerners had superiority in numbers at each surge of fighting. Given the way the Union column approached on one road and its disposition of forces, the Rebels were able to attack the Federals piecemeal, one or two units at a time. The battle had lasted five hours, during which the Union suffered more than 1,300 military casualties plus the civilians, particularly Negroes, who were killed.[33] The battle at Marks' Mill was a twin to that of Poison Springs in tactics and results.

When Steele heard about Marks' Mill and its disastrous results, he was immediately forced to halt his waiting game. He had 15,000 men and 9,000 horses in a land of pine barrens and swampy river bottoms, a countryside devoid of forage. Although his generals disagreed on a course of action, Steele made up his mind that the only way to save his command was to evacuate Camden the next day and begin a retreat to Little Rock. The retreat took on the look of a rout, though more organized. Steele ordered everything that could not be carried by the troops to be destroyed—including, strangely, a large amount of hardtack and bacon that could not be distributed.[34] The men set out after dark on April 26 after fooling the Confederates into believing they were bedding down for the night. By midnight they had crossed the Ouachita and pulled up their pontoon bridge; they slept along the road where they stopped.[35]

At 9:00 A.M. on April 27 the Confederates entered the abandoned works at Camden. Smith had had no idea that Steele had left. His three infantry divisions from Louisiana all arrived late that afternoon but could not pursue because they had no pontoon bridges. Smith then sent Maxey's division back to the Indian Territory, believing it would not be needed. Marmaduke's cavalry crossed the Ouachita by swimming, but not until darkness fell. The next morning, Smith ordered his troops to begin bridging the river.

Steele was pushing his men as hard as he could; he chose the road to Jenkins' Ferry rather than the Pine Bluff road, allowing him to avoid the mudflats of the Moro Swamp. To lighten their loads, men threw away things they had previously thought important. Rumors were rampant that the Confederates had passed to their front and were waiting somewhere ahead. The Confederates, however, were having trouble of their own. Fagan could not find a place to cross the Saline River. The water had risen because of the almost constant rains, so he finally gave up and led his men to Arkadelphia on April 29 to find supplies. Southern Arkansas was equally inhospitable to both sides, Marmaduke, to Fagan's south, was pressing closer to Steele's column.

Steele reached Jenkins' Ferry that afternoon and found the Saline as unyielding as it had been for Fagan. He brought up the pontoons loaded on wagons and bridged the torrent, but it was after 4:00 P.M. when he began moving the wagons and artillery across the bridge.[36] The infantry and cavalry would cross last.

Meanwhile, Marmaduke was closing in on the Federal column. He began to skirmish the next morning, trying to hold the rear guard down until reinforcements would arrive. Churchill's division, the first of these, caught the Federal infantry on the west side of the Saline River.[37] The road leading to the ferry descended from a line of hills and bluffs into a narrow slit bordered on the north by a line of bluffs, a small bayou, and a canebrake. To the south were fields separated and ringed by timber. There was little area for either side to maneuver. In the fields close to the river the Union infantry felled trees to form an abatis and some contrived breastworks. The field of fire was less than a quarter-mile.[38] The fields were flooded with almost two feet of water. Across this swamp and into the abatis and breastworks was the only approach the Confederates could use.

Price ordered Marmaduke and Churchill to attack. This was done piecemeal, committing regiments individually because of the tight quarters.[39] The small bayou called Toxie Creek proved an added problem for the advancing Confederates. Steele's regiments, set as skirmishers across the stream, poured fire on the advancing Rebels. Smith decided there were not enough forces engaged, so he added all of Churchill's division and then Parsons's division. But the Confederates did not realize that Steele had not yet been able to cross his infantry in bulk over the Saline and that they were fighting the main force, not the rear guard. Both divisions were forced to retreat in the withering fire coming from their front and their right flank. Between a fog and the smoke of both muskets and

Brigadier General John Marmaduke. Library of Congress, Prints and Photographs Division, LC-B8172-1979

artillery, visibility was poor. Both Price and Smith told the two divisions to pull back. At about the same time, Walker's division arrived, and Smith committed it to attack on the Union left; he wanted all three brigades to advance and overpower the Federal position. In this senseless attack, all three commanders were wounded, Randal and Scurry mortally.[40] As the Confederates fell back, Steele took the remainder of his forces over the river in three hours. The Union troops then pulled the bridge to their side and destroyed it.[41]

The track behind Steele's retreat was littered with wagons that had broken down and pack animals that had been freed because they were too weak to pull wagons or artillery limbers. Military equipment previously thought to be essential was discarded when it became a burden to the troops. Water had backed up from the Saline River into low areas on the eastern side as well, making some of the road chest-deep in water.[42] But the Union column kept moving throughout May 1 and did not stop that night but marched until 4:00 A.M. without a break.[43] The column was finally given a short break before dawn. Their meager food supplies had given out, and after an all too brief respite, Steele began the march again until that afternoon, when the men reached Benton. There a supply train from Little Rock met them, and Steele halted for the remainder of the day and evening.[44] The next morning the lead elements of the column moved into Little Rock before noon. The hard march had brought the Union troops to safety. They believed that the Confederates would try to engage them in another battle, but Smith, without pontoon bridges, was unable to pursue them.

Smith and Price each showed very poor judgment in their tactics at Jenkins' Ferry. (Hindsight shows Marmaduke by far the most capable Rebel leader.) Confederate casualties were listed as 800 to 1,000 killed, wounded, or missing of 6,000 committed.[45] Union casualties were approximately 700 killed, wounded, and missing.[46] In all, Confederate losses in the Arkansas campaign were reported as 2,300 to the Union's 2,750.[47] Steele had a huge loss in matériel, including 635 wagons, 2,500 mules, and nine artillery pieces.[48] The Confederates, who did not travel with large trains, lost only thirty-five wagons and three field pieces.[49]

Smith moved his army back to the little village of Tulip, located near the Jenkins' Ferry battlefield. On the night of April 30 both Scurry and Randal died of their wounds and were buried in the village graveyard. For the next three days the army encamped while Smith pondered what to do. On May 3 he ordered Tappan's, Churchill's, and Walker's divisions to return to the town of Taylor.[50] They would not reach their Louisiana and Texas comrades in time to assist them in the pursuit of Banks.

NOTES

1. O.R. 34, 246, 519, 547, 576.
2. JCCW, 154–57.
3. O.R. 34, 657, 692.
4. A. F. Sperry, *History of the 33d Iowa Infantry Volunteer Regiment* (Des Moines, IA, 1866), 62–65 (hereafter cited as *33d Iowa*).
5. O.R. 34, 673, 679, 821; pt, 3, 77–78; Sperry, *33d Iowa*, 66.
6. O.R. 34, 821–22; Sperry, *33d Iowa*, 66.
7. O.R. 34, 821–22.
8. O.R. 34, 660, 675, 693, 780, 822–25; pt. 3, 77–78; Sperry, *33d Iowa*, 67.
9. Sperry, *33d Iowa*, 68.
10. O.R. 34, pt. 3, 77–79.
11. Johnson, *Red River Campaign*, 178.
12. Sperry, *33d Iowa*, 68–72; O.R. 34, 675, 687, 780, 824–25.
13. Sperry, *33d Iowa*, 72; O.R. 34, 687, 780, 824–25.
14. Taylor, *Destruction and Reconstruction*, 176; O.R. 34, 545–46.
15. O.R. 34, 571–72.
16. Taylor, *Destruction and Reconstruction*, 180.
17. O.R. 34, 481.
18. Blessington, *Walker's Texas Division*, 243–44.
19. O.R. 34, 743–44.
20. Ibid., 848–49.
21. Ibid., 744–45.
22. John M. Harrell, "Arkansas," in *Confederate Military History*, 12 vols. (Atlanta, 1899), 10:250.
23. O.R. 34, 844.
24. Ibid., 746.
25. Harrell, "Arkansas," 10:250.
26. Ibid., 661–62.
27. Ibid., 663.
28. O.R. 34, pt. 3, 267–68.
29. O.R. 34, 781; pt. 3, 267–68; Sperry, *33d Iowa*, 83.
30. O.R. 34, 712–13.
31. Ibid., 34, 789, 794, 835–36.
32. John N. Edwards, *Shelby and His Men; or, The War in the West* (Cincinnati, OH 1867), 279; O.R. 34, 668.
33. O.R. 34, 713.
34. Sperry, *33d Iowa*, 85; O.R. 34, 680.
35. Sperry, *33d Iowa*, 86–87; O.R. 34, 688.
36. O.R. 34, 677.
37. Ibid., 782, 799–800.
38. Blessington, *Walker's Texas Division*, 249; Sperry, *33d Iowa*, 90–91; O.R. 34, 782, 800, 802, 809, 815, 817; Harrell, "Arkansas," 265.

39. *O.R.* 34, 801–2, 829–30.

40. Ibid., 556–57, 677, 725–26, 817; Comte de Paris, *History of the Civil War in America*, 4 vols. (Philadelphia, 1875–1888), 4:557.

41. *O.R.* 34, 668, 670, 677, 690.

42. Sperry, *33d Iowa*, 94–95; *O.R.* 34, 670, 678, 680–81.

43. Sperry, *33d Iowa*, 97; Johnson, *Red River Campaign*, 201–2.

44. Sperry, *33d Iowa*, 96–98; *O.R.* 34, 393–94.

45. *O.R.* 34, 557.

46. Ibid., 34, 758.

47. Ibid., 34, 770–71, 779–80.

48. Harrell, "Arkansas," 255.

49. Ibid.

50. Blessington, *Walker's Texas Division*, 260; *O.R.* 34, 482.

CHAPTER NINE

KATABASIS

PORTER LEFT GRAND ECORE on the morning of April 7 with a much smaller but still powerful fleet. The slowly dropping water level, emerging sandbars, and maps showing the river ahead to be narrow and winding forced him to leave the *Eastport* behind. Its length and draft made the great ironclad a liability; shallow-draft vessels were his only viable option. He chose his vessels for the final sprint to Shreveport for their firepower and their ability to navigate the tight meanders of the unpredictable river.

The monitors *Osage* and *Neosho* each carried two 11-inch naval smoothbore guns in a single turret mounted at the bow and one 12-pounder smoothbore cannon. The monitors were sister boats, identical with the exception of the gun ports mounted at the stern of the *Neosho*. They were the only sternwheel monitors built during the war. Each was 180 feet long and weighed 523 tons but needed only four and one-half feet of water to stay afloat. The monitor's turrets carried an incredible six inches of armor plate. The appearance of decks sloping to the sides and running just above the waterline gave them the nickname of "Turtle Backs." With huge turrets in the bow and massive armored engine houses in the stern, the vessels tended to be unwieldy and difficult to steer in tight places.[1]

The only ironclad in the force that was not a monitor was the *Chillicothe*, a hybrid propelled by two sidewheels and two screw propellers. It also carried two 11-inch smoothbore guns and one 12-pounder smoothbore cannon. Its weight was 395 tons and length 162 feet, but it required almost seven feet of water to get underway.[2]

The *Lexington*, constructed in 1860, was one of the oldest warships in the inland fleet. A timberclad sidewheeler, it was 177 feet long, weighed 362 tons, and had thick layers of wood as protection from enemy guns. Its own guns were two 8-inch smoothbore, one 32-pounder, two 30-pounders, and one 12-pounder howitzer. The *Lexington* required six feet of water to keep it afloat.[3]

Porter also selected two tinclads, vessels with thinner armor, usually one-half to three-quarters of an inch thick. The *Fort Hindman* was a sidewheeler, weighed 280 tons, was 150 feet in length, and carried two 8-inch smoothbore and four 8-inch rifled cannons. Amazingly, it drew only two feet, four inches of water.[4] The *Cricket*, a sternwheeler, weighed 178 tons, was 154 feet in length, and carried six 24-pounder howitzers for armament. It had a draft of four feet.[5] Porter picked the *Cricket* as his flagship.

The *William H. Brown,* a tinclad that saw service as a dispatch vessel. It was lost during the campaign. Naval Historical Center photo NH 60352

The remainder of the U.S. Navy's contingent consisted of the tugs *Dahlia* and *William H. Brown* and the supply transport *Benefit*. Of the three, the *William H. Brown* was the only one armed, mounting two 12-pounder cannons. Large for a tug, it was often used as a dispatch boat.[6]

These navy vessels guarded and herded the army's transports, at least twenty vessels. The quartermaster's boats held supplies for the main column and 1,600 of A. J. Smith's men of the Seventeenth Corps under Brigadier General T. Kilby Smith, who had armed most if not all of these boats with army field cannons mounted on the decks. He had also placed bales of cotton and sacks of oats on the decks from behind which his men could fire in relative safety. Among the transports was Banks's headquarters boat *Black Hawk*, which Porter detested as an insult to his own favorite command vessel, the *Black Hawk*.

The transport *Black Hawk*, General Banks's command vessel. Admiral Porter considered the use of this boat an insult. Miller, *The Photographic History of the Civil War*, 6:223

The fleet headed north and reached Campti at five o'clock that first afternoon. The next morning, as the force got under way, the transport *Iberville* ran aground almost immediately and wedged itself so tightly in a sandbar that it took several hours to get afloat. The water level was dropping at a steady rate. As Porter passed north of the Grand Ecore hill complex and the mouth of Bayou Pierre, he had no way of knowing that the river had been starved for water by the Confederate destruction of the Tone's Bayou dam on March 18.

Once the *Iberville* had been pulled off the bar, the fleet slowly ascended the river, the crews calling out the locations of snags in the channel bottom. Remnants of the Great Raft still remained in the river north of Natchitoches, and some were now emerging with the subsiding water level. Travel was slowed to just above steerageway in the now gentle current. The fleet reached the town of Coushatta and the mouth of Bayou Coushatta or Coushatta, Chute, at 6:00 P.M. Kilby Smith sent a brigade ashore to guard the fleet from attack, and it took two prisoners.

The large tinclad *Black Hawk*, Admiral Porter's flagship. Library of Congress, Prints and Photographs Division, LC-B816-3140

At nine o'clock on the morning of April 8 the fleet headed north again, moving in single file up the narrow, winding river. Porter saw the river road that Banks could have used and the fields of corn and herds of cattle upon which the army could have subsisted.[7] Other than the small band of Confederates at Coushatta, there was no opposition. The day passed uneventfully, as did April 9. At 2:00 P.M. on April 10 the fleet reached the mouth of Loggy Bayou—or what Porter believed to be Loggy Bayou, but this body of water was not the stream shown on his map.[8] Lake Bistineau, lying to the east of the river, was one of several lakes that had been found by the Great Raft. Of three outflows that connected it to the Red River, the southernmost was Coushatta Chute. The other two were channels of Loggy Bayou. The Union maps were not correct in the positions or names of these streams; in fact, Porter did not know specifically where he was. In his *Naval History of the Civil War* the admiral wrote that he reached Springfield Landing, his rendezvous point, within an hour of his appointed time.[9] Springfield Landing is four miles west of the Red River. In his official report he said he reached Loggy Bayou.[10] In his *Incidents and Anecdotes*, Porter stated that he reached the mouth of the Shreveport River, a stream that does not exist.[11] We may never know just how far north he went. If the water level was sufficiently deep for his convoy to make it, he may have traveled another four river miles and anchored opposite a small stream one mile south of the foot of Scopini's cutoff. He may have been as close as two miles south of Tone's Bayou or as much as four to five miles below it.

In any case, while anchored opposite the stream, Kilby Smith sent a landing party to scatter some Confederates who were watching them. Then, after traveling another mile, Porter and Smith saw a sight that halted any further progress. Porter described it in a letter to General Sherman.

FLAG-SHIP CRICKET, *OFF ALEXANDRIA, LA.,*
April 16, 1864.

> Maj. Gen. W. T. SHERMAN,
> *Comdg. Mil. Div. of the Miss., Nashville, Tenn.:*
> When I arrived at Springfield Landing I found a sight that made me laugh; it was the smartest thing I ever knew the rebels to do. They had gotten that huge steamer, New Falls City, across Red River, 1 mile above Leggy [sic] Bayou, 15 feet of her on shore on each side, the boat broken down in the middle, and a sandbar making below her. An invitation in large letters to attend a ball in Shreveport was kindly left stuck up by the rebels, which invitation we were never able to accept. . . .

DAVID D. PORTER,
Rear-Admiral.[12]

While Porter began working on the problem of moving the *New Falls City*, Kilby Smith landed troops to secure the position. Seeing Confederates out in the open and watching them, both sensed something was wrong. Porter told Smith: "Banks has been defeated or we wouldn't see those men here. If Banks was still advancing, the outposts would keep on the main road to Shreveport. If defeated, the enemy's look-outs would be watching for our arrival, and be ready to turn their whole force upon us."[13] Shortly after this Captain William Andres of the Fourteenth New York Cavalry rode up with fifty of his troopers and told them of Banks's defeat on April 9. He carried with him several dispatches and specific verbal orders for Kilby Smith to return to Grand Ecore.[14] No mention was made of Porter's fleet.

The huge transport *New Falls City*. The Confederates wedged the vessel across the Red River to block the Union fleet. *Courtesy of Joseph Merrick Jones Collection, Manuscripts Department, Howard-Tilton Memorial Library, Tulane University, New Orleans, Louisiana*

Smith and Porter decided that they must both return to Grand Ecore before the Confederates could bring their artillery to the banks of the river and effectively blockade them, a move that could easily lead to either the capture or the destruction of the fleet. Porter ordered additional artillery placed on the upper decks of the transports, and more barricades of any materials available were made to provide firing positions for the infantrymen. Now the fleet began the arduous downstream passage from the deepest penetration ever made into the Red River valley by Federal forces.

The fleet was in a difficult position. From the time they entered the Narrows, the vessels had had to contend with the winding river and shallow channel. Now they were wedged bow to stern, with the *New Falls City* blocking them. The channel was so narrow that the largest vessels could not turn around but had to back down the river stern first for several miles.[15] The physical strains of this reverse movement over an extended course caused severe problems with steerage assemblies and major mechanical malfunctions. Snags in the channel and along the shore made the backward passage

Lieutenant Commander Thomas O. Selfridge, c. 1886. Naval Historical Center photo NH 2858

even more difficult. To make matters worse, the Confederates had hastily sent men and as much artillery as they could muster to high points along the banks north of Grand Ecore to harass the fleet.

Almost immediately the *Chillicothe* impaled itself on a submerged tree and was not able to move until the *Black Hawk*, using the *Chillicothe*'s hawser, was able to free the ironclad.[16] Patching the pierced hull halted the fleet for more than two hours. Other vessels suffered damage as rudders became unshipped and paddles were splintered. Then the *Emerald* ran hard aground. The Confederates began to rattle musket fire at the fleet, and the sound of minié balls careening off the hulls, casemates, and superstructure of the *Benefit*, *Black Hawk*, and *Osage* was ear-shattering.[17] These vessels responded to the ineffective long-arm fire with their 11-inch naval guns, which "must have been like hunting partridges with a howitzer."[18] When the fleet reached Coushatta Chute on the morning of April 12, the *Lexington* collided with the transport *Rob Roy*, spearing the latter's wheelhouse and launch and damaging its smokestacks.

The *Osage* was the first vessel to use a periscope in combat, at the Battle of Blair's Landing. Library of Congress, Prints and Photographs Division, LC-B816-3126

Later on the 12th the fleet approached Blair's Landing, which was due east of Pleasant Hill and approximately forty-five miles north of Grand Ecore. Since Green's cavalry had moved there to harass and, if possible, halt its progress, Porter's fleet, transports and armed vessels alike, passed the landing under cannon and small-arms fire.[19] Some personnel were wounded and vessels damaged by the Confederate artillery, which was well placed and concealed. Bringing up the rear of the flotilla were the tinclad *Lexington* and the monitor *Osage*. Strapped to the *Osage* to provide extra power was the transport *Black Hawk*. In making the tight turn above the landing, the *Osage* slewed and ran aground. Green and his 2,500 men, who were near the bank at this time, dismounted, tied their horses, formed into three ranks, and began pouring fire into the three boats. The *Black Hawk* took such devastating fire that forty soldiers on its decks had to be evacuated to the confines of the cramped metal hull of the *Osage*. All hands aboard followed. Later, Porter stated upon examination of the *Black Hawk* "that there was not a place six inches square not perforated by a bullet."[20]

Porter was fortunate that the unprotected wooden transports had already passed the landing, and if Green and his 2,500 men had had more artillery, the scene would have been much worse. Selfridge, commanding the *Osage*, wrote to Admiral Porter some sixteen years later, recalling the event as "one of the most curious fights of the war, 2,500 infantry against a gunboat aground."[21]

The *Osage* and the *Black Hawk* strapped together were still aground—their wooden surfaces riddled like Swiss cheese from musket and artillery fire—leaving the *Lexington* to carry on the fight. After an intense engagement of over an hour with no hint of the Confederates lessening the strength of their attack, the *Lexington* finally silenced Green's four-gun artillery battery with its 8-inch guns.[22] Shortly before that happened, the *Osage* managed to move from the bar on which it was grounded and cut the lines to the *Black Hawk*. Selfridge let the current move the boat close to the Confederates with no engines running, then brought one of his 11-inch guns to bear on the troops and, at a distance of only twenty yards, fired a load of grape shot and canister directly at the officer on horseback who had been urging his men on with fiery passion. This blast decapitated the unfortunate man—General Green himself. The Confederates broke ranks and moved away from the riverbank. There had been very few casualties, but Green's loss was catastrophic for Taylor.[23]

Porter kept the vessels moving past sunset and into the night—a very perilous journey with only torches and perhaps moonlight to light the way. Normally, the admiral did not take such risks, but the relative safety of the remainder of the fleet and the need to reach the support of the army to keep the Confederate army at bay were powerful incentives. The fleet finally anchored at 1:00 A.M. on the morning of April 13. Several transports had run aground during the night, and after dawn the next morning the quartermaster's boat *John Warner* went aground as well and delayed the progress of the fleet. As Porter made attempts to extricate the *John Warner* throughout the day, Confederate field pieces on a high bank fired at the vessels until *Osage* drove them off. The *Rob Roy* then lost its rudder and had to be placed under tow by the transport *Clara Bell*.[24]

The *John Warner* resisted all attempts to remove it from the sandy river bottom, so at daylight on the morning of the 14th, fearing

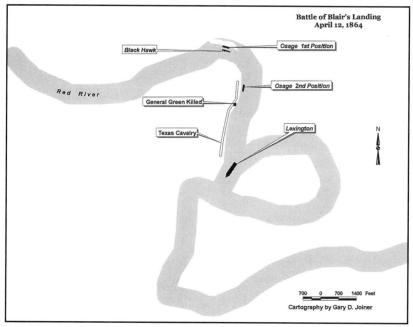

Map of the Battle of Blair's Landing, perhaps the most unusual battle in the Civil War, in which Texas cavalry fought heavily armed naval warships.

that the Confederates were preparing a trap, Kilby Smith ordered his transports and their protecting gunboats ahead to Campti. He left the ironclad *Fort Hindman* with the *John Warner* for protection. The next day the *Fort Hindman* managed to pull the vessel off the bar, and they both reached Grand Ecore on the 15th, where the fleet was safely under the army's guns. The navy was finally in contact with the army.

Banks's column was full of griping, angry men who believed that they had been betrayed by incompetent commanders. The words of improvised songs floated up and down the line. The chorus of one ditty, sung by Massachusetts troops to the tune of "When Johnny Comes Marching Home," included the line "We all skedaddled to Grand Ecore." The troops sometimes ended the bitter song with a yell of "Napoleon P. Banks."[25] The soldiers began referring to the commanding general as "Mister Banks," alluding to his lack of military training and his accession to the lofty rank of major general without ever having worn so much as a private's stripes.[26]

The column had covered the distance from Pleasant Hill to Grand Ecore in three days. Banks ordered the men to expand the outer perimeter of the Confederates' former defenses, where the army's 30,000 men were packed into a fortification of about six square miles. Believing that Taylor had 25,000 men to contest him, he ordered the remaining division at Alexandria under Brigadier General Cuvier Grover to come to Grand Ecore immediately.[27] Next, he sent a message to Pass Cavallo, Texas, instructing Major General John McClernand to strip his command of all but 2,000 soldiers and bring the bulk of his force to Grand Ecore. McClernand was to take over command of the Thirteenth Corps, replacing the wounded Ransom.[28]

Banks then reported to Grant the details of the campaign thus far. He made five major points: (1) Shreveport was the prime focus of the Confederate defenses; (2) Confederates were on the defensive; (3) Rebels had been planning an invasion of Missouri; (4) Steele's advance on the line he was using rendered Banks no assistance at all; and (5) gunboats were useless to the army, considering the shallow depth of the river.[29] He concluded by saying that he intended to advance on Shreveport using a different route. Just as this missive was completed, word came from Sherman demanding the return of A. J. Smith and his men.[30] Banks countermanded Sherman's order since he was senior to Smith's commander.[31]

Banks made an apparent effort to shift blame and bolster his own support—which was lagging among the troops and within his staff—by firing his chief of staff, Brigadier General Charles P. Stone, and replacing him with William Dwight.[32] He also relieved Albert Lee from command of the cavalry division and sent him to New Orleans.[33] With Lee was "Gold Lace" Dudley, who was relieved of command as well, and scathing letters were attached to both men's files.[34]

When Porter arrived at Grand Ecore, he visited Banks in his headquarters tent. The admiral found the general's accommodations well appointed, even opulent for field conditions. Banks was wearing a fine dressing gown, velvet cap, and comfortable slippers. He was reading *Scott's Tactics*, his usual nightly ritual.[35]

Banks made it plain that he considered he had won the Battle of Mansfield and that the subsequent fighting at Pleasant Hill had been simply a withdrawing action. He gave Porter the same excuse he had used with A. J. Smith, that he withdrew only for lack of water. The admiral reminded him that if so, he was only six miles from water at Mansfield. He left the general "under the delusion that he had won the battle of Mansfield, or Sabine Cross Roads, or whatever name that unfortunate affair was known by."[36] Totally disgusted with Banks and his excuses for retreat, the admiral later wrote "that he should have read it [*Scott's Tactics*] before he went to Sabine Cross Roads."[37] Porter told Banks that under no circumstance would the navy go back upstream.[38]

With the river falling rapidly at Grand Ecore, the fleet and the army were forced to withdraw from this region that had held so much promise for them. The army began marching along the river road to Alexandria. On April 16, with some navigation problems and further mechanical failures, the fleet proceeded downstream three miles with the *Eastport* in the lead. The Confederates, knowing that the fleet could return only on the same route it had taken north, in mid-March had placed six torpedoes below the ferry at Grand Ecore.[39] The *Eastport* struck one of these mines, and though the shock was felt by only a few people aboard, it took on water rapidly and came to rest on the bottom. Fortunately, the bottom was only a few feet at most below its keel, which settled in the soft sand.[40]

The *Eastport* thus became an obstacle less threatening than the *New Falls City* but potentially just as deadly since it blocked the passage of the fleet behind it. The pump boat *Champion No. 5* was used to bilge out the water. Then the guns were removed and placed on flat rafts towed by the *Cricket*. The captain, Lieutenant Commander Seth Ledyard Phelps, and his crew worked day and night to save the vessel and finally refloated it on April 21. Though grounding occasionally because it was still taking on water, the *Eastport* proceeded downstream another forty miles. Near the town of Montgomery, however, it ran into submerged snags on the 26th and became firmly stuck. The pump boat *Champion No. 5*, the *Champion No. 3*, and the *Fort Hindman* attempted to wrest the vessel free, but their efforts only worsened the situation. The captain of the *Fort Hindman*, Acting Volunteer Lieutenant John Pearce, and Phelps made several attempts to rock the *Eastport* free, but they were doomed to failure. Receiving news that the water level downstream was falling and knowing that the fleet was in danger of being bottled up behind the great ironclad, Porter ordered a ton of powder placed throughout the boat and available combustible materials packed into it. At 1:45 P.M. on April 26, the *Eastport* was destroyed.[41]

The vessels that had been aiding and guarding the *Eastport*—*Fort Hindman, Cricket, Juliet, Champion No. 3,* and *Champion No. 5*—then made their way downstream. Near the mouth of the Cane River, the Confederates had assembled four artillery pieces of Florian Cornay's battery with 200 riflemen from Polignac's division assisting. They heaped fire on the vessels and sank the *Champion No. 3.* Below its decks, more than 100 slaves being carried to freedom were scalded to death. The *Champion No. 5,* heavily damaged, was grounded and abandoned by its crew. The *Fort Hindman* (now commanded by Phelps), the *Cricket* with Porter aboard, and

The *Fort Hindman*, a small, but powerful, tinclad. Naval Historical Center photo NH 61569

the *Juliet* were severely damaged but passed through the gauntlet. A tribute to the ferocity of this attack is that in five minutes the *Cricket* was hit some thirty-eight times and suffered twenty-five dead and wounded—fully half of the crew. The *Juliet* also lost half its crew, with fifteen killed and wounded, and the *Fort Hindman* had three killed and four or five wounded.[42]

Porter, aboard the *Cricket*, displayed great personal bravery in keeping the tinclad in the fight. A shell hit the guns and killed the entire gun crew. Another eliminated the forward gun and its crew. Cornay's Confederates were pouring accurate fire on the gunboats.

A third shell hit the fire room, where the stokers kept steam pressure up in the boilers, killing all but one man. Porter gathered some refugee slaves that the *Cricket* had taken aboard, showed them how to fire a gun, and turned them into a gun crew to try to keep the Confederates' heads down long enough for the vessel to escape. He then went to the engine room and, finding the chief engineer dead, put the assistant engineer in charge and told him to get the steam pressure up. Porter then went to the pilothouse and discovered that another shell had wounded one of the pilots and that the remaining crew on the bridge were hiding. With his customary aplomb, Porter took charge of the *Cricket* himself and moved it past the battery that had nearly sent it to the bottom.[43]

The *Cricket*. It fought a vicious battle against Confederate artillery in which it suffered major damage. Naval Historical Center photo NH 55524

Porter's fleet limped into the northern approaches to Alexandria with the Red River falling rapidly. He had lost the most powerful ironclad in the fleet; two of his tug and pump boats had been sunk and three of his tinclads severely damaged. Most of the army transport vessels had received either mechanical or battle damage.

To make matters worse, the river had fallen a full six feet, trapping most of his fleet above the Falls.[44]

While the navy bumped and scraped its way along the sandy, rock-scattered river bottom, Banks was leading his men south toward Alexandria. The high bluffs of Grand Ecore did not directly connect to the river road. Four miles south of Grand Ecore lay Natchitoches, the oldest settlement in the Louisiana Purchase. From there the road, which ran along the Red River, crossed the Cane River. The channel of the Cane had once been the main course of the Red River; by 1864, however, the Red occupied another channel to the east, which the French explorers had named the Rigolet du Bon Dieu. These two channels ran roughly parallel for thirty miles before joining at Monett's Ferry. The river road followed the twisting channel of the Cane River and then added another fifteen miles to cross the island formed by the two streams. Had Banks taken an alternative route, traveling west to White's Store and then turning south, he would have left the safety of the fleet and reentered the "howling wilderness." At this stage of the campaign he wanted neither of those options. The road taken, however, afforded him little assistance from the fleet until he reached the ferry, for it followed a channel west of the river, which was not open to the naval vessels.

Banks placed A. J. Smith's division in Natchitoches between Richard Taylor and his army; Smith's men would be the last to leave. On April 21 at 5:00 P.M. the column began to move.[45] The men torched the few buildings in Grand Ecore.[46] Three brigades of cavalry, now allowed to perform their duties properly, screened the column. As twilight led to darkness, the cavalrymen burned homesteads and barns to light the way for the infantry and to exact some revenge. Following the cavalry came the infantry led by Grover's division, just arrived from Alexandria. Banks positioned the combined trains behind these fresh troops. Next came the remainder of the Nineteenth Corps, then the Thirteenth Corps. After the column had passed through Natchitoches, A. J. Smith's Sixteenth Corps and one brigade of cavalry brought up the rear.[47]

Banks received messages that Taylor was moving his forces south to cut the Union forces off at Monett's Ferry.[48] If the Confederates made a strong position at the ferry, the entire column would be cut off on the island between the channels and, possibly, forced to surrender. Banks therefore drove his men to reach the ferry ahead of the Confederates. Rebel soldiers cut trees to block the road ahead of the Union troops, slowing the column, and there were no large streams on the island from which the men could fill their canteens. The banks to the Cane River were steep and not easily traversed. The men were pushed to the limit of their endurance, with some staggering, some sleeping while marching, and officers often asleep in their saddles.[49] Then Taylor sent Green's cavalry, now under the command of Major General John Wharton, to harass the rear guard. Wharton's timely arrival not only saved Natchitoches from being torched by A. J. Smith's men, but his cavalry's adept hit-and-run raiding tactics added to the tense atmosphere of the Union column.[50]

Photograph of the fort complex at Grand Ecore, taken shortly after the Union occupation in 1864. Archives and Special Collections, Noel Memorial Library, Louisiana State University, Shreveport

As news of events at both the front and rear of the column moved quickly from unit to unit, the Union march took on the aura of a nervous herd of cattle ready to stampede. The angry troops devastated the countryside, leaving nothing of value in their wake. A. J. Smith's "gorillas" continued the manners they had learned in the Meridian campaign and destroyed everything in sight. Taylor later wrote that according to local residents, eastern troops under Banks tried to stop the westerners but were unable to do so.[51] The pattern of devastation continued to the end of the campaign.

The column pressed on through the night of April 21 and finally halted at 2:30 A.M. to allow the rear units to catch up. The lead elements had covered twenty miles in a little over nine hours. At 11:00 A.M. on April 22 the cavalry and infantry units took up the march again, just as the rear guard units were closing in on the column, giving Smith's troops time to rest before beginning the next leg of the march. The cavalry and forward infantry regiments encamped that night about three miles south of Cloutierville, just north of Monett's Ferry. As the men began to bed down, however, Banks received word from scouts that the Confederates were on his side of the ferry. At midnight he ordered Emory to take the entire army except the rear guard and secure the ferry landing. Banks also ordered A. J. Smith to send a brigade to assist Emory. Smith refused, stating that he could not spare any men.[52] Emory pressed forward and by 4:30 A.M. had driven the Confederate pickets across the river. But as dawn broke, Emory and his men could see what awaited them: across the river on a high and deeply wooded bluff the Confederates had mounted numerous cannon. The position overlooked any line of approach the Federals might take on that narrow tip of the island.

Taylor's troops—four batteries of artillery and 1,600 cavalry under Brigadier General Hamilton Bee—who had been sent to seal off the ferry, commanded the best ground for miles around.[53] Bee was ordered by both Taylor and Wharton to hold the ferry crossing and not let Banks escape. What Emory and his men did not know was that Confederate infantry under Polignac had secured the ford opposite Cloutierville and that other infantry units under Brigadier General St. John R. Liddell were in position at Colfax on the other side of the Red River. Wharton's cavalry was pressing A. J. Smith so hard that his men might not be able to hold the Confederates at bay; if the army were to retreat to Grand Ecore, they would be forced to fight every inch of the way.[54] All avenues of escape for the Army of the Gulf had apparently been blocked. Emory sent his cavalry forward, only to have them driven out of range by Rebel artillery. Next, he formed a line with his infantry to watch the Confederates and sent the cavalry to find another exit. None was found. Taylor had achieved his goal.

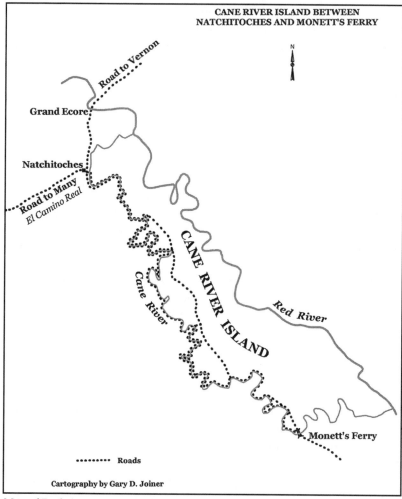

Map of Banks's retreat across Cane River Island.

Then some of the Union troopers approached a black man and asked him if there was a place to cross the Cane River other than the ferry. He spoke of a place two miles behind them and led them to a ford that was not covered by the Confederates.[55] Grover's division led by Brigadier General Henry Birge, Benedict's brigade now led by Colonel Francis Fessenden, and the remnants of the Thirteenth Corps were selected to make the flank attack. (Fessenden was the son of William Fessenden, a former senator from Maine and Lincoln's secretary of the treasury.) The Union troops under Birge made a long arcing loop around both the Cane River and the Confederates blocking the ferry position. They approached in line of battle with skirmishers deployed to their front. This was a difficult maneuver because the terrain was wooded and sometimes marshy. They emerged unseen onto a broad cotton field. After crossing the field, the Union troops climbed a wooded ridge, where their skirmishers encountered Bee's pickets. From this ridge, Birge and his men could see the main Confederate position, a quarter-mile ahead and across an open field. They could also look down at some of their own troops across the Cane River.[56]

Birge allowed Fessenden to prepare the attack. Benedict's old brigade held the right of the line and Birge's men the left. Cameron's division was held in reserve. Fessenden ordered the men to mount bayonets and wait to fire in volley to increase their effectiveness. The Union line moved forward, and Fessenden was one of the first casualties, suffering a wound to his right leg, which was later amputated. The line wavered as it descended the ridge and crossed a slough into a trapezoid-shaped field that forced the troops to crowd closer together. Reaching the foot of the ridge where the Confederates—Colonel George Baylor and the Second Arizona Cavalry—were lodged, the Union men charged. Seeing the size of the force to their front, the Rebels fell back to a line behind an overgrown fence, where they were joined by Colonel Isham Chisum Woods's Second Texas Partisan Rangers Cavalry. Baylor asked Bee for two regiments to plug a hole in his flank, but none was sent.

Birge halted his men, dressed their line, then rode with some of his staff to examine what lay ahead of them. As they went into a gully, they were hit by murderous artillery and small-arms fire whose location they could not determine. To save themselves, Birge and his party rode back through the line creating such confusion that the Union regiments simply hit the ground or broke and ran. Two regiments crossed into a ravine for cover.[57]

Emory, watching from across the Cane River, directed an artillery battery to provide fire support, then ordered his troops to make a feint as if forcing the ferry crossing in order to distract the Confederates. The ruse worked, and the Rebels were forced to split their artillery fire between Birge and Emory. Bee then received an incorrect message that his right flank was being attacked. There were no Federal forces there, but Bee concluded that Banks had outmaneuvered him and that the battle was lost. Bee ordered Baylor, who was expecting fire support, to retreat.

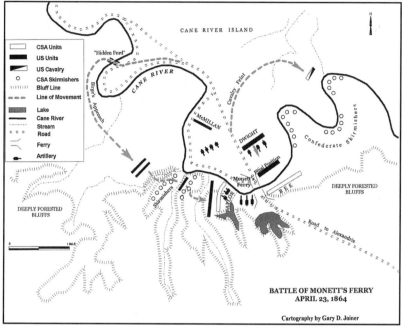

Map of the Battle of Monett's Ferry at the southern end of Cane River Island.

Taylor by that time was south of Cloutierville doing his best to pin down A. J. Smith. The Confederates there were making great progress, and Taylor believed that his trap was working.[58] But Bee's retreat left the ferry landing open. Emory crossed and ordered the cavalry division to chase Bee's men. Emory's troops took a wrong road and missed the fleeing Confederates.[59] Nonetheless, the road to Alexandria lay open for the Union column. A. J. Smith's men were the last to cross the river at 2:00 P.M. the next day. Wharton had driven them to the ferry just as Polignac joined up with Taylor. The Confederate forces were now at the narrow end of the island, and the Union forces were gone. In the running battles of April 22 and 23, Union losses were 300 killed, wounded, and missing; Confederate losses were less than half that. Bee had suffered only fifty casualties.[60]

Taylor censured Bee and later fired him. Kirby Smith and Bee's peers defended him, but his premature action in retreating forces the tactical blame squarely on him for the battle's loss.[61] Ultimately, perhaps, the blame can be equally placed on Kirby Smith, who removed three divisions of infantry to chase Steele in Arkansas and thus left Taylor with inadequate resources to trap Banks. Taylor did not have enough men to keep the Union from creating a bridge-head at the ferry. Emory could have forced it by the next day, especially with Birge cooperating in a flanking maneuver.

The Union column marched on to Alexandria, the lead elements entering the town on the afternoon of April 25.[62] At the rear of the column, A. J. Smith's men scorched the earth around them and arrived the next day. As they marched in, hordes of runaway slaves entered with them, freed from the torched plantations along the river. Franklin had issued orders against looting, pillaging, and burning, but the charred ruins of the plantations and homesteads north of Alexandria told a different story.

NOTES

1. Silverstone, *Warships of the Civil War Navies*, 149; *O.R.N.* 26, xvi–xvii, 51, 59–60; *JCCW*, 275–76; Johnson and Buel, *Battles and Leaders*, 4:366; H. Allen Gosnell, *Guns on the Western Waters* (Baton Rouge, LA, 1949), 15; Francis T. Miller, ed., *The Photographic History of the Civil War*, 10 vols. (New York, 1911), 5:145.

2. Silverstone, *Warships of the Civil War Navies*, 153.

3. Ibid., 158–59.

4. Ibid., 168.

5. Ibid., 170.

6. Ibid., 183.

7. *O.R.N.* 26, 60.

8. *O.R. Atlas*, pl. 52; LaTourette Map.

9. Porter, *Naval History*, 502.

10. *O.R.* 34, 380.

11. Porter, *Incidents and Anecdotes*, 232.

12. *O.R.* 34, pt. 3, 172.

13. Porter, *Naval History*, 502.

14. *O.R.* 34, pt. 3, 98–99; *O.R.N.* 26, 51, 60, 789; *JCCW*, 203.

15. Newsome, *Experience in the War*, 126.

16. Robert L. Kerby, *Kirby Smith's Confederacy: The Trans-Mississippi South, 1863–1865* (Tuscaloosa, AL, 1972), 309; Abstract log of USS *Chillicothe*, March 7–June 8, 1864; *O.R.N.* 26, 777–78.

17. *O.R.N.* 26, 778, 781, 789; *O.R.* 34, 633.

18. Johnson, *Red River Campaign*, 211.

19. Taylor to Walker, April 9, 1864, Walker Papers; *O.R.* 34, 570–71; Anne J. Bailey, "Chasing Banks Out of Louisiana: Parsons' Texas Cavalry in the Red River Campaign," *Civil War Regiments* 2, no. 3 (1992): 219.

20. Porter, *Naval History*, 512.

21. Selfridge, *What Finer Tradition*, 102.

22. Porter, *Naval History*, 512–13.

23. *O.R.N.* 26, 49, 55; *O.R.* 34, 172–204, 571, 633.

24. *O.R.* 34, 382.

25. John Homans, "The Red River Expedition," in *Papers of the Military Historical Society of Massachusetts*, 13 vols. (Boston, 1895–1913), 8:85–86.

26. Hoffman, *Camp, Court, and Siege*, 97; Sprague, *13th Connecticut*, 190; Edwin B. Lufkin, *History of the Thirteenth Maine Regiment* (Bridgton, ME, 1989), 87 (hereafter cited as *13th Maine*); George W. Powers, *The Story of the Thirty-Eighth Regiment of Massachusetts Volunteers* (Cambridge, MA, 1866), 133 (hereafter cited as *38th Massachusetts*).

27. *O.R.* 34, 186.

28. *O.R.* 34, pt. 3, 128, 592.

29. *O.R.* 34, 185, 187–88.

30. *O.R.* 34, pt. 3, 24; *O.R.* 32, pt. 3, 242.

31. *O.R.* 34, pt. 3, 175, 265–66.

32. Irwin, *19th Corps*, 327; Scott, *32d Iowa*, 230.

33. *O.R.* 34, pt. 3, 211, 294, 259.

34. *JCCW*, 17.

35. Porter, *Incidents and Anecdotes*, 235–36.

36. Ibid.

37. Ibid.; Porter, *Naval History*, 517.

38. *O.R.* 34, 190.

39. Ibid., 505; *O.R.N.* 26, 62.

40. *O.R.N.* 26, 62.

41. Ibid., 72–77.

42. Ibid., 26, 76.

43. Porter, *Naval History*, 523–23.

44. Ibid., 524.

45. *O.R.* 34, 310, 428; pt. 3, 222, 244; Irwin, *19th Corps*, 328; Sprague, *13th Connecticut*, 192.

46. Powers, *38th Massachusetts*, 136–37; Sprague, *13th Connecticut*, 192; Lubbock, *Six Decades in Texas*, 539.

47. *O.R.* 34, 310, 428; pt. 3, 222, 244; Irwin, *19th Corps*, 328; Sprague, *13th Connecticut*, 192.

48. *O.R.* 34, 190.

49. Sprague, *13th Connecticut*, 193; D. H. Hanaburgh, *History of the One Hundred and Twenty-eighth Regiment, New York Volunteers* (Pokeepsie [*sic*], NY, 1894), 103 (hereafter cited as *128th New York*); Williams, *56th Ohio*, 87–88; Lufkin, *13th Maine*, 87–88.

50. Lubbock, *Six Decades in Texas*, 540; Pellet, *114th New York*, 229; *O.R.* 34, 581.

51. Taylor, *Destruction and Reconstruction*, 193–94.

52. *O.R.* 34, 262, 394–95, 460; Ewer, *3d Massachusetts*, 164.

53. *O.R.* 34, 580; Taylor, *Destruction and Reconstruction*, 180.

54. *JCCW*, 15, 34–35.

55. Sprague, *13th Connecticut*, 195; J. T. Woods, *Services of the Ninety-Sixth Ohio Volunteers* (Toledo, OH, 1874), 74 (hereafter cited as *96th Ohio*).

56. Sprague, *13th Connecticut*, 195–96.

57. *O.R.* 34, 434; Sprague, *13th Connecticut*, 198–200.

58. Lubbock, *Six Decades in Texas*, 539.

59. Clark, *116th New York*, 170; Ewer, *3d Massachusetts*, 166.

60. *O.R.* 34, 190, 432–35, 580, 611.

61. Ibid., 580, 611–15; Taylor, *Destruction and Reconstruction*, 152.

62. Sprague, *13th Connecticut*, 201.

Chapter Ten

Colonel Bailey's Dam

Banks arrived in Alexandria only vaguely realizing the political firestorm in which he was involved. The campaign had begun five weeks earlier. In that short time, Grant had become general-in-chief, Halleck was chief of staff, and Sherman was making final preparations for his thrust into Georgia and the Carolinas. Banks's carefully worded messages to his superiors and to Lincoln and others, concerning tactical situations, had been mixed with exuberant exaggerations and expectations. He was not privy to conversations and letters exchanged among the people with whom he was communicating. Nor was he aware of newspaper reports and letters from within his own command condemning his actions.[1]

Grant's orders to Banks of March 31 had been plainly stated. First, if Banks captured Shreveport, he was to hand over the city to Steele and let the navy handle the defense of the river. Second, with the sole exception of the Rio Grande River, Banks was to withdraw from every point he occupied on the Texas coast. Third, he was to reduce garrison posts and troop concentrations in order to compose a force of 25,000 troops to take Mobile. Banks received these orders on April 18, while the army was at Grand Ecore.[2] At about the same time, Banks's message of April 2 was telling Grant of his intention to chase E. Kirby Smith into Texas.[3]

That letter infuriated Grant. Such a move would mean that his timetable in the East would be delayed. He had planned for Mobile to be taken or at least attacked by May 1. Mobile was critical to the upcoming campaigns because it would tie down Confederate forces under Lieutenant General Leonidas Polk in Mississippi and Alabama and would keep them away from Sherman's path through Georgia. A Union failure to take Mobile would create another problem for Sherman. Once deep in Georgia, Sherman's supply lines would be rail-dependent and therefore in danger of being severed.

On April 17, Grant sent Major General David Hunter to Banks with a copy of his March 31 orders. Hunter was to make it very plain to Banks that Mobile was more important than Shreveport. If he found that Banks had taken Shreveport and gone on to East Texas, he was to order Banks to retrace his steps and prepare for the attack on Mobile.[4] Hunter arrived in Alexandria on April 27.

On April 18, other correspondence was generated between Secretary of War Stanton and the naval base at Cairo, Illinois, Porter's headquarters. Stanton was told of navy dispatches from Porter explaining that Banks had been defeated at Mansfield, had retreated to Pleasant Hill, and had won a battle there.[5] At that point no mention was made of the retreat to Grand Ecore. Stanton also received the first newspaper reports of the battles and immediately sent them, with the naval dispatches, to Grant. Shortly after doing so, Stanton received news from Cairo that Sherman's aide, Brigadier General John M. Corse, had arrived there with word from A. J. Smith that Banks had lost 4,000 men, sixteen guns, and 200 wagons and had retreated to Grand Ecore with his force in very poor condition.[6] He forwarded these reports to Grant as well. A furious Grant telegraphed Halleck that he wanted Banks removed from command and replaced by Major General J. J. Reynolds, then in command of New Orleans. Halleck took Grant's telegram to the president, who told the chief of staff to delay action on Banks's removal. Lincoln needed New England in the upcoming November elections, so firing Banks was politically out of the question.

On April 25, Grant issued an order countermanding his demand that A. J. Smith and his men be sent back to Sherman. He did so on the basis of reports from Porter to Secretary of the Navy Gideon Welles, purely to protect the fleet.[7] On the same day, Grant received an anonymous letter, apparently from an officer in the Thirteenth Corps, railing against Banks's deplorable mismanagement.[8] This was too much; on April 27, Halleck ordered Banks to turn over command to the next ranking officer, return to New Orleans, and carry out previous instructions for the attack on Mobile. The order was not delivered, however; it was apparently aboard the vessel that was sunk on the way.[9] Grant thereupon abandoned the attack on Mobile, realizing that troops from west of the Mississippi could not be feasibly moved in time to coordinate attacks. He next suggested that the Gulf region be reorganized and that Halleck take over command of the Army of the Gulf. Halleck declined, but Grant and Halleck both informed Banks that no troops were to be withdrawn from the region at that time.[10]

Lincoln's silence on Banks's removal certainly added to the delay in reallocating forces for the spring campaigns. Nevertheless, although no formal written communication exists, Lincoln must have agreed to the wishes of Halleck and Grant: on May 7, Major General Edward R. S. Canby was given command of the newly reorganized Military Division of West Mississippi, comprising the Departments of the Gulf and Arkansas.[11] A delicate balance was struck in this promotion. Canby was given broad discretionary powers in his command. Banks was to remain in command of the Department of the Gulf but as a subordinate officer to Canby. Banks's position would still carry the trappings of power, but that was only an illusion. Banks, of course, knew nothing of this; he was in Alexandria with his army, and most of the fleet was trapped above the Falls with Taylor and his Confederates at their heels.

Taylor was in a peculiar position. With only 6,000 men, he had surrounded an army of 31,000 men, eighty cannon, and a huge fleet of warships. Banks had pulled everyone he could into Alexandria and had begun fortifying the town, leaving the interior of Louisiana devoid of Union forces. Taylor had cavalry patrols operating at Fort DeRussy and on Bayou Teche. He positioned artillery batteries at various points on the river below Alexandria and waited for the divisions that had been diverted to Arkansas to return, but they never arrived.

J. A. A. West's battery was sent to David's Ferry, located on the Red River about thirty miles below Alexandria, where the artillerymen almost immediately engaged and burned the transport *Emma* on May 1.[12] On May 4 they attacked and captured the *City Belle* on its way to Alexandria with reinforcements (and Grant's orders). Of the 700 men of the 120th Ohio Infantry who were on board, about half were captured and the remainder killed or wounded.[13]

That same day, traveling downstream, the *John Warner* left Alexandria, joined by the tinclads *Covington* and *Signal*. The *John Warner* carried the men of the Fifty-sixth Ohio Infantry, who were leaving on veterans' furloughs.[14] The vessels received small-arms fire throughout the day. At night the small convoy tied up on the riverbank about twenty miles south of Alexandria. Confederates fired at the men as they ate their evening meal. Early the next morning they got under way, and at 4:45 A.M., as they reached Dunn's Bayou, the *Warner* was attacked by artillery and musket fire. The *Covington* and *Signal* fired back on the attackers, but the Confederate artillery disabled the *Warner*'s rudders, and the transport drifted to the bank. There, continued fire from artillery and Confederate cavalry pounded it into a floating pile of debris, and the Fifty-sixth Ohio, still aboard, was torn to shreds.[15] The *Covington* tried to torch the boat rather than allow it to be captured after the captain of the *Warner* raised the white flag, but the colonel of the Fifty-sixth Ohio pleaded with the party from the *Covington* not to burn it because 125 of his men lay dead or dying on the decks.

The *Covington*, which was destroyed in action below Alexandria during the campaign. Naval Historical Center photo from a copy at the Mansfield State Historic Site, Mansfield, Louisiana.

As the artillery from Dunn's Bayou poured more fire on the warships, the *Covington* and *Signal* tried to retire upstream, but the *Signal* lost its steering assembly and port engine. The *Covington* threw a towline and began pulling the other warship against the current. An artillery shell then hit one of the *Signal*'s steam pipes, and the crew believed the boilers were going to explode. The *Covington* cut it loose and tried to escape, but its rudder had been hit as well. The captain tied it to the opposite bank, and his crew returned fire for a short time, until they ran out of ammunition. The captain then ordered the guns spiked and set fire to the tinclad. The *Signal* was forced to surrender under the combined battery fire after the *Covington* began to burn. The Confederates reported that they drove off another gunboat that tried to offer assistance. The navy suffered more in losses to vessels and men that day than they had on April 22 below Grand Ecore.[16]

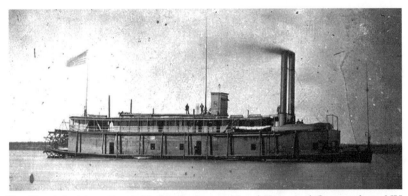

The *Signal*, lost in action with the *Covington*. Naval Historical Center photo NH 49978

They were not alone in their adversity. Inside the defensive perimeter at Alexandria, Porter was dealing with other problems, for the fleet was in desperate straits, trapped above the Falls. The water level had fallen until the sand and rocks of the Falls were showing as only damp indications of their usual treachery to mariners. The *Louisville* and its sisters needed seven feet to float, but the river level at the chute or navigable channel was only three feet four inches deep.[17] The transports and gunboats that had been left behind when the remainder of the fleet ascended the river had been ordered below the falls as the river level dropped, and the transports that had accompanied Porter upstream were ordered across as well. But potential disaster lay in the fact that the majority of the most powerful vessels were trapped above the rocks: the *Lexington, Osage, Neosho, Mound City, Louisville, Pittsburg, Carondelet, Chillicothe, Ozark,* and *Fort Hindman*.[18] If the navy retreated, these vessels would have to be destroyed. It was unthinkable to lose these very expensive and powerful boats, and their loss would badly damage or even destroy Porter's career. It was Porter's report to Gideon Welles that resulted in Grant's decision to keep A. J. Smith's men with Porter to protect the fleet.

The number of possible actions was limited if the fleet were to be saved. A huge number of men would be tied down at Alexandria waiting for the autumn rains to raise the river level, and that appealed to no one, particularly with Richard Taylor and his army nearby. The only other possibility was to force the water level to rise at Alexandria. This option was advanced by Lieutenant Colonel Joseph Bailey of Wisconsin, one of Franklin's engineers. Bailey had worked in the logging industry in Wisconsin and was familiar with the practice of building temporary dams in dry weather to increase water levels sufficiently to float logs downstream to sawmills. He had used the technique at Port Hudson to salvage two steamers the previous year. Having watched the water levels drop for three weeks, Bailey then suggested to Franklin that dams might be needed to float the fleet.[19] Franklin was favorably impressed but became distracted by command issues, and nothing was done. After the *Eastport* was destroyed, Franklin sent Bailey with a letter of introduction to Porter, but the admiral gave little credence to an idea from an army officer to save his fleet.

The ironclad *Carondelet*. Naval Historical Center photo NH 63376

Franklin, too, was an engineer, however, and appreciated Bailey's approach, so he once again attempted to convince Porter, now at Alexandria. By this time Porter's options were even more limited, and the water level was lowering with each passing hour. On April 29, Bailey attended a meeting with Banks and Hunter, who had been in Alexandria for several days. Banks was interested because Hunter's message from Grant made it imperative that the army withdraw from central Louisiana as quickly as possible, but he could not afford to desert Porter with Hunter there watching him. Sherman's belief that Banks would leave the fleet stranded should the army be forced to leave might have become a reality had Hunter not been sent with the message from Grant. Hunter, though skeptical, agreed to Bailey's idea because Franklin promoted it.

Crew of the *Carondelet*. Miller, *The Photographic History of the Civil War*, 6:210

Unfortunately, the same day construction began, Franklin sought a leave of absence because of his wound and left Alexandria for convalescence.[20] His departure helped make Bailey's task of dam building more difficult than he expected. First, he had trouble securing work gangs; some regimental commanders thought the project a total waste of time.[21] Second, the site he chose for the main dam was wider than the stream above and below, 758 feet wide. The water level varied from four to six feet and as the dam was formed, the level rose and the current increased to ten miles per hour.[22] Third, building materials for the dam were not uniform. To get enough he disassembled buildings in Alexandria and across the river in Pineville (ironically including portions of Sherman's beloved Louisiana Seminary for Learning and Military Institute).[23] Bricks, stones, wall segments, even pieces of furniture were used. Soldiers from Maine, most of whom had been lumbermen, felled trees and chopped them to appropriate lengths. From the other side of the river, bricks and stones were gathered into barges to make cribs to meet the tree dam in the center. Construction of the dam became quite a spectacle, attracting the interest of the bored troops. It was built primarily by the Maine soldiers and members of the Corps d'Afrique.[24]

Union Quartermaster Corps transports at Alexandria. Library of Congress, Prints and Photographs Division, LC-B816-3120

Construction of Bailey's Dam at Alexandria. Miller, *The Photographic History of the Civil War*, 6:231

After a week of work, when the tree dam extended 300 feet from the western bank, four coal barges loaded with brick and stone were latched together and sunk to extend it farther. From the other side, the crib dam met the barges on May 8. The lightest-draft vessels, the *Osage, Neosho,* and *Fort Hindman,* floated to the area behind the dam. The others did not follow, even though the water was deep enough for them to do so. The ironclads were still filled with cotton, and removing it would have lightened them sufficiently to pass through the dam on May 8, but they were not willing to lose the white gold. The water level was rising significantly and exerting pressure on the cribs and barges. Finally, at 5:00 A.M. on May 9 the river pushed the center barges aside. Porter ordered the *Lexington* through the gap before the water level fell, and it managed to pull through with a full head of steam. The *Osage, Neosho,* and *Fort Hindman* followed with only the *Neosho* suffering minor hull damage from the rocks.[25]

Since the other vessels had not been moved down to the pool behind the dam, once the water level lowered again, they were unable to get through. Bailey immediately began repairs on the dam and decided that other structures called wing dams must be built to channel the water behind the main dam. This delay affected Banks's plan for evacuation on May 9, for by then, McClernand had arrived from Texas, giving Banks more troops to deal with. On May 11 he sent word to Porter that the navy must be ready to move its boats as soon as the wing dams were built. Porter believed that Banks was ready to bolt and leave the fleet. A. J. Smith assured the admiral that he and his men would remain, regardless of Banks's actions.[26]

Porter told Banks that once the river rose another foot, the boats could move, and the army would be free to leave. Porter was very condescending to Banks and treated him as he would a small child, even going so far as to say, "Now, General, I really see nothing that should make us despond. You have a fine army, and I shall have a strong fleet of gunboats to drive away an inferior force in our front."[27]

Porter began removing guns and iron plating from the ironclads to lighten their weight, placing armor and armaments on wagons as was the cotton, to be transported below the falls. Porter chose not to carry eleven 32-pounder smoothbore cannons but had them spiked and dumped into the river.[28] By May 11 the wing dams were complete, but water was still not rising sufficiently to navigate the vessels over the dam, so a bracket dam was hastily built. Two days later the water was high enough for the ironclads to shoot through the gap. By May 15, Porter had pushed his fleet out of the Red River and into the wide waters of the Mississippi. He wrote to his mother, "I am clear of my troubles and my fleet is safe out in the broad Mississippi. I have had a hard and anxious time of it."[29]

NOTES

1. *O.R.* 34, 211, 220, 221, 235, 244; pt. 3, 252–53; *O.R.* 32, pt. 3, 407, 420, 422, 437.
2. *O.R.* 34, 11, 206.
3. Ibid., 110–11.
4. Ibid., pt. 3, 190–92.
5. Ibid., 211, 220–21, 235, 244.
6. Ibid.
7. *O.R.N.* 26, 50–54.
8. *O.R.* 34, 181–85; pt. 3, 278–79.
9. *O.R.* 34, 474.
10. *O.R.* 34, pt. 3, 357–58.
11. Ibid., 491.
12. Taylor, *Destruction and Reconstruction*, 186; *O.R.N.* 26, 102.
13. *O.R.* 34, 475; Taylor, *Destruction and Reconstruction*, 186.
14. Williams, *56th Ohio*, 73.
15. *O.R.N.* 26, 113, 117–18; Williams, *56th Ohio*, 74–78.
16. *O.R.N.* 26, 114, 119, 123, 134; Taylor, *Destruction and Reconstruction*, 185–86; *O.R.* 34, 442, 475, 621, 623.
17. *O.R.N.* 26, 94; *O.R.* 34, pt. 3, 316; Silverstone, *Warships of the Civil War Navies*, 151–53.
18. *O.R.N.* 26, 94; *O.R.* 34, pt. 3, 316.
19. Johnson and Buel, *Battles and Leaders*, 4:358.
20. Surgeon's certificate and attached correspondence, April 30, 1864, Franklin Papers.
21. E. Cort Williams, "Recollections of the Red River Expedition," *Papers Read before the Ohio Commandery of the Military Order of the Loyal Legion*, 2 vols. (Cincinnati, 1888), 2:84.
22. *O.R.* 34, 403; Johnson and Buel, *Battles and Leaders*, 4:358.
23. *O.R.N.* 26, 130–31.
24. Ibid., 132; *O.R.* 34, 405.
25. *O.R.* 34, 209, 254; *O.R.N.* 26, 131.
26. *O.R.N.* 26, 140; Scott, *32d Iowa*, 250–51.
27. *O.R.N.* 26, 140–41.
28. Ibid., 132, 149; *O.R.* 34, 255; *JCCW*, 84; Williams, "Recollections," 115.
29. David Dixon Porter to his mother, May 18, 1864, David D. Porter Papers, Division of Manuscripts, Library of Congress, Washington, DC; *O.R.N.* 26, 130–35.

CHAPTER ELEVEN

REQUIEM FOR A BLUNDER

AFTER THE DAM BROKE on May 9, Banks had time to prepare for his departure in more detail. Evidently worried that A. J. Smith's "gorillas" might cause problems and tip off Taylor about the army's departure, he ordered Brigadier General Richard Arnold, his new chief of cavalry, to place 500 horsemen under "reliable" officers inside the town during the departure to prevent a conflagration. Smith's men were not pleased; Brigadier General Oliver Gooding was overheard to say, "This is just like old Banks."[1]

The first troops left Alexandria at 7:00 A.M. on May 13. A little over an hour later, with most of the column still in town, buildings began to burn. Some Union soldiers with buckets and mops were smearing a mixture of turpentine and camphene (a precursor to napalm) on buildings, and one was reported as saying they were "preparing the place for Hell!"[2] The town turned into an inferno. One civilian reported that the cavalry officers who were assigned to protect them were actually directing the burning. Even stout pro-Unionists, who had been under the protection of the army until then, saw their homes torched. People whose sons had just enlisted in the Union army were burned out, and they asked for refuge on the boats, knowing that their neighbors would seek retribution. Several on Banks's staff and the provost guards tried to extinguish the flames by using explosives but the sources were too numerous, and a wind fanned the conflagration. In three hours the entire center of town had ceased to exist.[3] Banks had not ordered the torching, but he certainly failed to halt it. Moreover, his ultimate purpose for *not* burning the town had not been accomplished: the flames could be seen for miles, and Taylor certainly knew the Union forces were on the move.

Banks set his usual order of march with the cavalry screening forward and to the flanks. Next came the Nineteenth Corps, the combined supply train, the Thirteenth Corps, and then Smith's Sixteenth and Seventeenth Corps units. The men torched buildings all along the road, and nothing was left usable for the people of the

169

region.[4] Taylor was doing his best with the forces at his disposal. His cavalry was harassing the column from both front and rear, and his men blocked the roads beginning twelve miles south of Alexandria, trying to buy time for reinforcements that never came.

The next day Banks's engineering troops and scouts cleared the road and spanned Bayou Choctaw with a pontoon bridge. That evening the troops bivouacked beside the wrecks of the *John Warner*, *Signal*, and *Covington* and saw their mail strewn over the ground.[5] On May 15 the column slowly traversed the Bayou Choctaw Swamp and ascended to the tablelands of the Avoyelles prairie. The lead elements were attacked several times by Wharton's cavalry. The Nineteenth Corps finally brought enough troops to the open country to push back the Rebels—who retreated to set up again farther down the road.

The head of the column entered the town of Marksville at nightfall. On the morning of May 16, Banks found that Taylor had drawn all his available forces to meet him six miles ahead at the village of Mansura. Using the buildings of the village as his center, he placed eight cavalry regiments on his right with nineteen cannon. Polignac and his infantry were on the left with thirteen guns.[6] Also on the left were two regiments of cavalry. About half the field guns now aimed at the Federals had been taken from them at Mansfield. The Union troops formed line of battle, and an artillery duel ensued. Taylor later said that it was a beautiful site (and sight), with lines of battle three miles long on prairie land as "smooth as a billiard table."[7]

Both sides recorded the beauty of the scene as regiments marched into order. Cavalry skirted about seeking a place to charge, and a myriad of silken flags fluttered in the late spring breezes. The air was filled with glittering accoutrements of war, and many diaries reflected the grandeur of the spectacle.[8] The Nineteenth Corps moved forward, but Taylor's formerly Union guns kept them at bay. The sporadic artillery duel lasted nearly four hours, until A. J. Smith's men were brought up from the rear, and the entire line moved forward at the pace set by the westerners. Taylor, confronted with 18,000 men moving against his 6,000, retreated, and there were few casualties.[9]

Banks pushed on to Bayou de Glaise. From there the road led to Moreauville, Yellow Bayou, Simmesport, Old River, and the Atchafalaya. The army was close to safety, even though Confederate cavalry was still vigorously aggravating and slowing down the rear guard. The Confederates also tried to attack the wagon train but had little success. When the lead elements arrived at Simmesport —or its charred ruins—they believed the campaign was over. The entire army drew up in and around the former town.

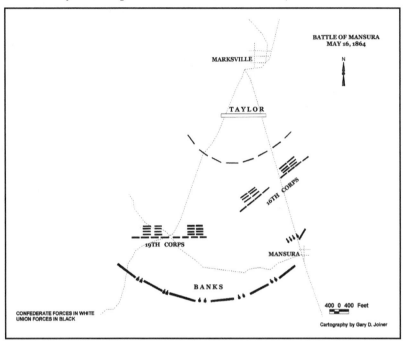

Map of the Battle of Mansura on May 16, 1864.

A. J. Smith, tired of Confederate cavalry harassing him while he guarded the tail of the column, had Mower return to Yellow Bayou with three brigades to push the Rebels back. Mower crossed the small bayou and, another two miles ahead, found Wharton's cavalry and Polignac's infantry drawn up in line of battle. Polignac attacked with artillery and then advanced his infantry toward Mower's men, who pushed them back and then withdrew; Mower was worried that he might be advancing into a trap. Polignac advanced again and was again repulsed. The fighting moved into a thicket of dry trees and brush, which caught fire. The Confederate artillery prevented Mower from giving chase. Polignac, who had about 5,000 men on the field to Mower's 4,500, lost 608 men killed, wounded, and missing; Mower lost 350.[10] Taylor simply did not have enough men to trap Banks, and the Battle at Yellow Bayou proved it. Mower's men could pridefully boast that they were the first in and last out in the campaign and had certainly seen more than their share of the fighting.

As the men of Banks's column came to the landing to leave the Red River country, they encountered high water, something they had missed during the entire campaign. Since pontoon bridges were not useful in the fast-flowing current, the army again faced the possibility of being trapped. It seemed as if the earth itself was on the side of the Confederates. But then Bailey, undoubtedly one of the most resourceful engineering officers in the Union army, made a floating bridge by anchoring transports side by side and lashing

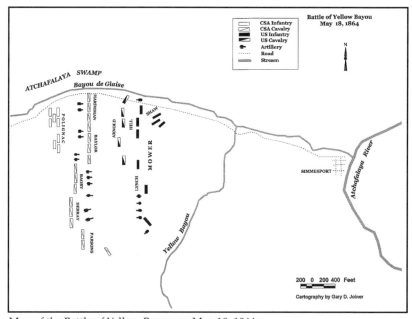

Map of the Battle of Yellow Bayou on May 18, 1864.

them together. Using them as a roadbed, he put planks across them, allowing the supply trains and artillery to cross the deep-channeled Atchafalaya while the infantry was ferried over in transports making bank-to-bank journeys. In this way the entire force was able to cross on May 19 and 20. Once the transports were unlashed and the anchors hoisted, there was no way for Taylor to pursue any farther.[11]

Edward Canby had arrived at Simmesport on May 18 and was waiting to inform Banks of the reorganization ordered by Washington. Banks returned to New Orleans and became primarily a political officer, writing reports and doing nothing that Canby did not approve.[12] In the fall he secured a leave of absence to go to Washington and tried to salvage his career. By that time, however, the presidential elections were over, and Lincoln had no reason to help him. He was picked to head the Reconstruction government in Louisiana for the president, and that put him in disfavor with the Radical Republicans in Congress.[13]

In December 1864, Congress convened the Joint Committee on the Conduct of the War to investigate the Red River expedition. Chaired by Ben Wade, it heard testimony from December 14, 1864, through April 21, 1865. Banks was the first in a long list of witnesses that read like a Who's Who of the Union side of the campaign. Porter, Franklin, Emory, Arnold, Lee, and other major commanders testified. Several of Porter's captains were called, including Selfridge and Breese. Members of Banks's staff, including Dwight and Drake, were questioned. Testimony was given by the river pilots Withenbury and John Martin and Banks's chief topographic engineer, John Clark. Halleck was the highest-ranking officer testifying.

The Radicals were out for blood, and Banks was a very easy target. Almost all who testified blamed him for muddled commands, paying too much attention to cotton stealing, and gross neglect in the conduct of the campaign. Since the committee members could delve into any matter of interest to them, they wanted to know who selected the order of march of the column on a daily basis; Franklin testified that it was Banks. They asked about the navy's role in cotton procurement and heard Porter piously wrap himself in the flag and the Naval Prize Law. Banks appears to have tried to answer questions with honesty and integrity; no one could make a case that he had personally gained from the campaign.

The Wade Committee published its findings and walked away in disgust; no direct action was taken against any of the officers. Lincoln sent Banks back to Louisiana to reorganize the government, but before he reached New Orleans, the president had been assassinated. Andrew Johnson was president, and harsh Reconstruction was the order of the day. In June, Banks resigned from the army and returned to Massachusetts.[14]

In Shreveport, when Kirby Smith returned from Arkansas believing that he had saved his department, Taylor could not stand the sight of the commanding general. On June 5 he wrote a letter to Kirby Smith that blamed Smith for his inability to capture the fleet and Banks's army; he asked for relief of command. Smith put Taylor under arrest five days later and sent a message to President Jefferson Davis regarding his actions. The same day, June 10, the Confederate Congress passed a joint resolution praising Taylor.[15] Troops loyal to Taylor almost came to blows with troops loyal to Smith. Taylor was promoted to lieutenant general and given the Department of Alabama, Mississippi, and East Louisiana. He surrendered that department at the end of the war. Shreveport, in 1865, was the last Confederate capital to fall. Kirby Smith, who had tried to reach Mexico to start the rebellion there, was captured at Galveston on May 25. Union troops entered Shreveport on June 6, just short of two months after Robert E. Lee surrendered at Appomattox.

What were the most significant effects of the Red River Campaign? Combined operations with the army and naval forces entered into a new phase; combined operations have since become a staple of American military strategy. Innovations in technology and in combat engineering were both elevated to new heights. Bailey's dam was a brilliant adaptation of logging industry techniques. Another innovation, its significance not recognized at the time, was the manner in which the *Osage* aimed the gun that killed Green: Selfridge used a periscope for the first time in battle to direct a weapon at an enemy. The device had literally been invented aboard the vessel a few days earlier.

The navy learned not to take inappropriately large vessels into tight quarters, regardless of their firepower potential. The army, by not giving clear authority to a single on-the-scene commanding officer or determining firm goals and objectives as a vital part of strategic planning, got a lesson in command and control. Battlefield intelligence and reconnaissance issues came to light during the congressional testimony, as did appropriate and inappropriate uses of cavalry, and questions of logistical support were closely scrutinized. Congressional oversight of military operations was affirmed, and the heat of public inquiry made military planners think twice before they committed to actions that had no clear operational or exit strategy. Economic gains were never again so blatantly emphasized over military objectives.

On the Southern side, Shreveport was spared the destruction that towns to the south, as well as in other states, suffered. It did not have to rebuild, as did Atlanta. Shreveport became the economic capital for the "Ark-La-Tex" region, a position the city retains. The former Confederate capital of Louisiana continued to be the second largest city in the state, behind Baton Rouge, until the last quarter of the twentieth century.

Harsh treatment of civilians during the campaign was exacerbated by harsh Reconstruction policies after surrender. Louisiana suffered under Reconstruction longer than any other Southern state, from the fall of New Orleans in 1862 to the final removal of Federal troops in 1877. The backlash against Union uniforms and later Federal occupation troops brought with it extreme conservatism, called Bourbonism, and radical underground groups such as the Ku Klux Klan. The barriers between the state's citizens truly began to fall only with federally forced integration in the 1950s and the Civil Rights and Voting Rights Acts of the 1960s.

The campaign that began with such promise ended with nothing to show for the great efforts made by both the U.S. Army and Navy. Wasted opportunities, too much bloodshed, and incredible blunders by Union and Confederate commanders alike all served to bury the campaign in the dustbin of history—witness the amount of literature other campaigns in 1864 have engendered versus the nearly total neglect of what happened during that long-forgotten spring in the interior of Louisiana.

NOTES

1. David C. Edmonds, *Official Report on the Conduct of Federal Troops in Western Louisiana, during the Invasions of 1863 and 1864, Compiled from Sworn Testimony under Direction of Governor Henry Watkins Allen* (Shreveport, LA, 1865), 72–73.

2. G. P. Whittington, "Rapides Parish, Louisiana—A History," *Louisiana Historical Quarterly* 18 (1935): 26–28.

3. JCCW, 335; Edmonds, *Report on the Conduct of Federal Troops*, 79; Whittington, "Rapides Parish, Louisiana," 26–28, 31–32, 37.

4. *O.R.* 34, pt. 3, 517, 558–59, 568; Bringhurst and Swigart, *46th Indiana*, 93.

5. Sprague, *13th Connecticut*, 207; Beecher, *114th New York*, 347–48.

6. *O.R.* 34, 593.

7. Ibid.

8. Scott, *32d Iowa*, 275; Sprague, *13th Connecticut*, 212; Ewer, *3d Massachusetts*, 181; Pellet, *114th New York*, 234; Bryner, *47th Illinois*, 114–15; Hanaburgh, *128th New York*, 114, Lufkin, *13th Maine*, 92; Clark, *116th New York*, 179–80. Shorey, *15th Maine*, 119; Powers, *38th Massachusetts*, 147–48; Beecher, *114th New York*, 349–51; *O.R.* 34, 425.

9. Scott, *32d Iowa*, 275.

10. *O.R.* 34, 304, 320, 329, 337, 347–48, 357, 364, 367, 370, 467, 594, 624, 631; Taylor, *Destruction and Reconstruction*, 191; Scott, *32d Iowa*, 259, 277.

11. *O.R.* 34, pt. 3, 644; S. C. Jones, *Reminiscences of the Twenty-second Iowa Volunteer Infantry* (Iowa City, 1907), 69.

12. Irwin, *19th Corps*, 347–48.

13. Harrington, *Fighting Politician*, 164; Lincoln, *Collected Works*, 8:121 n.

14. Harrington, *Fighting Politician*, 167–69.

15. *O.R.* 34, 597.

SELECTED BIBLIOGRAPHY

BIOGRAPHIES

Ambrose, Stephen E. *Halleck: Lincoln's Chief of Staff*. Baton Rouge: Louisiana State University Press, 1962.

Arceneaux, William. *Acadian General: Alfred Mouton and the Civil War*. Lafayette: Center for Louisiana Studies, University of Southwestern Louisiana, 1981.

Boggs, William R. *Military Reminiscences of Gen. Wm. R. Boggs, C.S.A.* Durham: Seeman Printery, 1913.

Casdorph, Paul D. *Prince John Magruder: His Life and Campaigns*. New York: John Wiley and Sons, 1996.

Dorsey, Sarah A. *Recollections of Henry Watkins Allen, Brigadier General Confederate States Army, Ex-Governor of Louisiana*. New Orleans: n.p., 1866.

Freeman, Douglas Southall. *R. E. Lee: A Biography*, 4 vols. New York: Charles Scribner's Sons, 1934–35.

Grant, Ulysses S. *Personal Memoirs of U. S. Grant*. New York: Da Capo, 1982.

Harrington, Fred Harvey. *Fighting Politician, Major General N. P. Banks*. Philadelphia: University of Pennsylvania Press, 1948.

Hearn, Chester G. *Admiral David Dixon Porter: The Civil War Years*. Annapolis, MD: Naval Institute Press, 1996.

Hollandsworth, James G., Jr. *Pretense of Glory: The Life of General Nathaniel P. Banks*. Baton Rouge: Louisiana State University Press, 1998.

Howe, M. A. DeWolfe, ed. *Home Letters of General Sherman*. New York: Charles Scribner's Sons, 1909.

Huffstodt, Jim. *Hard Dying Men: The Story of General W. H. L. Wallace, General T. E. G. Ransom, and Their "Old Eleventh": Illinois Infantry in the American Civil War (1861–1865)*. Bowie, MD: Heritage Books, 1991.

Jones, James P., and Edward F. Keuchel. *Civil War Maine: A Diary of the Red River Expedition, 1864*. Washington, DC: History and Museum Division, Headquarters, U.S. Marine Corps, 1975.

McClellan, George B. *McClellan's Own Story*. New York: C. L. Webster and Company, 1887.

Nicolay, John F., and John Hay. *Abraham Lincoln, a History*. New York: The Century Company, 1909.

Noll, Arthur Howard. *General Kirby-Smith*. Sewanee, TN: University of the South, 1907.

Parks, Joseph Howard. *General Edmund Kirby Smith, C.S.A.* Baton Rouge: Louisiana State University Press, 1954.

Parrish, T. Michael. *Richard Taylor: Soldier Prince of Dixie*. Chapel Hill: University of North Carolina Press, 1992.

Selfridge, Thomas O. *What Finer Tradition: The Memoirs of Thomas O. Selfridge Jr., Rear Admiral U.S.N.* Columbia: University of South Carolina Press, 1987.

Sherman, William T. *Memoirs of General W. T. Sherman Written by Himself*. 2 vols. New York: D. Appleton and Company, 1875.

Taylor, Richard. *Destruction and Reconstruction: Personal Experiences in the Civil War*. New York: Da Capo, 1995.

Thorndyke, Rachel. *Sherman and the Sherman Letters: Correspondence Between General Sherman and Senator Sherman From 1837 to 1891*. New York: Da Capo, 1969.

Vetter, Charles Edmund. *Sherman: Merchant of Terror, Advocate of Peace*. Gretna, LA: Pelican, 1992.

West, Richard, Jr. *The Second Admiral: A Life of David Dixon Porter*. New York: Coward McCann, 1937.

GENERAL

Andrews, J. Cutler. *The North Reports the Civil War*. Pittsburgh: University of Pittsburgh Press, 1983.

Badeau, Adam. *Military History of Ulysses S. Grant, from April 1861 to April 1865*, 3 vols. New York: D. Appleton and Company, 1881.

Basler, Roy P., ed. *The Collected Works of Abraham Lincoln*, 9 vols. New York: Rutgers University Press, 1953.

Bradford, James C., ed. *Captains of the Old Steam Navy: Makers of the American Naval Tradition 1840–1880*. Annapolis, MD: Naval Institute Press, 1986.

Canney, Donald L. *Lincoln's Navy: The Ships, Men, and Organizations, 1861–1865*. Annapolis, MD: Naval Institute Press, 1998.

Dana, Charles A. *Recollections of the Civil War With Leaders at Washington and in the Field in the Sixties*. New York: D. Appleton and Company, 1898.

Dimitry, John. "Louisiana," in vol. 10, *Confederate Military History*, 13 vols. Atlanta: Confederate Publishing Company, 1899.

Edwards, John N. *Shelby and His Men: or, The War in the West*. Cincinnati: Miami Printing and Publishing Company, 1867.

Gibbons, Tony. *Warships and Naval Battles of the Civil War*. New York: W. H. Smith., 1989.

Gibson, Charles Dana, and E. Kay Gibson. *The Army's Navy Series*, vol. 2, *Assault and Logistics: Union Army Coastal and River Operations, 1861–1866*. Camden, Maine: Ensign Press, 1995.

Glathaar, Joseph T. *Partners in Command—The Relationship Between Leaders in the Civil War*. New York: Free Press, 1994.

Gosnell, H. Allen. *Guns on the Western Waters*. Baton Rouge: Louisiana State University Press, 1949.

Greene, Jack. *Ironclads at War: The Origin and Development of the Armored Warship, 1854–1891*. Conshohocken, PA: Combined Books, 1998.

Hagerman, Edward. *The American Civil War and the Origins of Modern Warfare: Ideas, Organizations, and Field Command*. Bloomington: Indiana University Press, 1992.

Harrell, John M. "Arkansas," in vol. 10, *Confederate Military History*, 13 vols. Atlanta: Confederate Publishing Company, 1899.

Hoehling, A. A. *Damn the Torpedoes! Naval Incidents of the Civil War*. Winston-Salem, NC: John F. Blair, 1989.

Johnson, Robert U., and Clarence C. Buel, ed. *Battles and Leaders of the Civil War*. 4 vols. Secaucus, NJ: Castle, 1986.

Jones, Virgil Carrington. *The Civil War at Sea, July 1863–November 1865: The Final Effort*. New York: Holt, Rinehart & Winston, 1960.

Lord, Walter. *The Fremantle Diary: Being the Journal of Lieutenant Colonel James Arthur Lyon Fremantle, Coldstream Guards, on His Three Months in the Southern States*. Boston: Little, Brown and Company, 1954.

Luraghi, Raimondo. *A History of the Confederate Navy*. Annapolis, MD: Naval Institute Press, 1996.

McElfresh, Earl B. *Maps and Mapmakers of the Civil War*. New York: Harry N. Abrams, 1999.

Mahan, D. H. *A Treatise on Field Fortifications containing Instructions on the Methods of Laying Out, Constructing, Defending, and Attacking Intrenchments, With the General Outline Also of the Arrangement, the Attack, and Defense of Permanent Fortifications*. New York: John Wiley, 1863.

Melia, Tamara Moser. *"Damn the Torpedoes": A Short History of U.S. Naval Mine Countermeasures, 1777–1991*. Washington, DC: Naval Historical Center, 1991.

Military Analysis of the Civil War: An Anthology by the Editors of Military Affairs. Millwood, NY: KTO Press, 1977.

Miller, Francis T., ed. *The Photographic History of the Civil War*, 10 vols. New York: Review of Reviews, 1911.

Moore, Frank, ed. *The Rebellion Record: A Diary of American Events, With Documents, Narratives, Illustrative Incidents, Poetry, Etc.*, 12 vols. New York: D. Vann Nostrand, 1862–1871.

Musicant, Ivan. *Divided Waters: The Naval History of the Civil War*. New York: HarperCollins, 1995.

Olmstead, Frederick L. *A Journey Through Texas*. New York: Dix, Edwards, and Company, 1857.

Page, Dave. *Ships vs. Shore: Civil War Engagements Along Southern Shores and Rivers*. Nashville, TN: Rutledge Hill Press, 1994.

Paris, Comte de [Louis Albert d'Orléans]. *History of the Civil War in America*, 4 vols. Philadelphia: Porter and Coates, 1875–1888.

Perry, Milton F. *Infernal Machines: The Story of Confederate Submarine and Mine Warfare*. Baton Rouge: Louisiana State University Press, 1965.

Petrie, Donald A. *The Prize Game: Lawful Looting on the High Seas in the Days of Fighting Sail*. Annapolis, MD: Naval Institute Press, 1999.

Porter, David Dixon. *Incidents and Anecdotes of the Civil War*. New York: Appleton, 1885.

_____. *Naval History of the Civil War*. 1886. Reprint, Secaucus, NJ: Castle Books, 1984.

Ragan, Mark K. *Union and Confederate Submarine Warfare in the Civil War*. Mason City, IA. Savas, 1999.

Reed, Rowena. *Combined Operations in the Civil War*. Lincoln: University of Nebraska Press, 1978.

Schafer, Louis S. *Confederate Underwater Warfare: An Illustrated History*. Jefferson, NC: McFarland and Company, 1996.

Sherman, William T. *Report of Major General William T. Sherman*. Millwood, NY: Kraus Reprint Company, 1977.

Sifakis, Stewart. *Who Was Who in the Confederacy*. New York: Facts on File, 1988.

_____. *Who Was Who in the Union*. New York: Facts on File, 1988.

Silverstone, Paul H. *Warships of the Civil War Navies*. Annapolis, MD: Naval Institute Press, 1989.

Warner, Ezra J. *Generals in Blue: Lives of the Union Commanders*. Baton Rouge: Louisiana State University Press, 1993.

_____. *Generals in Gray: Lives of the Confederate Commanders*. Baton Rouge: Louisiana State University Press, 1993.

RED RIVER CAMPAIGN

Bailey, Anne J. *Between the Enemy and Texas: Parson's Texas Cavalry in the Civil War*. Fort Worth: Texas Christian University Press, 1989.

_____. *Texans in the Confederate Cavalry*. Fort Worth: Ryan Place Publications, 1995.

Bankston, Mary L. B. *Camp-Fire Stories of the Mississippi Valley Campaign*. New Orleans: L. Graham Company, 1914.

Barr, Alwyn. *Polignac's Texas Brigade*. College Station: Texas A&M University Press, 1998.

Bartlett, Napier. "The Trans-Mississippi," in *Military Record of Louisiana: Including Biographical and Historical Papers Relating to the Military Organization of the State*. New Orleans: L. Graham and Company, 1875.

Bearss, Edwin C. *A Louisiana Confederate: The Diary of Felix Pierre PochÈ*. Baton Rouge: Louisiana State University Press, 1972.

_____. *A Southern Record: The Story of the 3rd Louisiana Infantry, C.S.A.* Dayton, OH: Morningside, 1988.

_____. *Steele's Retreat from Camden and the Battle of Jenkins' Ferry.* Little Rock, AR: Eagle Press of Little Rock, 1990.

Beecher, Harris H. *Record of the 114th New York N.Y.S.V. Where It Went, What It Saw, and What It Did.* Norwich, NY: J. F. Hubbard, Jr., 1866.

Belisle, John G. *History of Sabine Parish Louisiana.* Many, LA: The Sabine Banner Press, 1912.

Bergeron, Arthur W., Jr. *A Guide to Confederate Military Units, 1861– 1865.* Baton Rouge: Louisiana State University Press, 1989.

Bering, John A., and Thomas Montgomery. *History of the Forty-Eighth Ohio Veteran Volunteer Infantry.* Hillsboro, OH: Highland News Office, 1880.

Blessington, J. P. *The Campaigns of Walker's Texas Division.* Austin, TX: State House Press, 1994.

Boggs, William R. *Reminescences of Gen. Wm. R. Boggs, C.S.A.* Durham, NC: The Seeman Printery, 1913.

Bridges, Joyce Shannon, ed. *Biographical and Historical Memoirs of Northwest Louisiana.* Nashville, TN: Southern Printing Company, 1890.

Bringhurst, T. H., and Frank Swigert. *History of the Forty-Sixth Regiment Indiana Volunteer Infantry.* Logansport, IN: Wilson Humphreys and Company Press, 1888.

Brock, Eric, and Gary D. Joiner. *Red River Steamboats.* Charleston, SC: Arcadia, 1999.

Brooksher, William Riley. *War along the Bayous: The 1864 Red River Campaign in Louisiana.* Washington, DC: Brassey's, 1998.

Burgess, Lauren Cook. *An Uncommon Soldier: The Civil War Letters of Sarah Rosetta Wakeman, alias Pvt. Lyons Wakeman, 153rd Regiment, New York State Volunteers, 1862–1864.* Pasadena, MD: Minerva Center, 1994.

Cardin, Clifton D. *Bossier Parish History: The First 150 Years, 1843– 1993.* Shreveport, LA: Aero Press, 1993.

Christ, Mark K., ed. *Rugged and Sublime: The Civil War in Arkansas.* Fayetteville: University of Arkansas Press, 1994.

Clark, Orton S. *The One Hundred and Sixteenth Regiment of New York Volunteers.* Buffalo, NY: Printing House of Matthews and Warren, 1868.

_____. *DeSoto Parish History: Sesquicentennial Edition, 1843-1993.* Mansfield, LA: DeSoto Parish Historical Society, 1995.

Coombe, Jack D. *Thunder Along the Mississippi: The River Battles That Split the Confederacy.* New York: Bantam Books, 1996.

Crandall, Warren D. *History of the Ram Fleet and the Mississippi Marine Brigade in the War for the Union on the Mississippi and Its Tributaries: The Story of the Ellets and Their Men.* St. Louis: Society of Survivors, 1907.

Edmonds, David C. *The Conduct of Federal Troops in Louisiana During the Invasions of 1863 and 1864: Official Report Compiled From*

Sworn Testimony Under the Direction of Governor Henry W. Allen, Shreveport, April, 1865. Lafayette: Acadiana Press, 1988.

Estaville, Lawrence E., Jr. *Confederate Neckties: Louisiana Railroads in the Civil War.* Ruston, LA: McGinty Publications, 1989.

Ewer, James K. *The Third Massachusetts Cavalry in the War for the Union.* Maplewood, MA: Historical Committee of the Regimental Association, 1903.

Flinn, Frank M. *Campaigning with Banks in Louisiana in '63 and '64 and with Sheridan in the Shenandoah Valley in '64 and '65.* Lynn, MA: Thos. P. Nichols, 1887.

Fordyce, Dr. Benjamin A. *Echoes: From the Letters of a Civil War Surgeon.* N.p., 1996.

Gosnell, H. Allen. *Guns of the Western Waters: The Story of River Gunboats in the Civil War.* Baton Rouge: Louisiana State University Press, 1949.

Grisamore, Silas T. *The Civil War Reminiscences of Major Silas T. Grisamore C.S.A.,* ed. Arthur W. Bergeron. Baton Rouge: Louisiana State University Press, 1993.

Gunby, A. A. *Life and Services of David French Boyd.* Baton Rouge: Louisiana State University Press, 1904.

Hanaburgh, D. H. *History of the One Hundred and Twenty-eighth Regiment, New York Volunteers.* Pokeepsie [sic], NY: Press of the Enterprise Publishing Company, 1894.

Heartsill, W. W. *Fourteen Hundred and 91 Days in the Confederate Army: A Journal Kept by W. W. Heartsill for Four Years, One Month, and One Day: or Camplife, Day-by-Day, of the W. P. Lane Rangers from April 19th, 1861, to May 20th 1865,* ed. Bell Irvin Wiley. Wilmington, NC: Broadfoot Publishing, 1992.

Hicken, Victor. *Illinois in the Civil War.* Urbana: University of Illinois Press, 1991.

Hoffman, Wickham. *Camp, Court and Siege: A Narrative of Personal Adventure and Observation during Two Wars 1861–1865, 1870–1871.* New York: Harper and Bros., 1877.

Irwin, Richard B. *History of the Nineteenth Army Corps.* Baton Rouge: Elliott's Book Shop Press, 1985.

Jeter, Katherine Brash. *A Man and His Boat: The Civil War Career and Correspondence of Lt. Jonathan H. Carter, CSN.* Lafayette: University of Southwestern Louisiana, 1996.

Johansson, M. Jane. *A History of the 28th Texas Cavalry, 1862–1865.* Fayetteville: University of Arkansas Press, 1998.

Johnson, Ludwell H. *Red River Campaign: Politics and Cotton in the Civil War.* Kent, OH: Kent State University Press, 1993.

Jones, James P., and Edward F. Keuchel, eds. *Civil War Marine: A Diary of the Red River Expedition, 1864.* Washington, DC: History and Museums Division Headquarters, U.S. Marine Corps, 1975.

Jones, S. C. *Reminiscences of the 22nd Iowa Infantry Giving Its Organization, Marches, Skirmishes, Battles, and Sieges, as Taken from the Diary of Lieutenant S. C. Jones of Company A.* Iowa City, IA: n.p., 1907; reprint, Camp Pope Bookshop, 1993.

Kerby, Robert L. *Kirby Smith's Confederacy: The Trans-Mississippi South, 1863–1865.* Tuscaloosa: University of Alabama Press, 1972.

Lubbock, Francis R. *Six Decades in Texas.* Austin,TX: Ben C. Jones and Company, 1900.

Lufkin, Edwin B. *History of the Thirteenth Maine Regiment.* Bridgton, ME: H. A. Shorey and Son, 1898.

Marshall, T. B. *History of the Eighty-Third Ohio Volunteer Infantry, The Greyhound Regiment.* Cincinnati: Eighty-Third Ohio Infantry Association, 1913.

Meyer, Steve. *Iowa Valor: A Compilation of Civil War Combat Experiences from Soldiers of the State Distinguished as Most Patriotic of the Patriotic.* Garrison, IA: Meyer Publishing Co., 1994.

Mills, Gary B. *The Forgotten People: Cane River's Creoles of Color.* Baton Rouge: Louisiana State University Press, 1977.

Newsome, Edmund. *Experience in the War of the Rebellion.* Carbondale, IL: published by the author, 1880.

Nichols, James L. *The Confederate Quartermaster in the Trans-Mississippi.* Austin: University of Texas Press, 1964.

Oates, Stephen B. *Confederate Cavalry West of the River.* Austin: University of Texas Press, 1961.

Pellet, Elias P. *History of the 114th Regiment, New York State Volunteers.* Norwich, NY: Telegraph and Chronicle Press Print, 1866.

Plummer, Alonzo. *Confederate Victory at Mansfield Including Federal Advance and Retreat to Natchitoches.* Shreveport, LA: Kate Beard Chapter No. 397, United Daughters of the Confederacy, 1964.

Powers, George W. *The Story of the Thirty Eighth Regiment of Massachusetts Volunteers.* Cambridge, MA: Dakin and Metcalf, 1866.

Robinson, Michael. *Gunboats, Low Water, and Yankee Inginuity: A History of Bailey's Dam.* Baton Rouge, LA: F.P.H.C., 1991.

Scott, John. *Story of the Thirty-Second Iowa Infantry Volunteers.* Nevada, IA, 1896.

Scott, R. B. *The History of the 67th Regiment Indiana Infantry.* Beford, IN: Herald Book and Job Print, 1892.

Shorey, Henry M. *The Story of the Maine Fifteenth Volunteer Infantry Regiment.* Bridgton, ME: Press of the Bridgton News, 1890.

Slagle, Jay. *Ironclad Captain: Seth Ledyard Phelps and the U.S. Navy, 1841–1864.* Annapolis, MD: Naval Institute Press, 1996.

Smith, Walter, G., ed. *Life and Letters of T. Kilby Smith.* New York: G. P. Putnam's Sons, 1898.

Soman, Jean Powers, and Frank L. Byrne, eds. *A Jewish Colonel in the Civil War: Marcus M. Spiegel of the Ohio Volunteers.* Lincoln: University of Nebraska Press, 1985.

Spencer, John. *Terrell's Texas Cavalry*. Burnet, TX: Eakin Press, 1982.

Sprague, H. B. *History of the 13th Regiment of Connecticut Volunteers*. Hartford, CT: Case, Lockwood, and Company, 1867.

Stanyan, John M. *A History of the Eighth Regiment of New Hampshire Volunteers*. Concord, NH: Ira C. Evans, Printer, 1892.

Stevenson, B. F. *Letters from the Army 1862–1864*. New York: Robert Clarke and Company, 1886.

Way, Frederick, Jr., ed. *Way's Packet Directory, 1848–1994*. Athens: Ohio University Press, 1994.

Weddle, Robert S. *Plow-Horse Cavalry: The Caney Creek Boys of the Thirty-Fourth Texas*. Austin, TX: Madrona Press, 1974.

Wells, Carol, ed. *Civil War, Reconstruction, and Redemption on Red River: The Memoirs of Dosia Williams Moore*. Ruston, LA: McGinty Publications, 1990.

Williams, E. Cort. "Recollections of the Red River Expedition," *Papers Read before the Ohio Commandery of the Military Order of the Loyal Legion*. Cincinnati: Robert Clark & Company, 1888.

Williams, Thomas J. *An Historical Sketch of the 56th Ohio Volunteer Infantry*. Columbus, OH: The Lawrence Press, 1899.

Winters, John D. *The Civil War in Louisiana*. Baton Rouge: Louisiana State University Press, 1963.

Woods, J. T. *Services of the Ninety-Sixth Ohio Volunteers*. Toledo, OH: Blade Printing and Papers Company, 1874.

Zeitlin, Richard H. *Old Abe the War Eagle: A True Story of the Civil War and Reconstruction*. Madison: State Historical Society of Wisconsin, 1986.

UNPUBLISHED DIARIES, MANUSCRIPTS,

AND PHOTOGRAPHS

Allen, N. S., Captain of Company A, Fourteenth Texas Infantry, Walker's Division, CSA. Diary, September 2–December 21, 1864. Archives, Louisiana State University, Shreveport.

Barron, Amos J. "A History of Pleasant Hill." Manuscript in Mansfield State Historic Site archives, Mansfield, Louisiana.

Boyd, David French. Letter to General Richard Taylor, CSA, April 14, 1864. Jackson Barracks Archives, New Orleans, Louisiana.

Carter, Jonathan H. "Carter Correspondence Book," manuscript. Division of Manuscripts, Library of Congress, Washington, DC.

David D. Porter Papers. Division of Manuscripts, Library of Congress, Washington, DC.

Dearman, Scott, Park Historian, comp. Order of Battle of the Confederate Army under Major General Richard Taylor at the Battle of Mansfield, April 8, 1864. Mansfield State Historical Site, Mansfield, Louisiana.

_____. Order of Battle of the Union Army under Major General Nathaniel Prentiss Banks at the Battle of Mansfield, April 8, 1864. Mansfield, Louisiana, State Historic Site.

Edwin M. Stanton Papers. Division of Manuscripts, Library of Congress, Washington, DC.

"Eli," sailor. Union Log Book, Alexandria to Shreveport, 1864. Collection of Jim Sandefur, Shreveport, Louisiana.

Fullilove, Tom, CSA. Diary, 1862–65. Collection of William Lane Stephenson, Shreveport, Louisiana.

King, William Henry, CSA. Diary: "Camp Life in the Civil War," 1862–65. Texas State Archives, Austin.

Knapp, Julius L., Company I, 116th New York Volunteer Infantry. Diary, January–December 1864. Collection of Jim Sandefur, Shreveport, Louisiana.

Lale, Max S. "New Light on Battle of Mansfield." Typescript. Archives, Louisiana State University, Shreveport.

Lord-Eltinge Collection. Photograph of the war fleet at Alexandria. Duke University, Durham, North Carolina.

McClung, R. L. "Three Years in the C.S. Army (P.A.C.S.)." Typescript, Mansfield State Historic Site, Mansfield, Louisiana.

Marston family diary in the collection of James Marston, Shreveport, Louisiana.

Mississippi Squadron Papers. Vols. 27–34, February–June 1864. Record Group 45, National Archives and Records Administration, Washington, DC.

Nathaniel P. Banks Papers. Microfilms at University of Texas, Austin. Original in the Essex Institute, Salem, Massachusetts.

Navy Yard Documents, Confederate Navy Subject File, Shreveport. Record Group 45, National Archives and Records Administration, Washington, DC.

Pearce, F. W., Second Maine Cavalry. Letter. Collection of Jim Sandefur.

Snyder, Perry Anderson. "Shreveport, Louisiana, during the Civil War and Reconstruction." Ph.D. diss., Florida State University, 1979.

Stewart, William H. Diary in the Southern Historical Collection, University of North Carolina, Chapel Hill, North Carolina.

Taylor, Richard, CSA. Letter to General John George Walker, April 9, 1864. John George Walker Papers, no. 910Z, Southern Historical Collection, University of North Carolina, Chapel Hill.

"Tom," Thirty-eighth Massachusetts Infantry. Letter, 1864. Collection of Jim Sandefur, Shreveport, Louisiana.

Wentworth, Thomas, Fifteenth Maine Infantry. Two letters, 1864. Collection of Jim Sandefur, Shreveport, Louisiana.

William B. Franklin Papers. Division of Manuscripts, Library of Congress, Washington, DC.

PERIODICALS

Bailey, Anne J. "Chasing Banks Out of Louisiana: Parson's Texas Cavalry in the Red River Campaign." *Civil War Regiments* 2, no. 3 (1994): 212–35.

Bee, Hamilton P. "Pleasant Hill—An Error Corrected." *Southern Historical Society Papers* 8 (1880): 184–86.

_____. "The Beginning of the End, A Greeting for the New Year." *Atlantic Monthly* 3 (1864): 112–22.

Benson, S. F. "The Battle of Pleasant Hill, Louisiana." *Annals of Iowa* 7, 500; *DeBow's Review* (Revised Series, 1866), 2:419.

Childers, Henry H. "Reminiscences of the Battle of Pleasant Hill." *Annals of Iowa* 7, 514–15.

Debray, X. B. "A Sketch of Debray's Twenty-Sixth Regiment of Texas Cavalry." *Southern Historical Society Papers* 13 (1885): 153–65.

Homans, John. "The Red River Expedition," in vol. 8, *The Mississippi Valley, Tennessee, Georgia, Alabama, 1861-1864*. Boston, MA, 1910. Papers of the Military Historical Society of Massachusetts, 13 vols., 1895–1913.

Joiner, Gary D., and Charles E. Vetter. " The Union Naval Expedition on the Red River, March 12–May 22, 1864. *Civil War Regiments* 4, no. 2 (1994): 26–67.

Read, Charles W. "Reminiscences of the C.S. Navy," *Southern Historical Society Papers* 1 (1876): 336–38.

Roper, Laura W. "Frederick Law Olmstead and the Western Texas Free-Soil Movement." *American Historical Review* 56 (1950–51): 58–64.

Van Dyke, Ben. "Ben Van Dyke's Escape from the Hospital at Pleasant Hill, Louisiana." *Annals of Iowa* (1906): 524.

Whittington, G. P. "Rapides Parish, Louisiana—A History." *Louisiana Historical Quarterly* 18 (1935): 26–28.

MAPS

"LaTourette's Map of Louisiana (undated), John Clark Collection, Cayuga County Museum, Auburn, New York.

"Lavender Soil Survey Map of 1906," Archives and Special Collections, Noel Memorial Library, Louisiana State University, Shreveport, Shreveport, Louisiana.

"Map of Mansfield Battlefield" (1864) by Major Richard Venable, CSA, Jerome Gilmer Papers, Southern Historical Collection, Wilson Library, University of North Carolina, Chapel Hill, North Carolina.

"Map of Pleasant Hill Battlefield" (1864) by Major Richard Venable, CSA, Jerome Gilmer Papers, Southern Historical Collection, Wilson Library, University of North Carolina, Chapel Hill, North Carolina.

"Pleasant Hill Battlefield" (No. 8) by Colonel John S. Clark (USA), John Clark Collection, Cayuga County Museum, Auburn, New York.

"Shreveport and Environs" (1864) by Major Richard Venable, CSA, Jerome Gilmer Papers, Southern Historical Collection, Wilson Library, University of North Carolina, Chapel Hill, North Carolina.

NEWSPAPERS

Bossier Banner (Benton, Louisiana) May 18–25, 1860.
Journalpage (Shreveport, Louisiana) November 25, 1995.
Mansfield Enterprise (Mansfield, Louisiana) May 17, 1977.
New York Times, October 30, 1862.
Philadelphia Press, April 10, 1864.

GOVERNMENT DOCUMENTS

Abstract Log, *USS Chillicothe*, March 7–June 8, 1864, Record Group 77, National Archives and Records Administration, Washington, DC.

Bounds, Steve, comp. "Casualty Lists of the Battle of Mansfield," Mansfield State Historic Site, Mansfield, Louisiana.

Caddo Parish (LA) Records, Conveyance Book N, folio 295.

Joiner, Gary D. "40 Archaeological Sites in the Red River Campaign," unpublished report for the Louisiana State Department of Culture, Recreation, and Tourism, Division of Archaeology, Baton Rouge, Louisiana, 1997.

Louisiana Legislature, Act 243 of the Louisiana Legislature, 1860.

Red River Campaign maps in Record Group 77, folios M72, M103-1 and M103-2, RG 77, National Archives and Records Administration, Washington, DC.

Shannon, George W. "Cultural Resources Survey of The Port of Shreveport-Bossier, Caddo and Bossier Parishes, Louisiana," unpublished report for the Caddo-Bossier Port Commission, Shreveport, Louisiana, 1996.

U.S. Congress. *Report of the Joint Committee on the Conduct of the War, 1863–1866: The Red River Expedition.* 1865. Reprint, Millwood, NY: Krauss Reprint Company, 1977.

U.S. Navy Department. *Dictionary of American Fighting Ships*, vol. 2. Washington, DC: Government Printing Office, 1963.

———. Naval History Division. *Civil War Naval Chronology 1861–1865.* Washington, DC: Government Printing Office, 1971.

U.S. Senate, *Senate Executive Documents*, 38th Congress, 2d Session, No. 2.

_____. *US Senate Documents*, 62d Congress, 3d Session, No. 987.

U.S. War Department, *Atlas to Accompany the Official Records of the Union and Confederate Armies*. Washington, DC: Government Printing Office, 1891–95.

_____. *Official Records of the Union and Confederate Navies in the War of the Rebellion*. 31 vols. Washington, DC: Government Printing Office, 1895–1929.

_____. *The War of the Rebellion: A Compilation of the Official Records of the Union and Confederate Armies*. 128 vols. Washington, DC: Government Printing Office, 1890–1901.

INDEX

Boldface page numbers indicate maps.

189